PERGAMON MANAGEMENT AND BUSINESS SERIES VOL 2

Editor: Lester M. Cone, Jr.
Marist College, New York

Encounters in Organizational Behavior: Problem Situations

Encounters in Organizational Behavior: Problem Situations

Robert D. Joyce

Principal, Innovative Management, Irvine, California
Supervisor, Management, and Professional Training
Douglas Aircraft Company
McDonnell Douglas Corporation
Long Beach, California

PERGAMON PRESS INC.
New York · Toronto · Oxford · Sydney · Braunschweig

Pergamon Press Offices:

U. K.	Pergamon Press Ltd., Headington Hill Hall, Oxford OX3 0BW, England
U. S. A.	Pergamon Press Inc., Maxwell House, Fairview Park, Elmsford, New York 10523, U.S.A.
C A N A D A	Pergamon of Canada, Ltd., 207 Queen's Quay West, Toronto 1, Canada
A U S T R A L I A	Pergamon Press (Aust.) Pty. Ltd., 19a Boundary Street, Rushcutters Bay, N.S.W. 2011, Australia
F R A N C E	Pergamon Press SARL, 24 rue des Ecoles, 75240 Paris, Cedex 05, France
W E S T G E R M A N Y	Pergamon Press GMbH, 3300 Braunschweig, Postfach 2923, Burgplatz 1, West Germany

First edition 1972

Fourth Printing 1975

Printed in the United States of America
08 017013 7 (H)
08 017116 8 (S)

To Dr. Manley Howe Jones who, while at the Illinois Institute of Technology, first introduced me to the managerial dilemmas of human behavior and...

To the thousands of executives, managers, and supervisors across the nation who have shared their ideas, experiences, concerns, and frustrations with me in their endless searches for human understanding...

I respectfully dedicate this book.

Contents

Contents

Preface

Encounters is an organized series of problem situations in individual and group behavior designed for use in undergraduate and graduate level courses in organizational behavior, organizational development, and industrial psychology. The problem situations can also be effectively used in business management courses involving managerial philosophies and practices, industrial relations, and basic supervision. They should also have value in many business and industrial manager development programs.

Like other management case study or critical incident collections, *Encounters* is primarily intended for use as an additional resource to the usual lecture and text format. Case studies are typically based on real situations, and this built-in reality tends to strengthen understanding of management theory and stimulate group discussion on a wide range of organizational problems. Materials similar in concept have been widely and effectively used for a number of years to supplement textbooks and formal classroom presentations, so little elaboration about the case study approach is necessary here.

Encounters may, in some instances, be used as the primary classroom text with resource readings drawn from the references after each problem situation. This approach allows the instructor unusual classroom flexibility since the cases need not be analyzed in any particular order.

Encounters differs in content from other casebooks. The problem situations in this book are about people at work and primarily about people who work in a larger organizational setting. It is about how they *feel* toward their jobs, their co-workers, and the organization they work for. This book is about people at various places along their respective work careers, their achievements, their moments of greatness, their aspirations, their individual weaknesses and frustrations in a complex work environment.

Encounters is also about how people *behave* at work and toward each other. In some situations we observe highly motivated, goal oriented behavior.

In others we note low levels of individual productivity, sagging group morale, lack of communication, petty bickering and divisiveness. At times it is the System which fosters specific individual and group behavior. In other instances it is individual behavior which alters the effectiveness of groups or the System itself. Because of this purposeful emphasis in the problem situations, *Encounters* should be particularly useful in any educational effort which has organizational behavior or organizational development as its focus.

The problems in *Encounters* have been drawn from a wide range of business, industrial, and governmental settings and reflect contemporary behavioral problems voiced to the author by thousands of managers and employees across the country. Some cases are textbook "models" about which much has been written; others involve emerging attitudes and behavioral patterns first now coming to the attention of scholars. All are reality based with content and detail altered to fit within the scope of this book.

It is worth noting that many situations or characters are not based on any one real incident or locale. They are *composite characterizations* in contemporary literature. Composites may be drawn from several real situations and focused into a single situation to prove the point or to condense needed detail into a shorter time frame.

I am particularly indebted to Dr. Lester M. Cone, Jr. who provided extensive editorial and content advice throughout the preparation of this book and to Miss Patricia Long, who not only typed all manuscript drafts, but offered countless suggestions for improvement. My thanks as well to Mr. Peter B. Lewin of Douglas Aircraft Company for reviewing the entire manuscript for clarity and continuity.

Lastly, it was my wife Vicki who encouraged me to write and to undertake this particular project. Now, after endless weekends of writing, I can finally appreciate the thankless role of the author's wife.

ROBERT D. JOYCE

Los Angeles, California
January 1972

Introduction

ABOUT THE PROBLEM SITUATIONS

The terms case study, problem situation, and incident, are used inter-changeably throughout this book. Although there are technical differences which can be drawn among them, I have chosen not to do so. Each situation or case was prepared to illustrate one or more specific behavioral problems with little regard for the number of words or material format. Some situations could be presented in as few as one or two pages while others required greater elaboration. However, the length of any particular problem situation is in no way related to the complexity of the issue it raises or the management dilemma it poses.

You will find extensive use of conversation in the problems. This is necessary in a book about the feelings and behavior of people. Instead of saying that a character, Eddie Campana, was frustrated and angry, we hear it in his own words when he says, "If Pardee is involved in the presentation to the Air Force, you can expect my resignation the next day!" You will be told little in third person narrative about how the characters feel at a given moment or why they behave as they do. *They will tell you about themselves*. They will explain their feelings, needs, and frustrations, and their perceptions of reality, truth, and logic. Often they will tell their perceptions of others and you will have to look beyond their personal value systems and biases to develop your own understanding of what is truth.

Expect little in terms of background descriptions. Whether a charac-ter is tall, short, fat, or thin is of only nominal concern except for a few specific instances. The places where the characters are located or where the action is occurring are also thinly described. Such descriptions add little to our understanding of the problem and your own mental image should be just as satisfactory.

Technical terms, methods, or procedures appear in some cases. These are included because they are either part of the problem or part of the normal language of the characters. The more complex ones and those which are colloquial to a given business are footnoted for your convenience.

I believe that abstract concepts are easier to understand, remember, and recall for later use when they are presented in a vivid, practical way. Toward this end I have attempted to create interesting characters as well as situations. Here are people who have strong feelings on many specific issues. Grant them their own biases and time to tell their story in their own personal way. Forgive them if they ramble in their discussions, overstate their pet gripes, or repeat themselves unnecessarily.

You are also unlikely to find Mr. Right and Mr. Wrong in most of these cases. Viewpoints vary and the vast majority of management decisions are not made on the basis of right or wrong or on hard, factual data, but on an imperfect composite of facts, feelings, and opinions from many sources. Therefore, in the majority of these cases, each character will believe he is "right" and behave accordingly.

Many of these problem situations are open-ended; that is, they do not necessarily end at a point which will satisfy you. This was purposely done in most instances to present the dilemma without offering solutions. In other situations, several solutions are purposely offered with the expectation that the reader will ponder the implications of each alternative.

The case, *What Makes Fawcett Late?*, was submitted by H. "Blackie" Shanlian of Lockheed Aircraft Company, Burbank, California. Two cases, *Metro City Health Department* and *The Plight of Ralph Cummings*, were prepared by Don. H. Wheeler, Assistant Professor, Braniff Graduate School of Management, University of Dallas, Irving, Texas. Mr. Shanlian is a perceptive manager concerned with the most effective use of human resources and is typical of those who shared their experiences with me to make this book possible. Mr. Wheeler is a talented young instructor whose students reap the benefits of his military and industrial background.

I wrote the other problem situations. Now that the collection is finished, I must confess it is difficult in case writing to avoid the "carbon copy complex," in which each case study begins to sound much like the one before. I have attempted to circumvent this by altering use of first and third person writing, narration forms, and settings. On this, you will have to judge my success.

ABOUT THE SPECIAL PROJECTS

One or more Special Projects are included at the conclusion of each problem situation. These vary considerably in scope from relatively short classroom activities to rather complex research assignments. Use of the Special Projects is optional and may depend largely upon the academic preparation and work exposure of the participants.

The projects are intended to be natural extensions of the discussion question format to make the ideas presented in the problem even more reality oriented. By further exploring the concept in another setting (such as small group analysis and classroom presentations) or matching theory with practice (such as discussions with the Manager of Personnel) the participant should develop significantly greater insight and perspective on the situation.

Projects may be undertaken after analysis of any given problem situation or assigned as term projects to specific persons at the outset of the course. I leave their use and modification to the imagination of the innovative classroom instructor.

ABOUT THE REFERENCES

General References

There are many fine texts with recent publication dates related to the general themes of Organizational Behavior, Organizational Development, Industrial Psychology, and Human Relations. The scope of most of these is so broad that, generally speaking, some information has been included which touches upon the central idea of most cases in this volume. For the convenience of the reader I have compiled these comprehensive texts into a single list titled General References. The subject index of each can serve as the basis of determining the topic coverage of an idea presented in any specific case.

Selected References

Following every case is a list of books and articles which are oriented toward the central idea or problem. In some instances an entire book has been devoted to the subject. Articles in academic and industrial journals which treat the subject from varying points of view are also included. These will all be noted in the Selected References.

Some references after a problem situation may be broader in scope than the problem itself. The title will usually be a reasonable guide to scope. Consider these as references to the entire section and use them accordingly.

I have chosen to include a subheading called *Anthologies* in the Selected

References. Anthologies or selected readings collections are republished articles which the editors feel are valuable as classroom supplements. These recent anthologies are more easily available than the original article in most instances and so I have emphasized their use as information sources.

Availability and date of publication were also the keys to my choice of readings from academic and trade journals. This eliminated many interesting articles from more obscure or aging sources but should reduce student library frustration. One exception to this is certain references to "classic" articles in easily available publications such as the *Harvard Business Review*. Another exception is the use of references from *Innovation*. This is a relatively new publication and may not be available at smaller libraries. The articles though are of unusually high quality and well worth the effort to seek them out.

Communication and Productivity | **1**

"Well something is wrong," replied Croft, "because everything is falling through the cracks lately. I feel I'm not getting through to the staff and, somehow, they aren't telling me everything they should."

PETER CROFT
Everything Is Falling Through the Cracks

INTRODUCTION

Why do we fail to communicate as individuals? What barriers do we create to shut off other people? What can be done to increase openness and frankness in an organization? What are the problems in communicating when there are differences in status or hierarchy? How does distance or remoteness complicate the process?

Cases in This Section

My Door Is Always Open

The door is open but few come in ... an example of psychological barriers to communication. Many things should be said ... problems to be resolved ... how many headbeatings can one man survive? How do you tell the man what he's doing to himself and the organization?

Everything Is Falling Through the Cracks

Two top executives come to the realization that problems exist in their organization ... bickering and distrust at the top ... Is there a way to reverse the trend ... or have we already started?

Eureka, I'll Call it the Wheel!

Months of work yield a valuable result for the organization and the mathematician is eager to share his discovery . . . ho hum . . . the wheel has already been invented. Is there any way to avoid senseless duplication of effort?

The Tale of the Gordian Knot

Shattered morale and a new manager enters the scene. What will he say to inspire the depressed marketing group? A strange tale with an unusual ending. What is the new man really like?

Dear Home Office: Do You Read Me?

An insurance executive questions whether a specific report is used at home office and decides to find out. A poke at the excesses in various organizational systems.

Metro City Health Department

A respected management consulting firm analyzes three distinct levels of management with not so surprising results . . . each is protecting his own interests and has distorted perceptions of the others. What can be done?

MY DOOR IS ALWAYS OPEN

Author's note.   This case is a sad but necessary way to introduce this book of behavioral situations. It is about a manager who wishes to communicate with his people and be effective with them, but who creates psychological barriers in the process. It is sad because the manager cannot correctly perceive the effects of his words and their implied threats. It is necessary because open or authentic communication between people is fundamental to a study of individual and organizational relationships. Lastly, in this case we sense a small feeling of guilt, for there is a bit of this behavior in all of us. And, like Steiner, we cannot see the truth.

Setting.   The Production Manager's Office
Participants.   Gilbert Steiner — Production Manager
              Harold Terry — Production Scheduler
Time.   Monday morning

STEINER: Good morning, Hal. Have a nice weekend?
TERRY: Great, Mr. Steiner . . . took the family to the beach.
STEINER: Fine weekend for it . . . bet your kids enjoyed it.
TERRY: They certainly did. My oldest boy loves the ocean.
STEINER: Billy?
TERRY: (*surprised*) Yes, Billy. I didn't know you knew his name.
STEINER: You probably told me once.
TERRY: You have a good memory.
STEINER: Thank you. Frankly, it's something I developed a long time ago. It's good management practice to get to know a little about your employees . . . their families . . . it brings you closer to them.
TERRY: I can't argue with that . . .
STEINER: Sounds a little phony at first . . . I mean a man could sound like a fool overplaying the concerned boss and carrying on about an employee's arthritic dog, Jasper . . . but I mean real interest and concern in the man and his family.
TERRY: I'm sure it pays dividends in employee loyalty and productivity.
STEINER: It certainly does. When you become a supervisor, I'm sure you'll realize it even more . . . (*pause*) Well, we'd better get started before the week is over.
TERRY: Right. I've already checked the Final Assembly Department, and we should be able to ship the Fedderson order by Wednesday and the A-B-N Industries order by Thursday or Friday.
STEINER: Good. I'll hold you to that . . .
TERRY: We do have a couple of problems though which I want to talk to you about.
STEINER: Yes?
TERRY: We can't ship to Ellis Industries as planned this week because . . .
STEINER: (*angrily*) What?
TERRY: The parts we need still haven't arrived . . .
STEINER: Dammit, man! You told me that last week didn't you?
TERRY: Yes, I did but . . .
STEINER: And do you recall what I told you?
TERRY: You said it was my responsibility to make sure the parts came in.

STEINER: And you blew it!

TERRY: Well, I did review the problem with Purchasing and they suggested . . .

STEINER: To hell with Purchasing! Those paperwork clerks only help foul up things worse. You should have contacted the vendor directly and . . . (*pausing and composing himself*) Look Hal, you're a big boy. I don't have to do your job do I?

TERRY: Of course not, Mr. Steiner.

STEINER: Then you will get those parts this week won't you?

TERRY: Yes, I'll get the parts.

STEINER: And you'll ship by Friday?

TERRY: We'll ship by Friday.

STEINER: (*smiling*) Good. Management by results is the only thing that counts . . . don't you agree?

TERRY: Yes sir.

STEINER: (*serious*) Look, Hal, I guess I come down hard on you sometimes but it's because I expect a lot from you. How can you grow without challenge . . . without difficult objectives to reach?

TERRY: I suppose you're right.

STEINER: I know I'm right. It's a philosophy I learned from my father years ago . . . results count, not words.

TERRY: True.

STEINER: Anything else I should know? I don't care for lots of detail but, at the same time, a man can easily get cut out of the communications loop if he gets too far from the action. And I don't like to get cut out of the loop.

TERRY: Not really. Everything else is moving according to schedule. (*pauses*) The people in Shipping are a little upset though over the late Friday afternoon shipping schedules and were asking me if we in Manufacturing might not work out a more sequential shipping schedule. I thought that was information we could use, particularly with the planned production increase for next quarter . . .

STEINER: Ignore them. Those guys are always complaining and they'll bend your ear all day if you let them. That's not information Hal, that's *noise* you're getting. When a shipping clerk stops complaining it means he's dead.

TERRY: Yes sir.

STEINER: Anything else?

TERRY: No. As far as I know we've covered everything.

STEINER: Hal, you know I like you. You've got tremendous potential in this department. I want to help you learn this business inside and out . . . I want to see you grow and develop . . .

TERRY: Yes?

STEINER: Well, what I mean is . . . don't be reluctant to come to me if you have any problems which I can help you with . . . anything that you want to sit down and talk about . . . my door is always open.

TERRY: Thank you, Mr. Steiner. (*turns to leave*)

STEINER: About that Ellis order . . . you did hear me didn't you?

TERRY: Yes sir, I heard you. We'll ship by Friday.

Setting.   The Waterfountain

Participants.   Harold Terry — Production Scheduler
Phil Siegel — Production Foreman

Time.   A few minutes later

SIEGEL: (*at fountain*) Hi, Hal. Didn't see you behind me.

TERRY: Move over, man. I've got some pills to take.

SIEGEL: Headache?

TERRY: (*taking aspirins*) You wouldn't believe . . .

SIEGEL: I can guess. You've just had your Monday morning head-beating from Steiner.

TERRY: Right.

SIEGEL: Why do you take it? Why don't you tell the bastard off?

TERRY: I need my job. Why don't you?

SIEGEL: I need my job, too. But, I don't have to go in to see him and ask for it like you. When Steiner wants me for something he has to find me out in production and ask. I'm not trapped in his office with regular scheduling reports.

TERRY: But you always handle him so well. I get all torn up inside because I can't communicate with him.

SIEGEL: You're doing it all wrong. First, never tell him *anything* he can use against you. Never volunteer information, pal.

TERRY: You mean *lie* about problems?

SIEGEL: Who said lie? I just said don't volunteer any information. What Steiner doesn't know won't hurt you.

TERRY: And the second thing?

SIEGEL: If he asks a question, answer it exactly as he asked it. You'll stay out of trouble that way.

TERRY: I don't follow you.

SIEGEL: When he says, Siegel do you have any problems? I say no sir, Mr. Steiner, no problems at all. You see, he's saying that he doesn't want you to have any problems so I agree with him and he's happy.

TERRY: And if you do have a problem?

SIEGEL: I get a friend to help me fix it. I have friends in every department.

TERRY: What if it needs Steiner's attention?

SIEGEL: Boy, you are naive! Most everything is done without Steiner now. He's a title; not the real thing! He cut himself off from the organization long ago.

TERRY: It's sad. It really is. I respect the man. He's very intelligent and he's worked so hard to get where he is ... and I know he's trying ... he really does want to communicate ... I'm sure he doesn't consciously intend to put everyone down the way he does ... but that's how it usually comes out.

Discussion Questions

1. What is an open door policy in management?
2. Why does an open door policy usually fail to achieve its stated purpose?
3. Why does Steiner fail to see the results of his discussions with subordinates?
4. What is wrong with the way in which Siegel responds to Steiner?
5. What are the long term implications for:
   (a) Steiner?
   (b) The organization?
6. Is there any way to reach Steiner; that is, to let him know how he is cutting himself out of the communication loop?
7. Can an employee "level" with his boss?
8. Why is it difficult to "level" with the boss?
9. Why is it difficult to "level" with anyone on subjects of mutual concern? (e.g. on problems in which each has an emotional stake as opposed to "chit-chat.")
10. Define and discuss:
    (a) Authentic or open communication.
    (b) Responsible feedback versus criticism.
    (c) Non-verbal communication.
    (d) Power, status, and ease of communication.
    (e) Hidden agendas.
    (f) Transactional analysis.

Special Projects

1. Clearly, Steiner provokes counter-productive behavior in his own organization. Most of us are guilty of the same thing to greater or lesser degrees. What is the common problem or problems we share? Brainstorm thoughts on this for fifteen to twenty minutes and try to develop the fundamental issues.
2. Prepare and present an analysis of this case based upon an understanding of the work of Carl Rogers and others regarding techniques for developing openness and trust in groups and organizations.
3. Prepare and present an analysis of this case based upon an understanding of the new psychiatric technique known as *transactional analysis* as developed by Eric Berne, Thomas Harris, and others.

Selected References

Books
Berne, E. *Games People Play*. New York: Grove Press, Inc., 1964.
Harris, T. A. *I'm OK — You're OK*. New York: Harper & Row, 1969.
Jones, M. and Jongeward, D. *Born To Win*. Reading, Massachusetts: Addison-Wesley, 1972.

Anthologies
Effective Communication on the Job. New York: American Management Association, 1963.
　　Gray, R. D. "What Your Boss Wants to Know," p. 125.
Hampton, D. R., Summer, C. E., and Webber, R. A. (Eds.). *Organizational Behavior and the
　　Practice of Management*. Glenview, Illinois: Scott, Foresman and Company, 1968. Berne,
　　E. "Games," p. 380.
Huseman, R., Logue, C., and Freshley, D. *Readings in Interpersonal and Organizational Com-
　　munication*. Boston, Massachusetts: Holbrook Press, Inc., 1969.
　　Rogers, C. R. "The Characteristics of a Helping Relationship," p. 269.
　　Wicksell, M. J. "Talking It Over *Is* Important," p. 234.
Leadership on the Job. New York: American Management Association, 1966. Sayles, L. "On-the-
　　Job Communication: Why Isn't It Easier?" p. 37.
Leavitt, H. J., and Pondy, L. R. (Eds.) *Readings in Managerial Psychology*. Chicago, Illinois:
　　University of Chicago Press, 1964.
　　Gibb, J. R. "Defensive Communication," p. 191.
　　Rogers, C. R. "A Process Conception of Psychotherapy," p. 251.
　　Zalkind, S. S., and Costello, T. W. "Perception: Implications for Administration," p. 32.

Articles
Bennett, C. C. "Secrets Are for Sharing," *Psychology Today*, February 1969, p. 30.
Burke, R. J., and Wilcox, D. S. "Effects of Different Patterns and Degrees of Openness in
　　Supervisor-Subordinate communications on Subordinate Job Satisfaction," *Academy of
　　Management Journal*, September 1969, p. 319.
Meyer, H. "If People Fear to Fail, Can Organizations Ever Succeed?", *Innovation*, Number
　　Eight, 1969, p. 56.
Slote, W. H. "The Self-Destructive Manager," *Innovation*, Number Sixteen, 1970, p. 16.

EVERYTHING IS FALLING THROUGH THE CRACKS[1]

Peter Croft, president of Hovall Chemical Company, recalled a presentation by a panel of personnel specialists he had heard while attending the annual Drug and Chemical Wholesalers convention in Chicago the prior month. It was common practice at this trade conference to conduct several special interest group meetings for representatives of the numerous member firms. Some of these sessions dealt with the organizational and management side of chemical wholesaling and Croft attended these sessions

[1]Originally appeared in somewhat longer form under the title, "Hovall Chemical Company" in *How to Develop and Train Your Own Managers*, (1971). Reprint permission is greatly appreciated from Management Information Center, Inc., Miami, Florida.

whenever possible. He felt it important to pick up any good new management ideas he could at these sessions, ideas he might be able to implement in his own organization.

As a former salesman with several companies in the wholesale chemical business and later, even as general sales manager of Hovall, Peter Croft had little experience with the business management side of a company. When retiring company president and founder, Harry Hovall, picked him as his successor, Croft knew that he was a "fish out of water" who would have to do his homework to make good in this position.

And, for the most part, he had done well. Sales and profits increased for five straight years under Croft's management. Croft successfully negotiated to have Hovall represent three major manufacturers on an exclusive basis. Territories were expanded, the sales force was upgraded, and both profit sharing and stock option plans were introduced for key sales and administrative executives. Considering his early feelings of inadequacy about his transition from salesman to executive, Croft guessed that he had done fairly well after all.

But in the last two years Croft's "magic" did not seem to work. Two of the best Hovall lines fell on hard times as competitors offered new and better products. In retrospect, Croft felt he should have seen the phaseout of these products and made arrangements for marketing alternatives. Worse yet, no one else in the company saw (or mentioned) the need for a thorough product line review. Now the competitive edge was lost.

Moreover, cost of sales, marketing expenses, and administrative costs were rising at a time when the chemical manufacturers were in the process of negotiating lower representatives' commissions on their products. Hovall was in the middle of a fee-cost squeeze.

The loss of key sales, reduced commissions, and increased costs had clearly affected executive morale and performance. At the last management meeting Croft was dismayed at the amount of petty bickering around the conference table. Capable professionals who had worked with each other for an average of five years were now frequently in conflict, blaming others for company problems.

So as Peter Croft thought of the panel presentation on Organizational Effectiveness, he realized that the speaker might have been talking about Hovall when he said:

> The new competitive edge will not be product or territory. The new competitive edge will be the effective use of human resources within the entire company, the use of hitherto unused talent. Some firms will, through mutual trust, open and frank communications, support of associates' activities, and the release of creative potential in the entire team,

overcome even the greatest external market difficulties and succeed. Problems will be turned into challenges and overcome. Cooperation and synergism will replace self-glorification and empire building.

Unfortunately, in some other firms, executives will continue to mistrust each others' intentions, fail to work through differences of opinion, and unknowingly stifle creativity and innovation. These are the firms which will face ever increasing competitive and financial problems because they will fail to recognize their basic problems and dissipate their energies fighting elusive windmills.

The words haunted Peter Croft. Was Hovall a company which promoted secrecy, inhibited creativity, and stifled open and authentic communications? It was easy to say no. To admit to these behavioral patterns, Peter Croft knew that he would have to implicate himself as part and parcel of the problem. Well, he thought, there was no time like the present to find out.

He phoned his vice-president of marketing, Max Gebhardt, and asked if he was free to come over to his office for a short conference. When Max arrived, they sat down to coffee and Croft posed a question to his long time friend and associate.

"Max, have you read that book about all executives being incompetent?"

"Yes, I have, but...," replied Max curiously.

"Well, do you believe that?"

"I suppose there's a lot of truth in it."

"How about here in our company? Max, are we incompetent at the executive level?"

"You're joking of course."

"No, Max, I'm serious as hell!"

Max Gebhardt could immediately see the obvious soberness being displayed by his boss. Croft was leading up to something important. Max hesitated and pondered his answer.

"No, Pete, I wouldn't say we're incompetent—individually or as a team. We've made some serious mistakes, especially in recent months, but I'd say that we're probably more experienced and capable than any of our competitors."

"Well, something is wrong," replied Croft, "because everything is falling through the cracks lately. I feel I'm not getting through to the staff and, somehow, they aren't telling me everything they should."

Max Gebhardt sipped his coffee and then carefully placed the half empty cup on the desk in front of him.

"Pete, I'm relieved to hear that you feel we have problems. For some time I've felt you might be refusing to acknowledge that they exist," Gebhardt continued.

"We're like a lot of other firms. We have our share of suspicions, anxie-

9

ties, fears, and personal frustrations which are hidden most of the time on the job. When business is good and profits are high these feelings remain in the background. Now, when conditions are tight, I think tensions rise, conflict increases, and productivity drops."

"Would you say that's our situation now?" asked Croft.

"I would."

"And how do you suggest we go about changing it?"

"I think we already are," replied Gebhardt.

Discussion Questions

1. What did Gebhardt mean by his last statement?
2. Gebhardt also said, "When business is good and profits are high these (anxieties, suspicions) feelings remain in the background. Now, when conditions are tight, I think tensions rise, conflict increases, and productivity drops." Do you agree or disagree? Why?
3. Is Peter Croft to blame for this problem? Explain.
4. Behavioral scientists agree that the common attitude held in many organizations of *I Win—You Lose*, must be replaced by an attitude of *I Win—You Win* among personnel. Explain this statement and relate it to this case.
5. What should Croft and Gebhardt do next?

Special Project

Divide the class into sub-groups of 4–5 each. Have each group develop a plan by which this work team can develop better internal communications and improve productivity. Discussion groups should avoid generalities and platitudes and develop a specific, implementable plan of attack which will likely be supported by the entire Hovall team.

Allow 30–45 minutes for preparation in class (or do as an out-of-class assignment) and have each group orally offer its plan to the entire class.

Selected References

Books

Bennis, W. G. *Organization Development: Its Nature, Origins, and Prospects*. Reading, Massachusetts: Addison-Wesley, 1969.

Likert, R. *New Patterns of Management*. New York: McGraw-Hill, 1961.

McGregor, D. *The Human Side of Enterprise*. New York: McGraw-Hill, 1960.

Peter, L. J., and Hull, R. *The Peter Principle*. New York: William Morrow, 1969.

Schein, E. H. *Organizational Psychology*. Englewood Cliffs, New Jersey: Prentice-Hall, 1965.

Anthologies

Hampton, D. R., Summer, C. E., and Webber, R. A. (Eds.) *Organizational Behavior and the Practice of Management*. Glenview, Illinois: Scott, Foresman and Company, 1968. Tannenbaum, R., Weschler, I., and Massarik, F. "Sensitivity Training for the Management Team," p. 539.

Huseman, R., Logue, C., and Freshley, D. *Readings in Interpersonal and Organizational Com-*

munication. Boston, Massachusetts: Holbrook Press, Inc., 1969. Lee, I. J. "They Talk Past Each Other," p. 24.

Leavitt, H. J., and Pondy, L. R. (Eds.) *Readings in Managerial Psychology.* Chicago, Illinois: University of Chicago Press, 1964. Schelling, T. C. "Bargaining, Communication, and Limited War," p. 422.

Articles

Davis, S. "Building More—Effective Teams," *Innovation,* Number Fifteen, 1970, p. 32.

Herman, S. M. "What Is This Thing Called Organization Development?" *Personnel Journal,* August 1971, p. 595.

Levinson, H. "A Psychologist Looks At Executive Development," *Harvard Business Review,* September–October 1962, p. 69.

Margulies, N. "Implementing Organizational Change Through an Internal Consulting Team," *Training and Development Journal,* July 1971, p. 26.

Morse, J. J. and Lorsch, J. W. "Beyond Theory Y," *Harvard Business Review,* May–June 1970, p. 61.

Zeyher, L. R. "Improving Your Three-Dimensional Communications," *Personnel Journal,* May 1970, p. 414.

EUREKA, I'LL CALL IT THE WHEEL!

"I accomplished a rather incredible feat the other day: I invented the wheel! As startling as that may seem, my name will never appear in history books. When I proudly displayed my wheel, I was told it had already been invented!

"Overly dramatic? Overstated? A case of sour grapes? Not at all. For all practical purposes I *did* re-invent the wheel last week and there was no reason for it . . . no reason at all!

"I was really steamed up when I found out about it. I was ready to march into the office of the Director of Operations to tell him that his 'superb' organization had invented two wheels . . . simultaneously! Bob O'Brien, my supervisor, talked me out of it. O'Brien argued that there were enough small differences between the two to justify the separate developments. Besides, O'Brien added, there was no reason to make waves now that the work was completed. Lastly, O'Brien said it was an inevitable occurrence . . . impossible to avoid in a large, complex operation such as ours.

"It's true that our operation is quite complex. We design and build commercial and military aircraft pilot training simulators. Most people think of an aircraft simulator as a simple closed container with a control stick. That was true years ago when airplanes were simple machines but now nothing could be further from the truth.

"Today a simulator cockpit is identical to the real bird and we can train pilots to fly jet aircraft without ever leaving the ground. When the cabin door is closed and our programmed computer begins to simulate reality,

11

the pilot might as well be in the sky. We can duplicate any and all motions, sounds, and, even smells of the real plane. It's probably one of the most complex businesses in the world today.

"And, we're large too. Over three thousand people work at our huge, sprawling two story facility. I suppose size is part of the problem.

"But inventing two wheels at the same time can't be blamed on complexity or size of the organization. We've got a communications problem and I think it has to do with the way in which we've organized our project work.

"The entire first floor of the building, other than administrative and staff support operations, is devoted to commercial simulator operations. Here we design and build simulators for the commercial jetliners. The second floor is devoted to simulator design for military aircraft.

"Now that seems like a perfectly logical way in which to organize, since the commercial work stresses lower unit costs and the military work stresses extreme reliability. And, to an outsider walking past the endless rows of desks, I guess we would appear to be quite efficient.

"The problem is duplication. The same basic design problems exist in both the military and commercial areas. Mathematicians, engineers, designers, and computer programmers on the first floor have counterparts on the second floor!

"I don't mean to imply that our top management staff is composed of idiots. They see the design and development similarities but feel the two areas are *so* specialized and have their own unique design requirements that the partial duplication is necessary. But specialization can be carried only so far and that's how the wheel got invented twice last week.

"I'm a mathematician assigned to the commercial operation. Recently I was asked to solve a series of airport approach problems given various trajectory angles, speeds, wind velocities, and body loads. It was a difficult problem and, even with the help of our scientific computer, it took ten weeks to complete. I was pretty proud of myself when I finished the project and had validated the equations.

"A day or so later I made it my business to look up my counterparts in the military operation to show them my results. I had asked Weller and Grimshaw to meet me for lunch in the cafeteria and I brought along a summary of my work.

"Weller and Grimshaw were very polite. Weller nodded continuously as I talked on (my enthusiasm was obvious), and Grimshaw glanced at my notes as he was eating his soup. Then, the bombshell!

"Grimshaw said that I should have checked with them first . . . that they had essentially developed the same data a month earlier and had computerized the problem. We both had invented the wheel!"

Discussion Questions

1. Who is at fault here:
   (a) The mathematician? Why?
   (b) Weller and Grimshaw? Why?
   (c) Bob O'Brien? Why?
   (d) Top management? Why?
   (e) The method of organization? Why?
   (f) Largeness and complexity? Why?
2. Define the fundamental problem which exists in this case and develop specific ways in which it can be improved.
3. Now, re-examine the problem. Is duplication of effort the problem or is it a symptom of yet another, broader problem? If so, what is it? Explain.
4. Much has been written about management information systems. How could an M.I.S. assist in keeping this situation from occurring?

Special Project

You are the Director of Operations and have just been informed of this communications problem. You are disturbed and decide to develop methods or techniques to keep it from happening again.

Using separate discussion groups of 4–5 persons each, develop a specific plan for the Director of Operations. Allow 30–45 minutes for small group discussion and at least an equal amount of time for oral presentation to the entire class. What similarities exist among the suggested plans?

Selected References

Anthologies

Huseman, R., Logue, C., and Freshley, D. *Readings in Interpersonal and Organizational Communication.* Boston, Massachusetts: Holbrook Press Inc., 1969.
   Crook, R. B. "Communication and Group Structure," p. 389.
   Timbers, E. "Strengthening Motivation Through Communication," p. 203.
   Walton, E. "Motivation to Communicate," p. 247.
Koontz, H., and O'Donnell, C. *Management: A Book of Readings.* New York: McGraw-Hill, 1968.
   Daniel, R. "Management Information Crisis," p. 519.
   Melcher, A., and Beller, R. "Toward a Theory of Organizational Communication," p. 496.
   Stewart, J. "Making Project Management Work," p. 202.
Leavitt, H. J., and Pondy, L. R. (Eds.). *Readings in Managerial Psychology.* Chicago, Illinois: University of Chicago Press, 1964. Jackson, J. M. "The Organization and Its Communication Problems," p. 486.

Articles

McGrath, T. "Management Information Systems: It's All In the Tailoring," *Innovation*, Number Thirteen, 1970, p. 44.
Mason, R. "Management Information Systems: What They Are, What They Ought To Be," *Innovation*, Number Thirteen, 1970, p. 34.

THE TALE OF THE GORDIAN KNOT

To say that the Marketing Department at Blanchard Manufacturing Company was demoralized would, most certainly, be an understatement. The morale decline had started almost two years ago as the market for barber chairs (the firm's major product line) began to decline. Retail barbers were suffering from changes in men's attitudes about hair styles. Few new shops were opening and many established barbers were cautious about remodeling their shops during an industry recession.

But the devastating blow for Blanchard occurred ten months ago when a Japanese manufacturer, Toyo-Satumi, introduced a high-quality barber chair into the American market at slightly more than two thirds the cost of the equivalent Blanchard chair. The move was unexpected, swift, and comprehensive. Toyo-Satumi had carefully established a large dealer network, promoted heavily within the trade and, within months, made significant inroads into traditional Blanchard markets.

Morton Feinstein, then the Director of Marketing, was summarily terminated for having failed to anticipate or have knowledge of the planned move by Toyo-Satumi. Feinstein was well liked by the marketing staff who viewed his dismissal as a pure case of company "scape goat."

Feinstein was replaced by his assistant, Larry Golden. Golden, an unimaginative paper shuffler, muddled and further confused the staff for several months before he resigned under top management pressure. For the last two months the position of Marketing Director has been open. Owen Blanchard, the president, has been personally covering the position while actively shopping for a high powered marketing man to head the department.

Today was the big day. Owen Blanchard smiled broadly as he personally introduced Harvey Grainger to the marketing staff and extolled Grainger's past marketing accomplishments in other industries.

The staff anxiously waited to hear what Grainger would say . . . to find out what kind of person he was and what direction he would move the stalled department. Blanchard then turned the group meeting over to Grainger.

"Ladies and gentlemen," said Grainger, "in a very short period of time I will be better acquainted with each of you and your respective roles in our mutual marketing effort. I am new to Blanchard and an unknown quantity to most of you. Let me take a few moments to give you a better idea by illustration of my way of working, my 'style' so to speak."

Grainger continued, "There is an old legend from Greek mythology about a small village which was constantly under attack by local barbaric tribes. The problem was one of leadership. There were sufficient men in the village to successfully ward off the attacks but the men were disorganized and ineffective. There was no one person or symbol around which they could rally.

"One year a stranger by the name of Gordias came to their village and provided leadership when the village was next attacked. A grateful village honored Gordias by naming him king for life.

"Gordias was a wise man. He knew it was a change in attitude among the men which had saved the village and not his sword alone. He decided to provide the village with a symbol of unity and strength which would bind them together even after his eventual death.

"And so a chariot was moved to the outskirts of the village and Gordias took a very long rope and tied a large knot around the yoke of the chariot. When he finished, he had fashioned the most complex knot known to man. No ends of the rope showed to even indicate how one might begin to unravel it. He named it the Gordian Knot.

"Then he proclaimed, 'My leadership of this village is hereby established and will remain so in perpetuity through my descendants. This village shall never be ruled by anyone else unless he has the great wisdom to untie the Gordian Knot. If he can do this he is truly fit to become your leader.'

"Many years passed and Gordias eventually died. His son ruled after him and his son after that. There was never again so great a leader but the village remained secure for, although many knew of the legend, no one could ever untie the Gordian knot.

"One day the army of Alexander the Great marched to the edge of the remote Asian village. Alexander asked the meaning of the strange knot tied to the chariot yoke and was told of the legend.

"Alexander stared at the knot for some time but did not attempt to untie it. Then he unsheathed his sword, raised it above his head, and slashed the knot to its very core! 'Thus do I untie the Gordian Knot' he proclaimed and marched his army into the village."

There was complete silence when Grainger finished. Then he added, "Symbols of strength will not stop us. We will cut through to the very core and march on!"

Later in the hallway, three marketing people discussed their reactions to Grainger's speech:

"What do you think of Grainger?" asked one.

"Don't know for sure, but I get the feeling he's action oriented," said the second.

"But I read in his remarks that it might get a little bloody if you stand in his way," said the third.

"Well," asked one, "what kind of a leader was Grainger trying to tell us he is? I got the impression that he's a hard headed pragmatist."

"Time will tell," said the second, "but a more descriptive word might be *dictator*."

"Or maybe that he's a Greek God," offered the third with tongue in cheek.

Discussion Questions

1. What did Grainger imply through the legend of the Gordian Knot?
2. What type of leader is Grainger likely to be? Do we have sufficient information?
3. Was this a realistic approach for the new Director of Marketing? Explain.
4. Parables, analogies, and other animate and inanimate comparisons can help a leader communicate with his people. If poorly done, the reverse can be true.
   (a) What are your feelings in this specific case?
   (b) Can you cite similar uses of comparative techniques which helped or hindered communication? The classroom lecture is usually rich in such examples.

Special Project

Assume you have just been named Director of Marketing for the Blanchard Manufacturing Company and are about to meet your personnel for the first time. Owen Blanchard has explained the impact of foreign competition, sluggish sales, and the low morale of your staff. How should you react at your first encounter with them?

This problem can best be analyzed in small groups of 4–5 participants. Allow 20 minutes for analysis and about 5 minutes for an oral report from each group.

Selected References

Books
Bennis, W. G. *Changing Organizations*: *Essays on the Development and Evolution of Human Organizations*. New York: McGraw-Hill, 1966.
Pigors, P. *Effective Communication on the Job*. "Meaning and How We Can Share It." New York: American Management Association, 1963.

Anthologies
Hampton, D. R., Summer, C. E., and Webber, R. A. (Eds.). *Organizational Behavior and the Practice of Management*. Glenview, Illinois: Scott, Foresman and Company, 1968.
Argyris, C. "Personality and Organization," p. 138.
Dearborn, D. C., and Simon, H. "Selective Perception," p. 162.
Huseman, R., Logue, C., and Freshley, D. *Readings in Interpersonal and Organizational Communication*, Boston, Massachusetts: Holbrook Press, Inc., 1969.

Hayakawa, S. I. "How Words Change Our Lives," p. 12.
Nirenberg, J. S. "Communicating for Greater Insight and Persuasiveness," p. 239.
Potter, C. J. "Persuasiveness—Powerful Tool," p. 252.
Rogers and Farson. "Active Listening," p. 480.
Leavitt, H. J., and Pondy, L. R. (Eds.). *Readings in Managerial Psychology*. Chicago, Illinois: University of Chicago Press, 1964. Hovland, C. I. "Studies in Persuasion," p. 179.

Articles
Harley, K. "Team Development," *Personnel Journal*, June 1971, p. 437.
Maugham, I. "Building An Effective Work Team," *Training and Development Journal*, January 1971, p. 20.

DEAR HOME OFFICE: DO YOU READ ME?

Charles (Hap) Clonninger is an outstanding life insurance salesman — he knows it and his company knows it. His monthly total of policies written in dollar value consistently places him in the top ten percent of all company agents. And, the more he sells, the easier it becomes. As Hap (for Happy), himself put it some time ago, "Sales build confidence in a man and confidence in himself is what motivates a man to do still more. It just builds and builds."

Clearly, Hap Clonninger is a highly motivated and productive insurance agent. The company has recognized Hap's contribution over and above the usual generous sales commissions. For example, in the past three years, Clonninger has received:

1. A two week, all expenses paid trip for himself and his wife to Nassau in the Bahamas as one of the top ten producers for the year.
2. A weekend in Mexico City (paid, of course) for top dollar sales in the month of January.
3. Free tickets to numerous theatrical and sports activities.
4. A weekend in Pasadena, California, for the annual Tournament of Roses Parade and two tickets to the Rosebowl Game.
5. Numerous sales citations and plaques which are prominently displayed in his downtown Atlanta office.

Hap Clonninger has also been recognized by industry professionals outside his company and he was recently elected to the position of Vice-President, Georgia Chapter, of the Insurance Executives Association.

Clonninger thoroughly enjoys his work and claims he wouldn't trade places with anyone. "I don't really think of myself as a salesman," he often says, "I prefer to think of myself as someone who helps people build their estates . . . a sort of financial planner and advisor. It's very satisfying work and I can immediately see the rewards for my efforts."

It seems, though, that no job is perfect in every respect and there is one part of his work which does irritate Hap Clonninger: a required company report in narrative form on sales prospects.

"That damned report kills a whole day each month!" says Clonninger. "Imagine, *an entire day* a month filling in six pages of questions in straight narration on how I propose to close sales for the next month.

"I mean, I can see the company's point of view, particularly with new and inexperienced salesmen. A detailed form such as this one forces a new man to work out a sales plan for the coming period. It helps the man because it transforms fuzzy or vague ideas in his head into a workable plan on paper. The form also helps the company because it shows that the agent really does have a well defined sales plan. It also can serve as a basis for monitoring his progress . . . how well he actually does compared to what he said he would do.

"But that monthly Sales Plan really doesn't have any value to the company or to me as far as my efforts are concerned. It probably has little or no value to any other top agent either. We've got so many deals cooking all the time that we don't bother to work from a plan.

"One month, about a year ago, I didn't send in the report for the first time since I've been an agent for the company. I thought if nothing was said I'd skip it from then on. Wow! You'd think I'd committed grand larceny! I received formal notices from two vice-presidents and several more lower level bureaucrats about the omission and so I figured it wasn't worth fighting the system . . . I'd continue submitting sales plans as in the past.

"Some time later though it occurred to me that the *only time* I had heard any feedback about my monthly report was in the month that I failed to turn it in! *At no other time in recent years could I recall anyone commenting on or questioning my sales plan.*

"Four months ago, on the day of the report, I was feeling pretty good. I had just sold a big policy to a supermarket executive and was in no mood to write the report. But, conditioned by years of compliance, I started plugging away at it.

"About halfway through, on page 3 or 4, I suddenly wrote, 'If anyone has bothered to read this far, I, Hap Clonninger, will personally buy him a martini.' You know, I didn't have to buy a single martini . . . and that report crosses at least four desks!

"The next month I wrote in the middle of the text, 'This report has been prepared by the world's greatest insurance salesman.' Again, no response from home office.

"Still there was the possibility that the report was being read but that my remarks were being ignored as whimsey. So, I decided last month to really test the system. On page 2 under the heading of New Prospects, I wrote:

> 'Edgar Millikan (company president) is a
> dirty old man and a poor insurance risk.'

Would you believe that I got no response? Nobody reads the monthly report . . . *nobody* . . . but, if I don't turn one in . . . Wow!

Discussion Questions

1. Discuss Hap Clonninger's primary feelings about his job in terms of recent behavioral and motivational research.
2. How do you feel about Hap Clonninger's behavior relative to the monthly report?
3. What should be his proper course of action regarding this report?
4. One school of thought holds: Make the system idiot-proof. If people can foul it up in some possible way they surely will. Discuss.
5. Another school of thought holds: True, people often foul up the system but usually only because the imposed system has been so poorly designed that such behavior can be expected. Discuss.

Special Project

Have participants review existing organizational rules, regulations, policies, and procedures with which they are familiar and, as an outside assignment:
1. Write out a specific existing regulation or procedure which they feel has built-in features which *has or might* induce behavior contrary to its original intent.
2. Prepare an analysis of why they feel this is the case and what probable forms of contrary or negative behavior might result. Document with actual occurrences if possible.
3. Re-write the rule or regulation to:
   (a) Still maintain its original intent.
   (b) Provide a better basis for positive behavior or improved behavior.
4. Submit this as a formal class project.

Selected References

Books
Fleishman, A. *Sense and Nonsense In Communication.* San Francisco: International Society for General Semantics, 1971.
Townsend, R. *Up The Organization.* New York: Alfred A. Knopf, 1970.

Anthologies

Effective Communication on the Job. New York: American Management Association, 1963.
Emory, D. "How to Plan Your Communications," p. 71.

Hampton, D. R., Summer, C. E., and Webber, R. A. (Eds.). *Organizational Behavior and the Practice of Management.* Glenview, Illinois: Scott, Foresman and Company, 1968. Leavitt, H. "Perception: From The Inside Looking Out," p. 155.

Huseman, R., Logue, C., and Freshley, D. *Readings in Interpersonal and Organizational Communication.* Boston, Massachusetts: Holbrook Press, Inc., 1969.
Boynton, R., and Wright, D. "Communication Gap: Is Anybody Up There Listening?" p. 448.
Planty, E., and Machaver, W. "Upward Communications: A Project in Executive Development," p. 122.
Townsend, L. A. "A Corporate President's View of the Internal Communication Function," p. 169.

METRO CITY HEALTH DEPARTMENT

The growth of Metro City during the past two decades has generated the need for continuously expanding public services. As in other cities, tax revenues are generally insufficient to provide all the services demanded by the community. The City Health Department, one of the public agencies most affected by the scarcity of public money, recently felt it might improve the quantity and quality of its required operations at existing funding levels by improving managerial and operating efficiency.

This suggestion for improving efficiency was presented at the monthly executive board meeting by the Department Director. All members of the board agreed that further efficiencies were possible. Indeed, outside critics of governmental operations, notably the largest Metro City newspaper, had frequently cited the City Health Department for specific instances of mismanagement and bureaucratic red tape. Before the meeting adjourned, a committee was appointed to select an independent management consulting firm to review and make recommendations as to how the Metro City Health Department could make the necessary operational changes to provide those public services required of it within the current budgetary limitations.

At the next meeting of the executive board, the committee submitted its findings as to the availability and projected costs for the services of four prominent management consulting firms. The committee's recommendation was, in view of their findings, that the firm of Barton, Bastine, and Bowditch should be contracted to perform this task. This firm had successfully performed on assignments with public service organizations in other major United States cities and the committee was confident that they would be able to provide the desired guidance in this instance as well. The executive board approved the recommendations of the selection committee and the contract was awarded to Barton, Bastine, and Bowditch.

On the first of May, a management evaluation team headed by Daryl Bowditch began its study of the City Health Department. The first task was to analyze the operations of the department and to compare its growth rate, expansion of services offered, and budgetary increases to the changes in city population over the last two decades. Second, a comparison of the services being offered by the Metro City Health Department would be made to those offered by health departments in other cities of similar size throughout the United States. Third, an audit of "management attitude" would be used to determine the validity and nature of apparent management inefficiencies.

After several months study, Daryl Bowditch reviewed a rough draft report on all three phases of their work. The first two phases were a confirmation of the feelings of the executive board. The third phase was somewhat of a surprise.

Phase 1   Services and Costs Relative to Population Trends

The consultant analysis of departmental operations revealed that the primary function of the City Health Department is the rendering of services directed toward the prevention of disease. In this capacity, the department coordinates the activities of several official and unofficial agencies which are also directly concerned with disease prevention.

The study also indicated that many of the department's programs are educational in nature—informing the public of potential health problems, the possible dangers, symptoms, and general methods of prevention. Activities include food, meat, and milk inspections, vector control,[1] air and water pollution, and others. An extensive program of services for the economically depressed includes direct medical services for prenatal care, pediatrics, dental health, tuberculosis control, and control and care of venereal disease. The drug abuse problem has also become a major program from the standpoint of education as well as treatment.

Phase 2   Comparisons With Other Cities

Analysis of the programs offered by the City Health Department revealed that the services offered in Metro City do not differ appreciably in

[1]Vector in biology is an insect or other organism that transmits a pathogenic fungus, virus, bacterium, etc.

scope or quality from those offered in comparable cities in other parts of the country.

The findings of the evaluation team relative to the growth rate of the department in proportion to the cities' growth and the expansion of services with time indicated that there was no major disparity between Metro City and others. The team recognized that it certainly would be easier for the department to function more effectively with greater human and financial resources. The findings were, however, that the present level of approximately three hundred employees, mostly professional and technical, and an annual budget of 18.5 million dollars was minimally adequate to deliver the required services.

Phase 3   Management Audit

The third phase of the Barton, Bastine, and Bowditch study involved an audit of management attitudes. The technique used to gather data for this portion of the study was to personally interview all members of each of the three levels of management starting from the Assistant Directors down. Seventy personal (and confidential) interviews were conducted. The major purpose of these interviews was to determine how each level of management viewed itself and the other two levels. Upon completion of the interviews, the team members compared notes and selected one statement characteristic of the views of the entire class of management toward the other classes. These summary statements were:

Top Management's View of:
  A. *Top Management:* "We are doing a beautiful job considering the handicap of a tight budget and incompetent personnel with whom we must operate."
  B. *Middle Management:* "Our big problem is uncooperative and incompetent middle management. Why can't these managers do what we want?"
  C. *First-Level Supervision:* "These people are lackadaisical but do an acceptable job under the circumstances."

Middle Management's View of:
  A. *Top Management:* "These people are unorganized and confused. They have no long range plan nor firm objectives or goals. They float with the tide."
  B. *Middle Management:* "We are ambitious and try to function effectively

without knowing what top management wants or expects. We are conscientious but need guidance. We wish we could really measure the results of our operation."

C. *First-Level Supervision:* "These people are lackadaisical but can get the job done if we stay after them."

First-Level Supervision's view of:

A. *Top Management:* "They do a fair job but they don't appreciate our efforts or understand our problems."

B. *Middle Management:* "They don't appreciate our efforts and should use some of our solutions rather than think up their own. We wish they would make up their minds as to which direction we are going. If they want good solutions, they should at least consult with us."

C. *First-Level Supervision:* "We do a good job when you consider the handicaps of the system. It is difficult to see the results of our efforts, much less measure them. No wonder we're glad when five o'clock rolls around each day."

Daryl Bowditch approved the report and had it typed in final form for presentation to the executive board.

Discussion Questions

1. How would you present the findings of the management evaluation team to the executive board?
2. Is there any likelihood that quality or quantity of service can be improved as a result of the information derived from this study? Explain.
3. Develop your own analysis of the managerial effectiveness of the three levels of management in the Metro City Health Department.
4. How can these contradictory views by each management level be altered?
5. Are the views expressed by the various levels of management typical of other businesses or isolated to this case? Explain.
6. Develop a long-range solution which will ease the management problems presently faced by the Metro City Health Department.

Special Project

Given the communications problem which exists in the Metro City Health Department, what can be done to improve future relations among the management levels?

Using either a small discussion group or role play techniques, have several class members define the basic issues involved here and have them reach consensus[2] on a *specific plan of action* to improve future relationships.

[2]Consensus is defined in the case situation, *Let's Take a Vote.*

Alternate. Have the above work submitted by each participant as a formal, written class project.

Selected References

Books

Beckhard, R. *Organization Development: Strategies and Models*. Reading, Massachusetts: Addison-Wesley, 1969.

Blake, R. R., and Mouton, J. S. *The Managerial Grid*. Houston, Texas: Gulf Publishing, 1964.

Blake, R. R., Shepard, H., and Mouton, J. S. *Managing Intergroup Conflict in Industry*. Houston, Texas: Gulf Publishing, 1964.

Lawrence, P. R., and Lorsch, J. W. *Developing Organizations: Diagnosis and Action*. Reading, Massachusetts: Addison-Wesley, 1969.

Anthologies

Hampton, D. R., Summer, C. E., and Webber, R. A. (Eds.). *Organizational Behavior and the Practice of Management*. Glenview, Illinois: Scott, Foresman and Company, 1968.

Gouldner, A. W. "Some Functions of Bureaucractic Roles," p. 483.

Presthus, R. "Toward A Theory of Organizational Behavior," p. 467.

Thompson, V. A. "Bureaucracy and Bureaupathology," p. 224.

Huseman, R., Logue, C., and Freshley, D. *Readings in Interpersonal Communication*. Boston Massachusetts: Holbrook Press, Inc., 1969.

Fergason, G. "Keeping Management Informed," p. 163.

Wade, L. L. "Communications in a Public Bureaucracy: Involvement and Performance," p. 100.

Koontz, H., and O'Donnell, C. *Management: A Book of Readings*. New York: McGraw-Hill, 1968. Likert, R. "Measuring Organizational Performance," p. 608.

Articles

Fitzgerald, T. H. "In-House Education, Reconsidered," *Training and Development Journal*, July 1971, p. 2.

Gemmill, G. "Managing Upward Communication," *Personnel Journal*, February 1970. p. 107.

Kruger, D. H. "Functions and Problems of Middle Management," *Personnel Journal*, November 1970, p. 935.

Nadler, L. "The Organization as a Micro-Culture," *Personnel Journal*, December 1969, p. 949.

Wickesberg, A. K. "Communication Networks in the Business Organization," *Academy of Management Journal*, September 1968, p. 253.

CASE STUDY CROSS REFERENCE

Although located elsewhere in this book, the following problem situations are also valuable in the study of Section 1:

Leadership Styles and Techniques

"It is highly unusual for a group to meet for the purpose of solving real organizational problems without the leader and agenda having been developed in advance. Your frustration is common to leaderless groups at this point. What you are realizing is that *all groups* develop one or more leaders even when leadership is not externally imposed. I agree that something must be done about the leadership problem."

SAXBE
Now, About the Question of Leadership

INTRODUCTION

Why is one man effective as a leader and another not? What personal attributes or characteristics are involved in leadership? To what extent does the subordinate work group play a role in the success or failure of the leader? How are other environmental factors involved in leadership? How does leadership evolve? Are temporary or multiple leaders possible in a given organizational setting?

Cases in This Section

Now, About the Question of Leadership

A temporary work group must solve a problem . . . but who is to be the leader? The apparent leader declines . . . how should it be handled? What will be the operational rules?

The Secret of Bradford's Warehouse

It's no secret that Bradford's group has been successful...but why? What is there about Bradford which makes him so effective as a leader? Use of people, material resources, and methods are explored in this case ...plus a vocal objection to the miraculous Bradford method.

What's Wrong with Wong?

Three maintenance mechanics discuss the attitudes and actions of their new supervisor and former peer group member...a good guy goes bad... friend turns against you...is it inevitable or is it a matter of perception?

The Case of the Clandestine Coffee Break

A classic case of trying to beat the System when the System runs counter to the usual practices and norms...a failure in leadership or trouble-makers in the work group? Leadership style, effective communication, and resistance to change are involved.

The Fall of Bainbridge House

Sudden death of a leader has long lasting implications for his firm. The team was prepared...but for what? The effective use of human resources is explored.

NOW, ABOUT THE QUESTION OF LEADERSHIP

"I have no doubt that we have the ability to provide the kind of mail services people expect, but it will take time and money. And it will take renewed commitment and dedication on the part of all postal employees to make it work. In turn, the new U.S. Postal Service is going to do all it can to make work more satisfying and rewarding. This, I am certain, is the surest path to providing excellent service to the American people."

WINTON M. BLOUNT — Postmaster General
From an internal publication to
Postal Service employees
1971

Setting. The Superintendent's Office of a large modern postal facility. There is a large conference table around which a number of people are seated.

Participants. Eight men and two women — primarily postal supervisors, carrier route examiners, and finance personnel from various city locations. One person is a trainer-consultant. They are officially assembled as a problem solving team.

Cast

Name		Title	Basic Attitude
Wrigley	(M)	Superintendent	Strong opinions
Hernandez	(M)	Route Examiner	Enthusiastic
Evans	(M)	Assistant Superintendent	Positive but cautious
Blackman	(M)	Assistant Superintendent	Reserved but positive
McCleary	(M)	Finance Examiner	Humorous but positive
Lowell	(F)	Customer Service Representative	Concerned
Smith	(M)	Superintendent	Somewhat negative
Cline	(F)	Finance Examiner	Swings with the majority
Fisher	(M)	Route Examiner	Tired and somewhat bored
Saxbe	(M)	P.S.M.I. trainer[1]	Officially neutral

Time: Now

SAXBE: I believe everyone is here now and we might as well start the session. Can I assume everyone is acquainted?

   (*general chit-chat, smiles, two or three introductions and handshakes*)

SAXBE: This being the first of eight meetings we will have, let me take a moment to review where we have been and where we are going.

   As you are well aware, the United States Post Office Department, in existence for over 200 years, is currently being reorganized. On August 12, 1970, President Nixon signed into law the Postal Reorganization Act which made change finally possible. The Act allows us to modernize our operations and procedures under a new name, the United States Postal Service.

   Many of you have probably already felt the first implications of that change.

McCLEARY: (*laughing*) Yeah! They already got my boss to take an early retirement.

EVANS: And I hear that each postal facility will eventually become an independent operating unit . . . with a budget of its own.

---

[1]P.S.M.I. — Postal Service Management Institute.

29

HERNANDEZ: Right! We'll finally be able to see where we're making money and where we're losing it. With the cost center approach used by private industry, we'll be able to take action to eliminate high cost-low effectiveness areas and functions.

BLACKMAN: I've already noted an easing of the procedures we use to justify and acquire new capital equipment.

McCLEARY: (*facetiously*) How 'bout that! Talk about *radical* changes in the Service,[2] I hear that each station superintendent will even have a petty cash fund for minor station expenses!

WRIGLEY: The important thing is that the Postal Service will be able to operate like any other sensible business without being subjected to the whims and politics of Congress.

BLACKMAN: No longer will we be a political whipping boy.

HERNANDEZ: *Amen!*
(*general laughter and exchange of comments*)

SMITH: Don't hold your breath. They've talked about changes in the past . . .

HERNANDEZ: (*to Smith*) Come on, fella. You know they mean business this time.

SMITH: I hope so . . . it's just that I've heard those good words before . . .

SAXBE: We seem to be straying. Let's see if we fully know why we're here today. Mrs. Lowell, why don't you give us your understanding of the purpose of our sessions?

LOWELL: Well, as I understand it, part of the new Postal Service program is to provide postal managers and supervisors across the country with the new skills and techniques they will need to meet future managerial requirements.

SAXBE: Right.

EVANS: Aren't these the concepts we covered in our recent Phase I training program?

SAXBE: Right again. These fairly uniform one week programs designated T.E.A.M.[3] Phase I, emphasize leadership, team dynamics, problem solving, and methods improvement. The program is administered and conducted nationally by the Postal Service Management Institute of which I am a staff member.

CLINE: It was really an enjoyable week. I feel I learned a great deal about myself and others, particularly how leadership operates in a small group setting such as ours.

HERNANDEZ: Me too. It was really great!

SMITH: I thought it was a little long myself.

[2]The United States Postal Service.
[3]T.E.A.M. — Team Effectiveness Approach to Management.

30

SAXBE: Phase I programs are uniform and structured in their format and normally presented to groups of forty supervisors at one time. Remember, *no single course, class, or training program can ever meet everyone's needs or expectations.*

SMITH: Oh, I liked it all right . . . I just said it might have been shorter. I get tired of sitting.

LOWELL: (*changing the subject*) Today we begin Phase II . . . is that correct?

SAXBE: Yes. Do you understand the purpose of Phase II?

LOWELL: Not exactly. I heard we'll have no more lectures, that we now solve real problems as a small team.

WRIGLEY: Try this. Phase II is a series of eight meetings of approximately four hours each in which a group of 10 supervisors work together to help solve Postal Service problems and develop improved operating methods and techniques.

SAXBE: Not bad.

HERNANDEZ: It's our chance to think up new ways to cut costs or improve service. Don't we agree as a group on a problem which we know exists and then develop and submit a formal proposal for change?

SAXBE: Right. Special *Proposal Evaluation Committees* have been established to consider each of the proposals which will be developed by the many Phase II teams now in operation. If they favorably act on a proposal it will be submitted to local, regional, or national levels as most appropriate for final decision and implementation.

SMITH: But what if the Proposal Evaluation Committees don't do their job. Then our effort is wasted.

WRIGLEY: Not likely. The Proposal Evaluation Committees are made up of supervisors like yourselves and just as anxious for positive change as we are. I know if we come up with some good ideas they will help us push for implementation.
    (*momentary silence*)

SAXBE: I think you'll find that most persons will be acting as a team in this total effort. What do you think, Mrs. Cline?

CLINE: (*surprised*) Oh! I . . . ah . . . I agree with you and Mr. Wrigley.

McCLEARY: (*to Cline*) Thinking about what to fix for dinner tonight, Betty?
    (*general laughter*)

LOWELL: (*to McCleary*) I'd expect a statement like that from you, Bill McCleary. You're always making demeaning statements about women employees.

FISHER: (*to Saxbe*) Mr. Saxbe, do we do *this* for four hours? I don't know where we're going and I, for one, could sure use a cup of coffee.

31

SAXBE: The group can elect to break when it chooses. In fact, this group is what might be termed a *temporary organization* by behavioral scientists. We exist for a specific purpose and for a specific eight week period of time. After that, like all other Phase II problem solving groups, we will be officially disbanded. As such, we can establish all of our own rules such as our choice of problem, method of operation, and leadership.

BLACKMAN: I take it then, Mr. Saxbe, that you are not our leader?

SAXBE: No. As a representative of the Postal Service Management Institute, I am officially called a *facilitator*. It is your group, your problem, and your leadership responsibility.

EVANS: Exactly what is the role of a facilitator?

SAXBE: That depends largely on your group. Officially my concern is with *group process*; that is, how well you work together. I will help you to work better together if that appears to become a problem. I may possibly *intervene* or break into your discussion if I feel little or no progress is being made. Officially, I have little to do with group *content* or *problem content*. You are the experts regarding postal problems. I certainly am not. However, informally or unofficially, I will be happy to ask questions or check your thinking along this line as well.

LOWELL: You're an observer then on how well we do?

SAXBE: No. My job is not to judge, rate, or compare you to one another or to other groups. Think of me as an impartial resource person who is here to help.

CLINE: Sounds good to me.

SMITH: Seems to me that you've got the easy job Saxbe.

SAXBE: I do.

MCCLEARY: Hey Smitty. You know the old saying . . . the more money you make the less you have to do . . .

(general laughter)

FISHER: No one answered my question about breaks. This is the end of my duty tour[4] and normally I'd be on my way home to bed. I could really use some coffee!

WRIGLEY: I'm sure we all understand your problem, Mr. Fisher, and I suggest we take a break in a moment. First, though, I think we should do several important administrative things. While we were talking I jotted a few notes on paper.

(reading aloud from his notes)

1. Select a leader for the group:
   (a) Permanently for the eight meetings or . . .
   (b) Rotate leadership at each meeting.

---

[4]End of his work shift.

2. Have someone take minutes at each meeting and obtain copies for each of us.

3. Have each person comment on a particular Postal Service problem he or she knows to exist or an operating method which can be improved. We can write down all the problems and then get a consensus on the one or two problems which have the broadest appeal to the entire group. Clearly we can't work on them all.

4. Set objectives for each of our eight meetings and try to stick to them.

5. Have some oral or written critique at the end of each session to see how well we performed both in content and process. Perhaps Mr. Saxbe can help here.

(*momentary silence*)

HERNANDEZ: You've got it pretty well thought out, Mr. Wrigley. Why don't you be our leader. I'll nominate you.

CLINE: Sounds good to me.

FISHER: Are we going to do all of these things before we have coffee?

EVANS: I think we ought to at least resolve the leadership problem before coffee break. Then when we come back we can develop our official agenda.

BLACKMAN: Evans is right. Without some titular leader we'll be just spinning our wheels. Mr. Saxbe, you're here to facilitate ... what do you think?

SAXBE: It is highly unusual for a group to meet for the purpose of solving real organizational problems without the leader and agenda having been developed in advance. Your frustration is common to leaderless groups at this point. What you are realizing is that *all groups* develop one or more leaders even when leadership is not externally imposed. I agree that something must be done about the leadership problem.

FISHER: Well, let's get on with it then. I'm dying for a cup of coffee!

Author's Notes

1. All references to the United States Postal Service, the Postal Service Management Institute, and the Phase I and Phase II management training programs are true. Progress in problem solving and the implementation of less costly, more effective operating procedures by the new Postal Service is, in the view of the author, very encouraging. However, the Phase II team alluded to in this case is fictional as are their specific comments. The dialogue though is not atypical for a small group of people who are interacting in their first hour together.

2. Our hypothetical team is twice revisited in later sections of this book as they continue their problem solving activity:

   (a) In the Problem Analysis and Decision Making section the case titled, *Let's Take a Vote*, poses questions of procedure and technique in group decision making.

   (b) In the Personal Identity, Values and Ethics section the case titled, *Some People Just Don't Care Anymore*, examines two of today's most distressing work related behavioral problems:

      • Repetitive and unchallenging work.
      • Lack of personal identity with work.

Discussion Questions

1. Saxbe indicated that the existence of a group officially designated or created for the purpose of solving real organizational problems without a pre-established leader, agenda, or goal(s) is uncommon. Why? Discuss.
2. Must all groups have a leader? Explain.
3. How does leadership emerge or evolve in a small group?
4. What is the difference between a titular leader and the real leader in a group?
5. Can dual or multiple leadership exist in a work group? Explain.
6. Is dual or multiple leadership a short term phenomenon or can either be permanent in a given group? Explain.
7. Discuss the term *influence* as it relates to leadership.
   (a) What is formal influence?
   (b) What is informal influence?
8. Does the subordinate work group influence the leader? How? What are the implications of this upward influence?
9. Does the nature of the task to be performed have any bearing on the type (style) of leader the group should have to be most effective? Explain.
10. Explain the term, *power gap* as it applies to leaders and groups.
11. How should the hypothetical Phase II group proceed at this point?

Special Projects

1. Have participants list and discuss the building blocks upon which one establishes group leadership when it is not externally determined. For example:
   (a) Seniority?   (c) Charisma?
   (b) Expertise?   (d) etc.
2. Have selected class participants assume the roles of the postal personnel in this case. Seat them around a large table (preferable) or in a circle and have them read the case aloud. Then, have them extemporaneously continue the dialogue until they have selected a leader and settled other minor administrative matters. Other participants can act as observers and, after about 10–15 minutes, report orally on their observations. Place emphasis for observers on:
   (a) *Content.* What did they say? Was it logical?

(b) *Process*. What went on in the group? What helped the group and what hindered the group?

   If a leader is selected, what were the apparent grounds for his choice by the group? Is he or she a known leader in class?

Selected References

Books

Allen, L. A. *The Management Profession*. New York: McGraw-Hill, 1958, Chapters 1, 4.

Schein, E. H. *Process Consultation: Its Role In Organization Development*. Reading, Massachusetts: Addison-Wesley, 1969.

Walton, R. E. *Interpersonal Peacemaking: Confrontations and Third Party Consultation*. Reading, Massachusetts: Addison-Wesley, 1969.

Zelko, H. P. *The Business Conference: Leadership and Participation*. New York: McGraw-Hill, 1969, Chapters 3, 4, 8.

Anthologies

Hampton, D. R., Summer, C. E., and Webber, R. A. (Eds.). *Organizational Behavior and the Practice of Management*. Glenview, Illinois: Scott, Foresman and Company, 1968.
   Barnard, C. I. "The Theory of Authority," p. 451.
   Goldhammer, H., and Shils, E. "Types of Power and Status," p. 480.
   Kolb, H. D. "The Headquarters Staff Man in the Role of a Consultant," p. 518.
   Mechanic, D. "Sources of Power of Lower Participants in Complex Organizations," p. 425.
   Simon, H., Smithburg, D., and Thompson, V. "Authority: Its Nature and Motives," p. 461.

Leavitt, H. J., and Pondy, L. R. (Eds.). *Readings in Managerial Psychology*, Chicago, Illinois: University of Chicago Press, 1964.
   Henry, W. E. "Psychodynamics of the Executive Role," p. 112.
   Thelen, H., and Dickerman, W. "The Growth of Groups," p. 382.

Koontz, H., O'Donnell, C. *Management: A Book of Readings*. New York: McGraw-Hill, 1968.
   Jennings, E. "The Anatomy of Leadership," p. 453.
   O'Donnell, C. "The Source of Managerial Authority," p. 24.

Articles

Bennis, W. "I Say Hello, You Say Goodbye," *Innovation*, Number One, 1969, p. 3.

Joyce, J. R. "The Search for Leaders," *Personnel Journal*, April 1970, p. 308.

Reith, J. "Meetings Cost Money—Make Them Pay Off!" *Training and Development Journal*, October 1970, p. 8.

Wohlking, W. "Structured and Spontaneous Role Playing: Contrast and Comparison," *Training and Development Journal*, January 1971, p. 8.

Woody, R. H., and Woody, J. D. "Behavioral Science Consultation," *Personnel Journal*, May 1971, p. 382.

THE SECRET OF BRADFORD'S WAREHOUSE

"...when we are not in a hurry to get things done right, we overorganize, overman, overspend and underaccomplish."

DAVID PACKARD
Assistant Secretary of Defense
August 1970

Robert Bradford was obviously enjoying the press conference being held in his honor:

REPORTER 1: Mr. Bradford, were you surprised when the congressional committee investigating defense contracting procedures today singled out your operation and praised it as a model of efficiency?

BRADFORD: Yes, I certainly was. We in the aerospace business are used to criticism from the Congress and various defense agencies. It was a pleasant change to have one's company lauded for its achievements.

REPORTER 2: But Mr. Bradford, the congressional committee specifically alluded to Bradford's Warehouse in its published remarks and not to the Ingersoll-Standard Corporation as a whole. Indeed, other segments of your corporation have come under fire recently for extensive schedule slippages and cost overruns.

BRADFORD: I haven't seen the entire text of the committee report. If they specifically referred to the Warehouse, then I am certainly honored and share this honor with my entire design and production team.

REPORTER 3: Mr. Bradford, could you tell us exactly what is meant by the term, Bradford's Warehouse?

BRADFORD: Well, about seven years ago Ingersoll-Standard quietly received an Air Force contract for a classified tactical missile system. Even today I am unable to reveal the scope or nature of the equipment involved because of security reasons.

At the time the effort was so security sensitive that the Air Force wished to have the entire project handled in a separate physical area so that all persons without a need-to-know could be easily excluded. The Air Force was also extremely concerned about compressing the time schedule as much as possible.

Ingersoll-Standard responded by acquiring a nearby vacant production facility which, subsequently, became known as the Warehouse. It was staffed by a small, highly select team of professionals which achieved the results desired by the Air Force. Since that time the same basic team has been involved in several other aerospace programs operating from the same location.

REPORTER 2:   Mr. Bradford, you've mentioned the Warehouse several times but isn't the more usual term, *Bradford's Warehouse*?

BRADFORD: Yes, I suppose you're right. I've been the General Manager of the Warehouse operation since its inception and my name has become associated with it by many persons both inside and outside the corporation.

REPORTER 3:   The congressional committee noted the efficiency with which your people have developed complex systems. They said your operation had a remarkably good cost and schedule record which is inconsistent with the prevailing industry record. Would you comment on this?

BRADFORD: At the Warehouse we strive to meet or exceed all contractual requirements.

REPORTER 1:   Could you be more explicit? Exactly what is the secret of Bradford's Warehouse?

BRADFORD: There is no secret . . . just common sense. First, we're very selective in our use of talent. When a new project comes in we evaluate its manpower needs relative to our available talent. If necessary we "borrow" persons from other Ingersoll divisions. These persons are particularly selected for their past accomplishments, inventive ideas, ability to work rapidly, and their probable compatibility with existing Warehouse personnel.

Secondly, we use only a quarter to a third the number of people usually assigned to a project of equivalent magnitude. In this way we virtually eliminate job overlaps and work duplication. We stretch every bit of creative talent out of each person on the team. Decisions are made at the lowest possible level and formal meetings are kept to an absolute minimum.

We also demand and get maximum design latitude so we don't have to submit time consuming and costly engineering change proposals to the government every time we run into a design snag. We trust our designers and we expect the contracting agency to trust us to meet the design parameters as originally developed.

Lastly, we keep all paperwork to an absolute minimum. We have successfully refused to submit the normal twenty tons of progress reports on projects of this type. Instead we provide periodic reports of our own simplified design.

REPORTER 3:   Your critics say that your management methods are ruthless . . . that you run Bradford's Warehouse with an iron hand. It is also widely known that you refuse entry to anyone who is not part of the project team. It is even rumored that you refused a visit by a certain General because you felt the facility tour would waste too much time. Is this true?

> BRADFORD: Our work is best accomplished with as few "advisors" as possible ... whether part of our corporation or not. However, I recall no instance in which a high ranking government official with a need-to-know clearance was barred from the Warehouse. Now, regarding my ruthlessness, I suggest you talk to my people ...

The news of the congressional committee report had been received about noon ,and, at the request of local newspapers and the television stations, the press conference had been hastily called that afternoon at the Ingersoll Executive Briefing Room. Many company officials were on hand with Corporate public relations personnel being most visible.

Not all Ingersoll-Standard officials were elated by the publicity. One executive later confided the following information to a reporter with the explicit understanding that it was off-the-record and, if printed, a denial would be issued.

> Bradford's Warehouse has to be put in its proper organizational perspective. Their output represents less than 15 percent of the total of our aerospace operations. Fortunately, Bob Bradford has a direct telephone line to our president, Mr. Ingersoll. When Bradford wants something he simply phones Ingersoll and he gets it! This fouls up all other priorities and schedules and the rest of us make a poorer showing as a result. It's a classic case of the tail wagging the dog!
>
> Bradford indiscriminately "raids" other projects for people whenever he wants them. I've had several top designers stolen by Bradford. This leaves me with unfilled positions and further schedule delays.
>
> Bradford also consistently circumvents established procedures and someone else has to pick up the broken pieces he leaves along his path. For example, his engineers ignore the Purchasing Department and deal directly with vendors. You can imagine the problems that creates for others.
>
> Next, I suppose Harry Ingersoll will suggest that all managers employ the *miraculous* Bradford methods. That would be analogous to King Arthur asking the knights of the round table to establish priorities in a free-for-all with broadswords! If it comes to that, Ingersoll can expect my resignation. Extending the use of Bradford's management techniques to other parts of the company would signal the end for Ingersoll-Standard in the aerospace industry!

Discussion Questions

1. The congressional committee is obviously pleased with Bradford's Warehouse. Is this operation successful for the reasons stated by Bradford?
2. What is the validity of the comments made by the unnamed official?
3. Could the Bradford methods be successfully extended to other parts of the company?
4. What other problems are involved here?
5. How does your company organize to meet unusual project or product demands?

Special Project

In the real world of business and industry, managers seldom "fit" classic textbook leadership styles or patterns. Divide the class into sub-groups of 4–5 persons each and have each sub-group discuss the following:

1. What is Bob Bradford's leadership style as might be represented by:
   (a) Theory X – Theory Y (McGregor)?
   (b) Authoritative – Participative (Likert, others)?
   (c) Management Grid (Blake and Mouton)?
2. In what ways does Bradford appear to deviate from his predominant style?
3. How does (and how should) a manager alter his usual style to meet different environmental needs?
4. What are the dangers or fallacies of attempting to classify a manager according to a style of leadership? Of what value is a study of leadership style?

Allow 30 minutes for small group discussion and have one person in each subgroup report its findings to the entire class.

Selected References

Books
Bassett, G. A. *Management Styles in Transition*. New York: American Management Association, 1966.
Blake, R. R., and Mouton, J. S. *Building a Dynamic Corporation Through Grid Organization Development*. Reading, Massachusetts: Addison-Wesley, 1969.
Blake, R. R., and Mouton, J. S. *Corporate Excellence Through Grid Organization Development*. Houston, Texas: Gulf Publishing, 1968.
Blake, R. R., and Mouton, J. S. *The Managerial Grid: Key Orientations for Achieving Production Through People*. Houston, Texas: Gulf Publishing, 1965.
Drucker, P. F. *The Effective Executive*. New York: Harper & Row, 1966.
Jackson, T., and Spurlock, J. *Research and Development Management*. Homewood, Illinois: Dow Jones-Irwin, Inc., 1966, Chapters 2, 3.

Anthologies
Hampton, D. R., Summer, C. E., and Webber, R. A. (Eds.). *Organizational Behavior and the Practice of Management*. Glenview, Illinois: Scott, Foresman and Company, 1968. Gellerman, S. W. "The Competence and Power Motives," p. 118.
Huseman, R., Logue, C., and Freshley, D. *Readings in Interpersonal and Organizational Communication*. Boston, Massachusetts: Holbrook Press, Inc., 1969. Galbraith, J. R. "Influencing the Decision to Produce," p. 219.
Koontz, H., and O'Donnell, C. *Management: A Book of Readings*. New York: McGraw-Hill, 1968.
Koontz, H. "Challenges for Intellectual Leadership in Management," p. 647.
Tannenbaum, R., and Massarik, F. "Leadership: A Frame of Reference," p. 463.

Articles
Hodgetts, R. M. "Leadership Techniques in the Project Organization," *Academy of Management Journal*, June 1968, p. 211.
Morton, J. "The Manager as Maxwell's Demon," *Innovation*, Number One, 1969, p. 38.
Park, F. "With Your Money and My Brains," *Innovation*, Number One, 1969, p. 56.

WHAT'S WRONG WITH WONG?

It was brown-bag time for the night shift maintenance mechanics. Pike and Monico were already eating at a small work bench next to the parts storage bins when Hazard arrived.

"Where have you been?" asked Pike.

"Servicing the conveyor belts in department B-9," replied Hazard as he snapped open his lunch bucket and took out a sandwich.

"You did that last week," said Pike. "Isn't that a monthly preventative maintenance job?"

"I guess so," said Hazard, "but Jimmy Joe wanted me to re-check the bearings and look for belt wear."

"Please," said Monico, "let us speak more respectfully of our great leader. You know we should refer to him as Mr. James Joseph Wong."

"Oh, no," countered Pike, "I believe the master of night shift plant maintenance would prefer to be called General Wong."

"Most certainly, General Wong . . . the Oriental autocrat," said Monico, playing along.

Monico and Pike bowed their heads ceremoniously.

"I think you guys are being too hard on Jimmy Joe," said Hazard, between bites.

"Come on, Hazard," said Monico. "Face it. Ever since they promoted Wong to supervisor three months ago he's been different . . . a regular dictator."

"That's right," added Pike. "Wong was completely different when he was just one of us guys in maintenance. But he really began to give the orders the moment he took over."

Pike continued, "None of the old procedures were good enough for him. He had to re-schedule everything. Then he promised management even more output on our shift. He really changed when he was given more power."

"I've seen this before," said Monico. "Promote a good guy from the ranks and he turns on you. When a man gets a blue stripe[1] on his badge he's not the guy you used to know."

"Hey, that's clever. That's exactly how to describe Wong," said Pike smiling broadly. "Try this fellas . . . where's the Joe I used to know?"

[1]Blue stripe. In this instance a color pattern on a standard employee identification badge to draw visual distinction between supervisors and non-supervisors. Color coding of employee badges is quite common.

Monico and Pike roared with laughter and even Hazard smiled.

"I've got another," said Monico. "How about...what's wrong with Wong?"

"Crazy!" said Pike applauding.

"Well, I don't know," said Hazard, pouring coffee from his thermos, "I don't see Jimmy Joe that way. He's certainly nice to me and I don't feel I've been working any harder since he took over. In fact, I think Jimmy Joe has improved our operation. You have to admit it was a little sloppy when Haney ran it."

"You rate busting kids never seem to learn," said Pike shaking his head. "We have pre-set standards for charging our time which allow for emergencies you can't predict. So, even though battery replacement in a lift truck takes only twenty minutes, we charge thirty minutes. The extra time is for emergency repairs as they come up...that's what you and General Wong don't seem to understand about the maintenance business."

"Right," said Monico. "Wong is squeezing out all our emergency time to make himself look good at our expense. Boy, will it hit the fan around here the first time we have a major breakdown."

"I don't happen to feel that way," said Hazard finishing his coffee.

"I think the new standards are fair...they correct some excesses created by equipment changes over the years."

Hazard stood up and closed his lunchbox.

"Look you guys," he said, "I've got to get back to check that conveyor again. But if you're that upset about the rates why don't you talk to Jimmy Joe?"

"That won't do any good," said Pike, "He's locked in like granite."

"Can't talk to him about anything anymore now that he's such a big, important man," added Monico as Hazard left.

"Got time for a cigarette?" asked Pike.

Monico glanced at his watch. "Yea, I guess we have five minutes yet."

The two mechanics lit up and exchanged predictions about the coming Sunday's pro football schedule.

"Mind if I join you guys?" It was Wong holding a vending machine sandwich and a cup of coffee.

"No, not at all, Jimmy Joe," said Pike as he put out his cigarette. "But, I've got to get back out and finish that assembly department repair job."

"Me too," said Monico. "I'm behind schedule now."

James Joseph Wong ate alone.

Discussion Questions

1. What is the basic leadership problem(s) suggested by these discussions?
2. Is Wong overreacting to his new leadership responsibilities or has the group perception of him changed? Or both? Discuss.
3. What is the perception of Wong, the leader as seen by:
   (a) Pike and Monico?
   (b) Hazard?
   (c) Wong?
4. What is the proper leadership role for a supervisor who works with his former peer group?
5. What should the leader do when he finds himself alienated from part (or all) of his work group?
6. Discuss this case in terms of:
   (a) Organizational communication.
   (b) Leadership styles and techniques.
   (c) Team building.

Special Project

Assume you are James Joseph Wong, a qualified mechanic who has been promoted to supervisor. Departmental performance has been adequate but not outstanding. You supervise six competent mechanics, former peers, who like maximum autonomy in their work. They respect you as a mechanic but are unsure of you as a leader. Develop a leadership framework which you feel will be most appropriate:
   (a) Now (just after your promotion).
   (b) A year from now.
Are the styles different with time? Why or why not?

This project can be done in small discussion groups of 4–5 participants each or in large group discussion.

Selected References

Books

Knowles, H. P., and Saxberg, B. O. *Personality and Leadership Behavior*. Reading, Massachusetts: Addison-Wesley, 1971.

Tannenbaum, R., Weschler, I. R., and Massarik, F. *Leadership and Organization: A Behavioral Science Approach*. New York: McGraw-Hill, 1961.

Anthologies

Hampton, D. R., Summer, C. E., and Webber, R. A. (Eds.). *Organizational Behavior and the Practice of Management*. Glenview, Illinois: Scott, Foresman and Company, 1968. Tannenbaum, R., and Schmidt, W. "How to Choose a Leadership Pattern," p. 501.

Huseman, R., Logue, C., and Freshley, D. *Readings in Interpersonal and Organizational Communication*. Boston, Massachusetts: Holbrook Press, Inc., 1969. Schultz, R. S. "How to Handle Grievances," p. 310.

Luthans, F., and Wortman, M. S. *Emerging Concepts in Management*. Toronto, Canada: The Macmillan Company, 1969. Hunt, J. G. "Breakthrough in Leadership Research," p. 115.

Articles

Balk, W. L. "Status Perception of Management 'Peers'," *Academy of Management Journal*, December 1969, p. 431.

Bavelas, A. "Leadership: Man and Function," *Administrative Science Quarterly*, March 1960, p. 491.

Brianas, J. G. "Between Employees and Supervisors: Three Cases In Point," *Personnel Journal*, November 1970, p. 892.

Evans, M. G. "Leadership and Motivation: A Core Concept," *Academy of Management Journal*, March 1970, p. 91.

Fielder, F. E. "Engineer the Job to Fit the Manager," *Harvard Business Review*, September–October 1965, p. 115.

Gaedke, J. "A Style of Managing," *Personnel Journal*, May 1970, p. 404.

Grote, R. C. "Effect of Leadership Changes On A Work Group," *Training and Development Journal*, July 1971, p. 18.

O'Rourke, P. "You, Too, Can Help Your Group!," *Training and Development Journal*, March 1970, p. 40.

Wernimont, P. F. "What Supervisors and Subordinates Expect of Each Other," *Personnel Journal*, March 1971, p. 204.

THE CASE OF THE CLANDESTINE COFFEE BREAK

"As one of a number of rapid changes which occurred in our organization last spring, the coffee machines disappeared. Our new General Manager had embarked on an efficiency and cleanliness campaign which, I think, reached absurd proportions when he made that particular decision.

"He apparently felt that coffee in office areas was unsightly. Coffee drinking wasn't banned as such. Coffee was available for thirty minutes prior to the start of work (7:30–8:00 a.m.) in the employee cafeteria but was not to be taken to the workplace. Coffee was again available in the cafeteria at mid-morning (9:45–10:15 a.m.) and at lunch (11:30 a.m.–1:15 p.m.) but the same workplace coffee drinking restriction applied.

"What the General Manager did was to remove all coffee vending machines from the halls. We used to stop by these machines several times each day because they were so convenient, take coffee back to our desks, and sip it while we worked. Now, suddenly, the machines were gone.

"People like me, Phyllis Carter, so completely addicted to the hot caffeine brew, now had several unpleasant alternatives to face.

"I could:

1. Skip morning coffee (unthinkable!)
2. Drink my coffee in my car on way to work (unsafe).
3. Come to work early (UGH!) and have coffee in the cafeteria.
4. Walk to the cafeteria at break time (and use up most of my break time walking).

5. Have coffee in the cafeteria at lunch and discipline myself not to eat any fattening goodies (I preferred to stay at my desk during lunch and eat three or four diet cookies with coffee. It's hard not to eat when you see all that good food and I *really* have to watch my weight).

"I talked the problem out at length with the other girls in the typing pool. They agreed with me that none of these coffee break alternatives was very palatable (no pun intended). So we did the only reasonable thing a group of working girls could do under the circumstances. We chipped in and bought our own coffee maker.

"The system worked quite well . . . at least for a while. The obvious place to hide the coffee maker was in the office supplies storage area located in the far corner of the typing pool office. The storage area was partially walled off from the rest of our office by five foot metal partitions. This kept most of the unsightly paper supplies storage out of sight but still convenient for us.

"Rarely did a visitor go into the storage area. When someone needed paper or pencils or any other company supplied item they were supposed to ask Edna Frank and she would fill their request. Management liked this approach because Edna handed out pencils like she was paying for them herself.

"To be safe we hid the coffee maker in the small metal cabinet which served as a base for the mimeograph machine. It was a perfect place! We took out the paper supplies and re-shelved them elsewhere. There was room for the coffee maker plus extra coffee and cups. We ran the electric cord through a small hole at the rear of the cabinet to a nearby convenience outlet. With the cabinet doors closed nothing looked out of the ordinary . . . nothing at all.

"Before leaving work each day one of us would clean and add fresh water to the coffee pot. We thought that this would be the most difficult part since the pot had to be smuggled to the ladies' room or a nearby custodial closet sink. We soon found though that we didn't have to be quite so secretive; others were clearly looking the other way. Apparently we weren't the only ones who had the idea.

"First thing each morning we'd plug it in and, minutes later, coffee would be ready. There was room in the storage area for two stools and so we generally took our breaks right there; you know, in shifts so it would look like everything was normal in the area. As time passed most of us got bolder and began to drink coffee right at our desks. Although many supervisors came into our area each day, no one ever said anything about the coffee cups.

"Yesterday morning when I arrived at work, there was the General Manager in our area . . . holding the coffee maker! His message was short and simple . . . it goes or we go! It went. I still don't know who blew the whistle on us . . . probably that creepy custodian who's always trying to make a pass.

"Anyhow, this morning there was a memo from the General Manager to all personnel stating that all coffee pots were to be removed from the office by the end of the week. Any offender found next Monday or thereafter would be subject to a three day suspension or to termination for repeated violations.

"I'm thinking of bringing down a jar of instant coffee and buying one of those little heating coils used by travelers to boil water. That way I can make coffee for myself, one cup at a time. And I won't be breaking the new edict on coffee pots!"

Discussion Questions

1. The General Manager is reported to have said to his secretary, "Phyllis Carter is typical of those people who will do anything to beat the system. No matter what the rule is, she'll figure out some way to get around it. Some people are just that way." Discuss.
2. What other more reasonable approach could have been taken by Phyllis Carter and others in the typing pool rather than setting up a clandestine coffee break system?
3. What can we say about the leadership styles and methods of the General Manager?
4. It is often said that people resist change, even when change brings improvement. Discuss.
5. Another school of though contends that people do not resist change but that they often resist the methods that management employs to bring about change. Discuss.

Special Projects

1. Prepare and submit a well-documented research paper on the subject of *resistance to change*. You should include, but not be limited to, the following subtopics on resistance to change:

   1. Purpose of change unclear or ambiguous.
   2. Personnel not involved in planning.
   3. Work group norms or habits are ignored.
   4. Communication is weak or secretive.
   5. Appeal for change based on personal grounds.
   6. Fear of failure.
   7. No reward or incentive for change.

8. Excessive current work pressure.
9. Employees like the current methods or procedures.

2. Review leadership style concepts such as *Theory X and Theory Y* by Douglas McGregor, *Management Systems* by Rensis Likert, or *The Managerial Grid* by Robert Blake. Relate leadership styles as illustrated in this situation to a standard "style" as defined by McGregor, Likert, or Blake.

Selected References

Books
Adorno, T. W. *The Authoritarian Personality*. New York: Harper & Row, 1950.
Tannenbaum, R., Massarik, F., and Weschler, I. R. *Leadership and Organization: A Behavioral Science Approach*. New York: McGraw-Hill, 1961.

Anthologies
Huseman, R., Logue, C., and Freshley, D. *Readings in Interpersonal and Organizational Communication*. Boston, Massachusetts: Holbrook Press, Inc., 1969. Buchanan, P. C. "How Can 'We' Gain 'Their' Commitment?" p. 211.
Koontz, H., and O'Donnell, C. *Management: A Book of Readings*. New York: McGraw-Hill, 1968.
    Golembiewski, R. T. "Three Styles of Leadership and Their Uses," p. 475.
    Peck, G. A. "The Mechanics of Implementation," p. 156.
Leadership on the Job. Lazarus, S. "What to do When You've 'Goofed'." New York: American Management Association, 1966, p. 262.

Articles
Argyris, C. "Resistance To Rational Management Systems," *Innovation*, Number Ten, 1970, p. 28.
Colin, J. M. "After X and Y Comes Z," *Personnel Journal*, January 1971, p. 56.
Genfan, H. "Managing Change," *Personnel Journal*, November 1969, p. 910.
Lawrence, P. R. "How to Deal With Resistance to Change," *Harvard Business Review*, January–February 1969, p. 4.
Slote, W. H. "The Self-Destructive Manager," *Innovation*, Number Sixteen, 1970, p. 16.
(Staff) "Whips, Smiles and Other Management Tools," *Industry Week*, April 20, 1970, p. 35.

THE FALL OF BAINBRIDGE HOUSE

A year ago last July, Arthur Bainbridge carefully placed the ball on the seventeenth tee of the Carolina Valley Golf Course in surburban Raleigh, North Carolina, and took several practice swings. He wiped his brow and lowered his cap, shielding his eyes from the hot afternoon sun. Then, he dug in his spikes firmly, swung with unusual accuracy, and drove the ball into a very long high arc. It dropped just at the edge of the green and rolled within a scant yard and a half of the hole. While his golf partners applauded, Bainbridge threw both arms upward in sheer joy; then, without warning, he faltered and fell to the ground.

Bainbridge House began to die that very day although to outsiders it still appears to be well and flourishing. But to anyone familiar with the customs, traditions, and attitudes of the firm it is clear that it is unlikely to survive much longer.

Curiously, this is not the story of the indispensable man but rather of an unusual but not uncommon sequence of events which has brought the firm to near ruin.

Raised in a family of furniture builders, Arthur Bainbridge was a master furniture craftsman by his mid-twenties. He started his own firm a few years later and Bainbridge House soon earned the distinction of being one of the finest small furniture manufacturers along the Atlantic Seaboard. Bainbridge House had generally avoided fabrics and coverings and concentrated instead on a limited line of custom crafted wood tables, chairs, and decorative pieces.

Arthur Bainbridge was always aware that it took a number of skills to run his High Point factory and that he did not have them all. Over the years he hired a small, but efficient, front office staff and an excellent finance man, Jess Forster. Two master designers were brought in from larger firms nearby and the finest furniture builders in the business soon began to gravitate to Bainbridge House. A solid network of representatives placed the line in custom furniture houses across the country.

No, Arthur Bainbridge was not indispensable and did not intend to be. Drawing upon scholars from Duke University and North Carolina State, Bainbridge House developed a modest, but workable internal organizational development plan which became a model for graduate student analysis for several years. The small team was at least as strong and capable as any in the industry.

Charlotte Bainbridge, now the sole owner, ran the firm in absentia for six months. The existing management team functioned reasonably well after the sudden loss of the president but profits were cut sharply by a sudden drop in demand for custom specialty furniture.

An attorney, and long time family friend, advised Charlotte to sell Bainbridge House, which she finally consented to do. Jess Forster headed a small group of management personnel who attempted to obtain adequate financing for its purchase. They were successful in obtaining the necessary financial backing but unsuccessful in the purchase itself. With great reluctance, Charlotte Bainbridge accepted a significantly larger offer from a Boston financial conglomerate.

The new owners were noted for using a return-on-investment ratio for all of their holdings. Elston G. Springer, a vice-president, was assigned operating responsibility for Bainbridge House and began a series of moves to return it to an acceptable level of profitability.

In capsule form, the following happened:

First Quarter

1. Springer ordered two specialty "losers" cut from the line.
2. The marketing manager objected vigorously.
3. Austere budgets were imposed on all departments.
4. The office staff was reduced.
5. A loss in the prior quarter was partly offset by a small profit in the first quarter.

Second Quarter

1. Early retirements among the older, higher paid furniture builders and finishers were encouraged.
2. Capital equipment expenditures were deferred.
3. Jess Forster objected vigorously.
4. Several local suppliers were dropped in favor of a new low-bid procurement policy.
5. Second quarter profits were up sharply.

Third Quarter

1. Inspection standards were lightened to reduce the reject and rework rate.
2. The production manager submitted his resignation.
3. The *new* production manager instituted the design of a low cost furniture line using some molded plastic parts to replace traditional hand sculpturing.
4. Jess Forster left Bainbridge House to accept a management position with another firm.
5. Toughened inspection procedures were introduced after numerous field complaints.
6. Profits rose to record levels.
7. Elston Springer, lauded at Corporate for his achievement in "turning around" Bainbridge House, was dispatched to revive another "sick" acquisition.

Fourth Quarter

1. Turnover among craftsmen increased.

2. The new General Manager scrapped plans for the line of low-cost furniture.
3. Quality problems forced a new look at using local suppliers and materials.
4. An abortive attempt at unionization was made.
5. A personnel survey revealed that only 37 percent of those now with the company had been employed before Arthur Bainbridge died.
6. Eight major accounts dropped the Bainbridge House lines near the end of the quarter.
7. Profits were off from the second and third quarter levels but the General Manager was optimistic about the future.

Discussion Questions

1. This case is *not* about the loss of a capable leader. It is *not* a melodramatic plea for participative management. It is *not* a call for family firm togetherness. It is *not* about a few specific marketing and production blunders by an inept manager. What is it about?
2. Discuss the signals which a manager typically receives to let him know everything is going well (or conversely, not going well). Can the signals be contradictory? Explain.
3. Is this situation in any way analogous to that described in *The Case of the Clandestine Coffee Break*? How?
4. What form of leadership would have been most appropriate for the firm after the death of Arthur Bainbridge?
5. Discuss this case in terms of *human resource accounting* as described in *New Patterns of Management* or *The Human Organization* by Rensis Likert.

Special Project

Prepare and submit a well researched paper titled, *Human Resource Accounting: Is It Workable?*

Selected References

Books
Likert, R. *New Patterns of Management.* New York: McGraw-Hill, 1961.
Likert, R. *The Human Organization: Its Management and Value.* New York: McGraw-Hill, 1967.
Simon, H. *Administrative Behavior.* New York: Macmillan, 1963.

Anthologies
Hampton, D. R., Summer, C. E.., and Webber, R. A. (Eds.). *Organizational Behavior and the Practice of Management.* Glenview, Illinois: Scott, Foresman and Company, 1968.
    Guest, R. H. "Organizational Change: The Effect of Successful Leadership," p. 716.
    McGregor, D. "Management By Integration and Self Control," p. 510.
    O'Donnell, C. J. "The Source of Managerial Authority," p. 465.
Leavitt, H. J., and Pondy, L. R. (Eds.). *Readings in Managerial Psychology.* Chicago, Illinois: University of Chicago Press, 1964.

Bavelas, A. "Leadership: Man and Function," p. 200.
Leavitt, H. J. "Unhuman Organizations," p. 542.
Martin, N. H., and Sims, J. H. "Power Tactics," p. 217.

Articles
Allison, D. "Can A System Perform Like A Hero?" *Innovation*, Number Eight, 1969, p. 16.
Coleman, R. J., and Riley, M. J. "The Chief Executive: His Personality Characteristics and the Firm's Growth Rate," *Personnel Journal*, December 1970, p. 994.
James, J. "Training for Leadership," *Training and Development Journal*, May 1970, p. 34.
Paster, I. "The Indispensable Man," *Personnel Journal*, March 1970, p. 246.
Pyle, W. "Accounting For Your People," *Innovation*, Number Ten, 1970, p. 46.
Wright, R. "Managing Man as a Capital Asset," *Personnel Journal*, April 1970, ·p. 290.

CASE STUDY CROSS REFERENCE

Although located elsewhere in this book, the following problem situations are also valuable in the study of Section 2:

3

Problem Analysis and Decision Making

"I hardly consider myself an organizational dictator," continued Farraday, "but I periodically get feedback from within my organization that all major decisions take place in my office. To the contrary, I often feel that most major decisions have been made *before* they ever get to my office!"

JOHN FARRADAY
The Programmed Decision

INTRODUCTION

What is the nature of the problem? Is the problem correctly defined? What decision strategies or alternatives can be developed? Have all alternatives been explored and evaluated? Should the problem be handled by one person or should there be group consensus? How will those affected respond to the decision? How should the decision maker react to low levels of acceptance, negativism, or sabotage? How can individual and group commitment to a decision be effectively achieved?

Cases in This Section

Let's Take a Vote

An unstructured group looks at the decision making process . . . how is a decision to be reached . . . the democratic process questioned . . . the concept of group consensus.

Get Rid of Franklin!

Organizational changes . . . new organizational philosophies . . . supervisory promotions . . . schedule slippages . . . accusations and counter accusations . . . lack of facts . . . highly opinionated suggestions . . . power struggles . . . jealousies . . . guarded statements.

The Programmed Decision

Autocratic decision making re-examined . . . complex technology and decision making . . . too much data . . . lack of verification . . . trust and reliance on specialists . . . a view of decision making from the top of the organization looking downward.

Caldwell's Hatchet Man

Unprofitable operations in multi-division corporation . . . termination of division manager . . . new man in charge . . . severe changes in departmental operations . . . displeased department managers . . . selling a necessary but unpleasant decision . . . acceptance levels . . . commitment versus compliance.

Management by Rumor

Slow sales indicate possibility of employee layoffs . . . a rumor spreads . . . credibility of the rumor . . . poor morale . . . an official statement by top management . . . reactions to the decision . . . acceptance and commitment.

The Great Pizza Fiasco

Introduction of new product lines and new internal ideas . . . an incentive scheme . . . initial employee reactions . . . implementation problems . . . poor communications.

LET'S TAKE A VOTE

Author's note. This case can be studied independently or as a follow on to *Now, About the Question of Leadership*, presented in the Leadership Styles and Techniques section of this book. If used independently, participants should at least read the referenced case to provide proper background and perspective.

Setting. The Superintendent's Office of a large modern postal facility. There is a large conference table around which a number of people are seated.

Participants. Eight men and two women—primarily postal supervisors, carrier route examiners, and finance personnel from various city locations. One person is a trainer-consultant. They are officially assembled as a problem solving team.

Cast

Name		Title	Basic Attitude
Wrigley	(M)	Superintendent	Strong opinions
Hernandez	(M)	Route Examiner	Enthusiastic
Evans	(M)	Assistant Superintendent	Positive but cautious
Blackman	(M)	Assistant Superintendent	Reserved but positive
McCleary	(M)	Finance Examiner	Humorous but positive
Lowell	(F)	Customer Service Representative	Concerned
Smith	(M)	Superintendent	Somewhat negative
Cline	(F)	Finance Examiner	Swings with the majority
Fisher	(M)	Route Examiner	Tired and somewhat bored
Saxbe	(M)	P.S.M.I. trainer[1]	Officially neutral

Mr. Wrigley has been nominated and, by acclamation, elected permanent chairman (leader) of the Postal Service Phase II T.E.A.M. problem solving group. An hour has passed since his election and a subsequent coffee break. During most of that time each participant has been expressing his feelings regarding a problem to which the group should address itself. Blackman has been listing each problem with felt pen on a large flip chart.

The listed problems include:

1. **How to minimize dog bites to letter carriers.**
2. **Improve money handling skills of postal clerks at customer service windows.**
3. **How to prevent mis-sent mail to direct firm holdouts.[2]**
4. **Supervising younger employees who have different value systems.**

[1] P.S.M.I.—Postal Service Management Institute.

[2] *Direct firm holdouts.* To expedite processing and delivery of mail, the United States Postal Service urges large mailers (e.g. banks, department stores, insurance companies) to code return envelopes with postal box numbers or other visible identifiers so this mail can be easily separated from other mail.

This coded incoming mail is separated (held out) at a major postal distribution center and not "mixed" with other mail going to a local post office for delivery. In this way an additional handling is avoided. But, as developed in this situation and more fully in, *Some People Just Don't Care Anymore*, other problems can develop as a result of this mail processing technique.

5. **Better internal communication.**
6. **Reducing absenteeism.**

The group is now engaged in a problem census to determine which problem to select.

WRIGLEY: Well, so far we've agreed to eliminate numbers 1, 2, and 4 as problems this group would like to work to improve. Now then, let's take a straw vote on the remaining problems. How many would like to work on number 3, *How to prevent mis-sent mail to direct firm holdouts?*
(*counts raised hands*)
One . . . two . . . three . . . and I make four.
How about *Better internal communication?*
(*counts hands*)
One . . . two. Okay, reducing absenteeism?
One . . . two.

HERNANDEZ: Hey, who didn't vote?

EVANS: Saxbe and Cline.

SAXBE: The facilitator has no vote.

McCLEARY: (*smiling*) Stand up and be counted, Mrs. Cline.

CLINE: I hesitated because I think they are all very interesting problems and I'll go along with the majority.

HERNANDEZ: Well, that settles it . . . we'll work on mis-sent mail . . .

EVANS: (*upset*) Now wait a second! If we've been assembled to meet here four hours each week for eight weeks, I think we should tackle a really big problem like communication. Lord knows we need better communication!

LOWELL: I agree with Mr. Evans. Communication is a terribly important problem.

WRIGLEY: But, as stated, it's so vague. How do we begin to go about attacking the problem?

HERNANDEZ: It's like the weather. You can talk about it all you want but nobody's going to be able to do much about it.

SMITH: That's for sure!

FISHER: (*irritated*) Let's get on with it! We're not getting anywhere.

HERNANDEZ: Majority rules. We'll work on mis-sent mail.

SAXBE: (*breaking in on group discussion*) Since our purpose here is to better understand the nature of leadership and group process methods as well as solving a particular Postal Service problem, I feel I am justified in intervening at this point. Behavioral scientists agree that the majority vote or so called democratic process is generally better for obtaining personal decision commitment than, say, autocratic choice of the leader . . .

HERNANDEZ: That's what I just said . . . majority rules . . . we'll work on mis-sent . . .

SAXBE: (*interrupting Hernandez*) But majority rule, although a reasonable expedient for the sake of time, is not always the best way . . .

BLACKMAN: What other way is there?

SAXBE: Consensus. Although procedurally slower at first, it can often prove to be better than majority rule.

BLACKMAN: I don't see the difference.

SAXBE: Consensus is a working through of differences to ultimately arrive at a decision whereas the democratic vote has a tendency to arbitrarily cut off all objections, reasonable or not, at a fixed point in time. This can, often, suppress further involvement or commitment by someone whose views have been overruled or denied expression.

SMITH: Good grief! You mean we have to get *everyone* to agree before we move on? We'll be as deadlocked as a hung jury!

BLACKMAN: Exactly what are the implications of consensus to group progress, Mr. Saxbe?

SAXBE: Not nearly as bad as I have apparently made it appear. Your straw vote was procedurally sound. It showed where the majority stands on the issue. My only concern is that the minority should not now be arbitrarily shut off.

FISHER: You mean we keep talking until Evans wins us over to *his* point of view?

SAXBE: Not necessarily, although that could happen. We're not severely time limited. I prefer to see consensus within the group before moving on than to have us work on a democratically chosen problem and not have the full and active support of several persons.

WRIGLEY: I'm a little confused. What should we do next? What is my role as the leader?

SAXBE: I'd ask the group what they think.

WRIGLEY: Okay. (*to group*) Where do we go from here?

LOWELL: I still stand with Mr. Smith, but I do see that we will have some difficulty addressing ourselves to a problem as complex and vague as communication unless we break it down in some way. I suggest we ask our two members who voted for *reducing absenteeism* for their comments.

WRIGLEY: Good idea. Who voted for working on the absenteeism problem?

(*McCleary and Blackman raise hands*)

McCLEARY: Let's not fight, team. (*smiling*) I voted for absenteeism because I see it as a big problem. However, at the large mail processing and distribution centers, absenteeism could be job related ... that is, somehow tied in with carelessness and poor motivation. If I have to make a choice between the two, I lean toward working on the problem of mis-sent mail. (*pause*) Even in discussing that problem I'll still get in some shots at the absenteeism problem. (*general laughter*)

WRIGLEY: I think you're right, McCleary. I have a feeling that excessive absenteeism may well be a symptom of low job motivation. (*momentary silence*)

BLACKMAN: Well, I voted for absenteeism as well. I lean toward taking communication as our problem but it really is too vague as we've stated it up to this point. We'd really have to break it down.

HERNANDEZ: Hey! If we're going to take one aspect of improving communication, why not tie it in with the mis-sent mail problem? Maybe the clerks don't fully understand the implications when they don't "stick"[3] mail correctly? Maybe we have to communicate better or give them better instruction or training. Maybe mis-sent mail involves communication.

CLINE: That's a good idea Mr. Hernandez. I'll go along with that and support the mis-sent mail problem.

BLACKMAN: (*smiling*) I wouldn't want it to get around that I actually agreed on something with Hernandez (*a few chuckles*) but he does have a point. I'll go along with mis-sent mail.

WRIGLEY: All right, that makes seven who support the idea of working on the problem of mis-sent mail.

LOWELL: I really have no objections either, except that as a Customer Service Representative I have no knowledge of operations at the mail processing and distribution centers. I don't feel I will be able to contribute very much.

WRIGLEY: That's not really true, Mrs. Lowell. Some of us are too close to the problem and may not be able to see the forest for the trees. You can check our thinking by asking questions and by offering fresh and unbiased ideas.

LOWELL: You make my role sound very important, Mr. Wrigley. I'm glad we made you the leader. (*general laughter*) I only hope I don't ask too many dumb questions.

HERNANDEZ: (*emphatically*) There is no such thing as a dumb question. Right, Mr. Saxbe?

SAXBE: Right.
(*momentary silence*)

FISHER: Well, what do you say, Mr. Evans? You going to join us?

[3]*Sticking mail.* The process by which a mail clerk reads addresses from unprocessed mail and then sorts mail into organized bins or trays.

EVANS: The group has my support. I'm sorry if I was divisive and held up progress. It's just that I feel so strongly about the communications problem . . .

WRIGLEY: Not at all, Evans. All of us share your general sentiments.

McCLEARY: Hey, Evans, you can still get your shots in . . . like I'm going to.

WRIGLEY: (*summarizing*) It appears then that we have indeed reached a consensus that this group will work on the problem of mis-sent mail to direct firm holdouts.

LOWELL: Mr. Saxbe, is this what you meant by working through differences in arriving at a decision?

SAXBE: Essentially. It took a few minutes longer but the group is now more likely to make better progress from this point forward . . . and with everyone's active support.

CLINE: I think we really work well together.

SAXBE: You do. (*winking*) For all practical purposes I might as well go home.

FISHER: I'll buy that! I'd like to go home too.

Author's Note

Our hypothetical team is again visited in the Identity and Belonging section of this book. In the case titled, *Some People Just Don't Care Anymore*, we see them as they cope with two of today's most distressing work related behavioral problems:

- Repetitive and unchallenging work
- Lack of personal identity with work

Discussion Questions

1. In a group situation such as this where a decision is to be made, what are the wanted and unwanted consequences of:
   (a)   A leader imposed decision?
   (b)   A democratic (majority rules) decision?
   (c)   A decision by consensus?
2. Under what general conditions might a leader imposed decision be best?
3. Under what general conditions might a democratic decision be best?
4. Under what general conditions might decision by consensus be best?
5. Is consensus possible when the leader is not chosen by the group? Explain.
6. What is meant by the term, *pseudo-democratic meeting*?
7. It has been said that a group cannot effectively deal with problems of content until they have effectively resolved their process problems. Explain.

Special Projects

1. Review all statements made by participants and classify them as to whether they are:
   (a) *Primarily content statements.* Do the words deal primarily with the subject under discussion? Do they add to further understanding, clarification, or analysis of the subject?
   (b) *Primarily process statements.* Do the words deal primarily with the interaction of one participant with another? Do they deal with procedural or operational group problems?
2. Obtain a group process book and review sections which specifically cover the subject of individual role in group. Although classified somewhat differently in each text, you will find breakdowns of various roles individuals play in the group (meeting) process; roles which can either help or hinder group progress.

   Such roles are:

   > Energizer
   > Digressor
   > Blocker
   > Facilitator
   > Initiator
   > Summarizer
   > etc.

   Discuss in class the implications of playing each role and match roles to the statements characters made in this particular case.

Selected References

Books

Likert, R. *New Patterns of Management.* New York: McGraw-Hill, 1961.

Maier, N. R. F. *Problem Solving Discussions and Conferences: Leadership Methods and Skills.* New York: McGraw-Hill, 1963.

Maier, N. R. F., and Hayes, J. J. *Creative Management.* New York: Wiley, 1962.

National Training Laboratories. *Handbook of Staff Development and Human Relations Training*: Material Developed for Use in Africa. Institute for Applied Behavioral Science, National Education Association, Washington, D.C., 1967.

Anthologies

Huseman, R., Logue, C., and Freshley, D. *Readings in Interpersonal and Organizational Communication.* Boston, Massachusetts: Holbrook Press, Inc., 1969.
   Bales, R. F. "In Conference," p. 368.
   Heyns, R. W. "What Makes A Conference Tick," p. 356.
   Zelko, H. P. "When You Are 'In Conference'," p. 337.

Koontz, H., and O'Donnell, C. *Management: A Book of Readings.* New York: McGraw-Hill, 1968. O'Donnell, C. "Ground Rules for Using Committees," p. 278.

GET RID OF FRANKLIN!

The Franklin problem apparently started about the time that Harold Newland, president of Newland Electronics Corporation, issued this memorandum:

December 2

To: Staff
From: H. Newland
Subject: Organizational Changes

As you are all well aware, growth at Newland Electronics Corporation this past year has exceeded our planned estimates. Sales of our unique microswitches and relays have risen above the 15 million dollar level with anticipated sales to reach 18.5 million next year. This is a credit to our entire organization.

This growth will require several organizational changes if we are to continue our success pattern. Our new organizational structure will reflect additional specialization within our existing functional groups. For some it will be a blessing, since many persons will not be required to "wear as many hats as before."

Effective immediately, I will personally intensify our efforts in long range product and market planning. Mr. Charles Murphy will become Executive Vice-President, responsible for overall plant management. Mr. Martin Brown will now devote full time to our sales effort as Vice-President—Marketing. We are now seeking a qualified person to assume the position of Vice-President—Finance.

Dr. Arnold Wilson, who has provided much of our recent technological growth as Supervisor of the New Products Group, will become Vice-President—Operations.

Additional changes at other levels will be announced by Mr. Murphy as they are effected.

H. NEWLAND

The next memorandum was released two weeks later:

December 18

To: Staff
From: A. Wilson
Subject: Changes in the Operations Department

The following promotions are announced, effective immediately:

    Edward Bellman—Director of Manufacturing
    Robert Maxey—Director of Engineering
    Matthew Doyle—Supervisor of Product Engineering
    Thomas Carlson—Supervisor of New Products
    Harry Pleasant—Manufacturing Superintendent

The attached organization chart will now apply.

A. WILSON

Approved: C. MURPHY

It was March. Dr. Arnold Wilson had only been Vice-President—Operations, for two months, but it had seemed like a year. It was one thing to solve technical problems as he had been doing as former head of the New Products Group. Lately, however, it seemed as if all he did each day was listen to "people" problems. Now he had another problem.

Wilson was aware that there was some friction between Bill Franklin of Engineering Services and Matthew Doyle of Product Engineering.

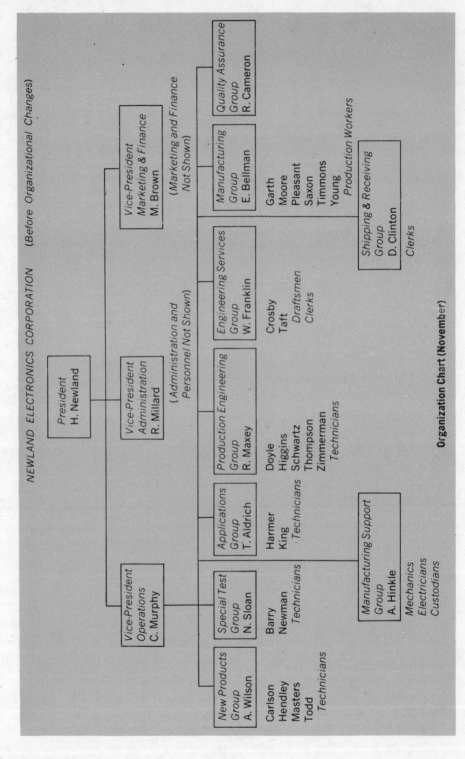

NEWLAND ELECTRONICS CORPORATION (Before Organizational Changes)

President
H. Newland

Vice-President
Operations
C. Murphy

Vice-President
Administration
R. Millard

(Administration and
Personnel Not Shown)

Vice-President
Marketing & Finance
M. Brown

(Marketing and Finance
Not Shown)

New Products
Group
A. Wilson

Carlson
Hendley
Masters
Todd
Technicians

Special Test
Group
N. Sloan

Barry
Newman
Technicians

Applications
Group
T. Aldrich

Harmer
King
Technicians

Production Engineering
Group
R. Maxey

Doyle
Higgins
Schwartz
Thompson
Zimmerman
Technicians

Engineering Services
Group
W. Franklin

Crosby
Taft
Draftsmen
Clerks

Manufacturing
Group
E. Bellman

Garth
Moore
Pleasant
Saxon
Timmons
Young
Production Workers

Quality Assurance
Group
R. Cameron

Manufacturing Support
Group
A. Hinkle

Mechanics
Electricians
Custodians

Shipping & Receiving
Group
D. Clinton

Clerks

Organization Chart (November)

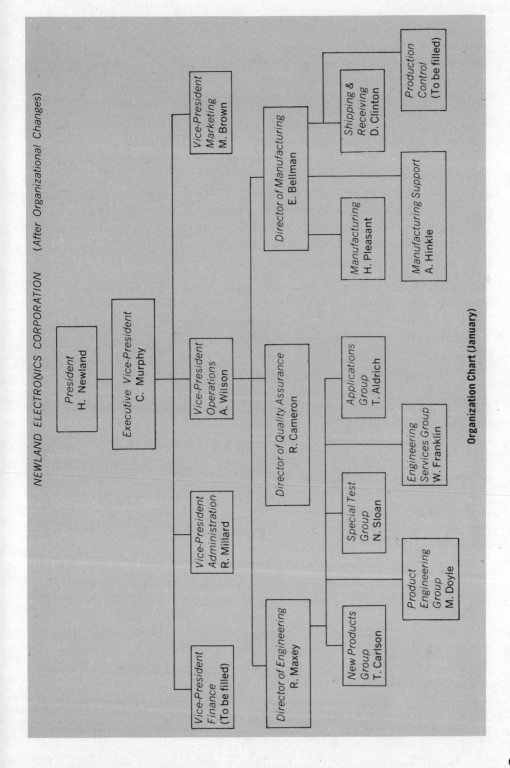

NEWLAND ELECTRONICS CORPORATION (After Organizational Changes)

Organization Chart (January)

61

Apparently the situation had worsened because both Doyle and Bob Maxey, the new Director of Engineering, came to Wilson's office this morning and demanded that Franklin be terminated.

Maxey and Doyle brought two charges against Franklin:

1. Franklin was not cooperating with Doyle's Product Engineering Group (production engineering). Drafting and technical writing support requests were constantly ignored. Projects were falling behind schedule.
2. Franklin personally was too young and inexperienced to handle this responsibility in a growing organization. He also was lacking in technical electronics know-how and preferred drinking coffee to learning his job. He ran his group like a kindergarten—all for fun and no effort.

Their proposal was to terminate Franklin or transfer him out of the Engineering Department. Maxey did not have authority to terminate a group supervisor and had brought the problem to Wilson.

Bill Franklin was twenty-nine and an Industrial Management graduate. He had spent two years in the Army and had been at Newland for three years. He started as an engineer in Product Engineering when the supervisor there was Milt Henry. Henry had liked Franklin, and when Henry decided to leave Newland, he suggested the creation of a new Engineering Services Group to provide technical writing, drafting, and related services to both the engineering and manufacturing areas. It was to be a talent pool on call when needed. Henry suggested young Franklin to head this new group and Franklin got the job.

Henry was not replaced from within. Instead, Charles Murphy selected Robert Maxey, a senior engineer from another small firm within the industry. Maxey was well qualified. He had a B.S. and M.S. in Electrical Engineering and twelve years experience. Maxey later brought in three engineers who had worked with him before . . . Doyle, Higgins, and Zimmerman. From almost that point on there was constant conflict between Franklin and Product Engineering, particularly Maxey and Doyle.

When Maxey and Doyle left, Wilson called Bill Franklin to his office. Franklin was enraged, but not surprised at the charges. He said that Maxey and Doyle told him they were taking the problem to Wilson.

Franklin claimed that over 70 percent of his technical writing and drafting effort was already being supplied to Product Engineering. The remainder was spread out thinly to all other user areas. He agreed he could use more draftsmen, but felt the problem was deeper than that. In

Franklin's opinion, Maxey and Doyle just had to have everything their own way. They were demanding a complete change in the drawing and specification numbering system. Franklin felt they wanted specifications systems like those used in their prior company. They were also purposely hypercritical of errors, and vastly exaggerated this as supposed incompetence. They really wanted control of drafting and specs by making it part of Product Engineering. Franklin felt this was coming and would not tolerate it.

He stressed his management ability as supervisor of the largest engineering group and felt his people were extremely loyal and hardworking, citing the facts that he had the lowest turnover and absentee rates in the entire plant.

Wilson suggested the possibility of a transfer to manufacturing but Franklin was cool to the idea. He felt it would be a demotion. Franklin offered his solution to the problem. "I'm doing my job like always. Get Maxey and Doyle off my back!"

Wilson decided to get more information from other likely sources. Ed Bellman had an opinion:

"Franklin is a bright young man. We all like him out here. I've heard he is technically weak, but he seems to be a good supervisor. I would consider him in floor supervision or for a spot in our new Production Control Group. I talked with him a few months ago, but he didn't seem very interested."

Wilson (*to himself*) —
Bellman is still miffed at being passed over for Vice-President—Operations. He is a good production man but lacks formal education. He would have difficulty managing my technical people.

Bellman (*to himself*) —
So, Ph.D. Wilson develops a product or two and they start grooming him for the top. I wonder how long he can work these problems out on his slide rule. The men's room scuttlebutt has it that the prima donna engineering types are looking to this Franklin decision as a test of Wilson's management ability. Good luck, Doctor Wilson.

Wilson conducted several additional discussions.

Carlson said:
"I've had no problems with Franklin, but then you (Dr. Wilson) did most of the liaison with him before your promotion. I don't think he fully carries his share though."

Sloan said:

"My complaint is a lack of technical writing. Franklin says it's getting diverted to Product Engineering. The work quality seems all right though. Mr. Maxey and Mr. Doyle are pretty sharp guys and are real assets to our company.

Aldrich said:

"Franklin is a friendly guy, but as an Industrial Management graduate, he just doesn't have enough technical background in electronics. Perhaps night school courses would help. I think the feelings of a new Engineering Manager should be given special consideration."

Cameron said:

"Franklin works relaxed . . . perhaps too relaxed. But he has management organization and personnel ability that puts most of us to shame. Several months ago I tried to talk two of his men into a transfer to Quality Assurance. I thought they would jump at the opportunity even though no raises were involved. Neither one left."

Wilson had been trained to be a logical person and was disturbed by the emotional way almost everyone had responded when the Franklin situation was discussed. Wilson wished he had more facts to work with but felt he had to take some type of action very soon.

Discussion Questions

1. What would you do if you were Wilson?
2. What comments can you make about the behavior of:
   (a) Maxey?   (b) Doyle?   (c) Franklin?   (d) Wilson?
3. Discuss the personnel effects of the organizational changes.
4. Is another organizational change in order?

Special Project

One effective way to analyze this case is to develop several possible alternative strategies which Wilson could take and evaluate each in terms of its positive and negative consequences to the individuals involved and to the organization.
Some alternatives are:

1. Terminate Franklin
2. Transfer Franklin to Manufacturing
3. Reorganize
4. and so forth

Using a separate sheet of paper for each alternative, write out the strategy in terms of a cause and effect relationship so that the wanted and unwanted consequences of each can be listed. Opinions, feelings, attitudes, and convictions have to be considered as well as the facts.

For example
   If I terminate Franklin, then . . . what will probably occur?

(CAUSE)   (EFFECTS)

Illustration

(CAUSE)
Alternative #1 If I (Wilson) terminate Franklin, then:

Wanted Consequences (EFFECTS)	Unwanted Consequences (EFFECTS)
1. Maxey and Doyle will be pleased. 2. I will be supporting a decision by a key manager. 3. I will look decisive. 4. Schedules may improve. 5. etc.	1. An employee with some known demonstrated capabilities will be lost. 2. Morale may decline. 3. A power play may develop. 4. Franklin will be unhappy. 5. etc.

Divide the class into groups of 4–5 and have each group do the following:

1. Brainstorm alternative approaches.
2. List and evaluate three or four fairly realistic alternative strategies as shown in the illustration.
3. Select an alternative as the decision of the group.

Allow one hour maximum for small group discussion and preparation, and then have a spokesman from each group present and defend their respective solutions to the entire class.

   Caution. It is *not* a truism that if more *facts* were available the decision (alternative selection) would be easy!

Selected References

Books
Jones, M. H. *Executive Decision Making*. Homewood, Illinois: Richard D. Irwin, Inc., 1957.
Kepner, C. H., and Tregoe, B. B. *The Rational Manager: A Systematic Approach to Problem Solving and Decision Making*. New York: McGraw-Hill, 1965.

Anthologies
Hampton, D. R., Summer, C. E., and Webber, R. A. (Eds.). *Organizational Behavior and the Practice of Management*. Glenview, Illinois: Scott, Foresman and Company, 1968.
   Gellerman, S. W. "The Competence and Power Motives," p. 118.
   Weber, R. A. "Innovation and Conflict in Industrial Engineering," p. 412.
Leadership on the Job. New York: American Management Association, 1966. Famularo, J. "Working With Other Managers," p. 291.
Leavitt, H. J., and Pondy, L. R. (Eds.). *Readings in Managerial Psychology*. Chicago, Illinois: University of Chicago Press, 1964.
   March, J. G. "Business Decision Making," p. 447.

Thompson, J. D., and Tuden, A. "Strategies Structures and Processes of Organizational Decision," p. 496.

Articles

Argyris, C. "Interpersonal Barriers to Decision Making," *Harvard Business Review*, March–April 1966, p. 84.

Delbecq, A. L. "The Management of Decision Making Within the Firm: Three Strategies for Three Types of Decision Making," *Academy of Management Journal*, December 1967, p. 329.

Kaufmann, F. "The Strategic Decision Makers," *Innovation*, Number Twenty, 1971, p. 18.

Lippitt, G., and Schmidt, W. "Crises in a Developing Organization," *Harvard Business Review*, November–December 1967, p. 102.

Meyer, H. "If People Fear to Fail, Can Organizations Ever Succeed?" *Innovation*, Number Eight, 1969, p. 56.

Strauss, G. "Tactics of Lateral Relationship," *Administrative Science Quarterly*, September 1962, p. 161.

THE PROGRAMMED DECISION

John Farraday, president of a medium sized science oriented company, was attending a management seminar for business leaders on how to improve organizational effectiveness. He sat quietly, taking notes, as several speakers in turn discussed the need for management to decentralize the decision making process within organizations in order to increase individual and group motivation as well as improve overall decision quality.

The last speaker of the day, Dr. Harlan Gould, an eminent professor of management, summed up the major points made during the entire program.

"We are at a place in our industrial technological development," said Dr. Gould, "where no one person, *even though an expert in his particular field*, can possibly have all the necessary information at his disposal to make a continuing series of reasonably correct technical and management decisions without the help of others. The message is abundantly clear for those among us who still insist on running an entire company or department by ourselves. We are courting disaster by doing so! The intelligent manager, both now and to an increasing degree in the future, will come to rely more and more on the assistance and advice of other personnel at all levels within the organization."

At the end of the formal presentation, questions were requested from the audience. Farraday lit a cigar and puffed slowly and thoughtfully while he listened to several minutes of questions and answers. Finally, he raised his hand.

"Mr. Farraday. Do you have a question?" asked Gould.

"Yes," Farraday replied, "but first I want to make sure that I fully understand the implications of the earlier remarks. My impression from the experts today is that the autocratic or authoritarian leader will *not* be successful and will *not* develop a successful, innovative organization, because he will inappropriately make too many of the major decisions by himself . . . effectively shutting off the information, ideas, and potential creativity of his subordinates. Am I essentially correct?"

"Yes, that is correct, Mr. Farraday," replied Dr. Gould.

"Well," said Farraday, "I agree with what has been said, but feel that we are not quite dealing with the organizational world as it really is. My experience indicates that, in a technically oriented organization, managers and supervisors *automatically* deal with peers and subordinates in a more interactive or participative manner rather than an autocratic manner with regard to complex problems and decisions.

Comments were quickly exchanged among other participants.

"Please, continue," said Dr. Gould.

"No disrespect intended toward any of the distinguished speakers," said Farraday, "but I am trying to match today's learning with my own experiences. Many younger technical and professional persons often claim that all major decisions are made by top management in a very autocratic and, often, arbitrary way. My experience indicates that complex decisions cannot be made without the information inputs of many people at all levels *regardless of the personal leadership attitudes of the boss.* Even the most autocratic leader recognizes and works within these groundrules, not because he necessarily wishes to do so, but because he has no effective alternative. *He is a victim of the complex technology of his own organization!*"

"I hardly consider myself an organizational dictator," continued Farraday, "but I periodically get feedback from within my organization that all major decisions take place in my office. To the contrary, I often feel that most major decisions have been made *before* they ever get to my office!"

"An interesting and most unusual observation," said Dr. Gould. "Can you give us an illustration?"

"I believe so," replied Farraday. "Last week, for instance, my Chief Engineer, Ed Hellman, came into my office to discuss several product design alternatives open to us to match recent moves by our major competitor. Each alternative involved the expenditure of a substantial amount of money, varying degrees of risk, and a number of other imponderables and unknowns.

"It was clear to me that Hellman had done his homework. He was amply supplied with charts, statistics, and projections prepared by his technical staff. I was overwhelmed by the mass of data . . . certainly more than I could assimilate in a reasonable period of time. I asked Ed if he had thoroughly reviewed all the information and he responded that he had checked all of the main points developed by his staff but could not *personally* authenticate any specific data. He quickly added that he had no reason to suspect that any of the information that had been developed was not correct.

"I reviewed the mass of information for a few minutes, asking a detailed question now and then, and finally asked Hellman point blank which alternative he would choose. He hesitated for a moment and replied that he favored Alternative C, which was the overwhelming choice of his staff."

Dr. Gould and most of the seminar participants appeared puzzled.

"Do you see what I'm getting at?" asked Farraday. "Complex decisions are rarely made at the top of the organization in an arbitrary and autocratic way. Instead, in reality, complex decisions are *approved at the top* using information which has been developed at successively lower levels and passed upward in steps through persons less familiar with the specifics of the problem. Gentlemen, *I was programmed from below to make the decision* and I contend that this is true of most managers today!"

Discussion Questions

1. John Farraday said that in a technically oriented organization managers and supervisors automatically deal with peers and subordinates in an interactive or participative manner rather than an autocratic manner on complex problems. Comment.
2. Farraday also said that the top manager is a victim of the complex technology of his own organization. Comment.
3. What do you think about the concept of programmed decisions?
4. Is there a flaw in Farraday's analysis? Explain.

Special Project

As an out of class assignment, have several persons study and later report on the reality of the programmed decision. This is best done by interviewing several managers, workers, or executives from technically oriented organizations.

Some students may have an advantage here through part-time employment or access to knowledgeable persons through friends or relatives. Taped interviews with classroom playback are excellent.

Caution. Make visit and interview arrangements well in advance. Be certain that the manager fully understands *in advance*:
   (a)   What you want.
   (b)   How much of his time will be involved.

(c)   How you will interview.

(d)   How the material will be used.

Don't violate your own groundrules. Send a thank you letter afterward. Tape recordings may not be advisable or even permissible under many circumstances. Clearly check before using tape recording techniques.

Selected References

Books

Odiorne, G. S. *How Managers Make Things Happen*. Englewood Cliffs, New Jersey: Prentice-Hall, 1961.

Ready, R. K. *The Administrator's Job: Issues and Dilemmas*. New York: McGraw-Hill, 1967.

Anthologies

Huseman, R., Logue, C., and Freshley, D. *Readings in Interpersonal and Organizational Communication*. Boston, Massachusetts: Holbrook Press, Inc., 1969.

   Planty, E., and Machaver, W. "Upward Communications: A Project in Executive Development," p. 122.

   Townsend, L. A. "A Corporate President's View of the Internal Communication Function," p. 169.

Articles

Gemmill, G. "Managing Upward Communication," *Personnel Journal*, 1970, p. 107.

Libaw, F. B. "And Now, the Creative Corporation," *Innovation*, Number Nineteen, 1971, p. 2.

Tribus, M. "The Power of Uncertainty In Organizations," *Innovation*, Number Fourteen, 1970, p. 2.

CALDWELL'S HATCHET MAN

> "Management often seriously underestimates the costs in time, energy, and money of ensuring that a decision is carried out when the commitment to it is low or absent."
>
> DOUGLAS MCGREGOR
> *The Professional Manager*, p. 190

Herbert Gates had been given the unenviable job of "turning around" the unprofitable Television and Stereo Division of Caldwell Industries. Ernest Caldwell, the president, had relied on Gates for numerous difficult corporate level staff assignments in past years and Gates had just completed two years as General Manager of Caldwell's Instruments Division.

When Caldwell proposed the assignment, Gates' first impulse was to turn it down. The Instruments Division was profitable and Gates was supported by several talented managers. Now fifty-five years old, Herbert Gates was beginning to enjoy the more relaxed pace of his job and an assignment as a "hatchet man" was hardly what he wanted at this point in his career.

In the end Caldwell prevailed as he always did. Caldwell admitted that he had no one, other than Gates, whom he could trust to bring the troubled Television Division back into the profit column. And, although unstated, Caldwell left no doubt that Gates was in line for the presidency of Caldwell Industries. Ernest Caldwell was due to retire and Gates had long held the hope that someday he would take Caldwell's place at the top.

The first requirement for Gates at the Television Division was to bring operating costs into line with the recently lowered division sales projections.

When departmental budgets for the fiscal year were prepared and approved four months earlier, they had been based upon an anticipated 20 percent increase. However, as of last month, actual sales had increased only 3 percent while engineering, factory, administrative, and sales costs had risen 24 percent on an average.

During his first week on the new job, Gates met the key department managers and generally familiarized himself with overall divisional methods of operation. Most of his time, however, was spent in closed sessions with the Comptroller, Norman Phillips, developing reduced departmental budgets which would ease the current financial crisis. At the end of the week, guideline budgets were established. These stated in maximum dollars the operating budget for each department. Gates chose not to decide which specific items would have to be deleted from each departmental budget to realize the new lower figures. None of the managers would like the austere budgets he was imposing but felt there would be fewer objections if each manager could decide where to make the necessary cuts in his own budget.

Gates' reception had been polite but cool. One thing was quite clear; to these managers he was Caldwell's hatchet man. That image would have to be erased in spite of the fact that his first major decision would be generally unpopular.

Long ago Gates had learned that it was one thing to order compliance to an unpopular decision and quite another to gain commitment to it. Ordered to do so, people will comply and go through the motions of implementing a decision. Their output though will generally be greater if they understand the reasons for the decision and put their support behind it.

Gates decided to call each manager individually to his office to announce the budget cuts. There, in a one-to-one setting, he could more appropriately respond to each man's reaction toward the sharp budget cuts and, hopefully, improve the commitment of each to the necessity of the action.

Gates summarized what little he knew of the men:

Ralph Keating—Director of Marketing.   Ralph was largely responsible for establishing the over optimistic sales projections although Ralph had commented to others that the sales estimates were forced on him by Arnold Miller, the former Division manager. Ralph is well educated, a family man in his middle thirties, and a "steal" from a west coast competitor two years ago. He is eager, aggressive, and pushed hard for the heavy advertising campaign which will now have to be sharply curtailed. He has been with four companies in related industries prior to coming to Caldwell Industries.

Marvin DeKalb—Director of Administration.   Marv is a nice guy who takes everything personally. The impending budget cuts will require personnel reductions and Marv will have to make many of the choices. Office and administrative costs will be slashed too, including DeKalb's proposed Personnel Training and Development program. In fifteen years with Caldwell, Marv has seen this before. Apparently, he still cannot get used to some facts of business life.

Dr. Milo Harrison—Director of Research and Engineering.   Milo has been controversial since he came to the Division three years ago. Arnold Miller met Harrison at a technical conference and, within three months, brought him in at the Director level. Before that he had spent most of his time in a "think tank" in Cambridge. There has been no question about Harrison's technical capabilities, but he is extremely self-centered. He tends to take much of the credit for his department's achievements as his own— much to the chagrin of several top engineers. Milo was given a free reign by Arnold Miller to develop an integrated solid state television chassis, and excessive costs in this area have been somewhat responsible for the current budget problem. Milo will have to trim Research and Engineering expenditures and make several design compromises. Milo also felt very close to Miller and was enraged when Miller was "allowed to resign."

Curtis Bacon—Director of Manufacturing.   Curtis has been with Caldwell Industries even longer than Gates. The two are casual friends though this is the first time they have worked together. Bacon started as a foreman on the portable radio line after World War II and simply outlasted everyone in the department. Bacon is a swell fellow, but no innovator. Engineering has to hound him endlessly to make cost cutting changes. Few layoffs are anticipated in Manufacturing but all overtime will

71

be cut. Some capital equipment expenditures will have to be deferred. Bacon once remarked to Gates, "We have a shakeup in the Television Division every six months. I got used to it a long time ago. It's usually the work of some young buck trying to impress Caldwell. They all end up as vague memories and I'm still here."

Norman Phillips—Comptroller. Norm has been with Caldwell only one year. Before that he was a senior Certified Public Accountant with the firm that serviced Caldwell Industries. Phillips is a realist and worked diligently with Gates in developing new budgets. Few persons in his area will be hurt by the cuts, but a lease agreement for a new computer is out. Phillips reluctantly blue penciled that item.

Discussion Questions

1. What is the difference between commitment and compliance?
2. What approach will probably be most successful with each of these managers:
    (a) Simple authority (Please do this)?
    (b) Easy proof (Conversational discussion)?
    (c) Hard proof (Preplanned, documented argument)?
    (d) Sanctions (Promises or threats)?
    (e) Other ways?
3. If hostility is encountered how should the manager respond?
4. It has been said that negative acceptance to a decision is rebellion or sabotage:
    (a) In what ways can a decision be sabotaged?
    (b) How can sabotage (sometimes done unconsciously) be prevented?
5. How should a manager deal with indifference (I couldn't care less about this) toward his decision?
6. In what other ways could Gates have handled this difficult problem:
    (a) Issue a memorandum? Discuss.
    (b) Call a group meeting? Discuss.
    (c) Other ways? Discuss.

Special Project

The concept of varying degrees of acceptance to any particular decision can be vividly portrayed in a role play situation. Have individuals assume the roles of:

> Herbert Gates
> Ralph Keating
> Marvin DeKalb
> Milo Harrison
> Curtis Bacon
> Norman Phillips

Allow time for each to become comfortable with his role before starting. A pony will help keep most persons in their role during discussion and can be prepared in advance.

Then, set up several successive one-to-one decision confrontations between Gates and the other men. Have others observe and feed back information on how well Gates won over (improved the acceptance level and increased the commitment of) the various men.

Alternate. Use 10 players with 5 assuming the role of Herbert Gates. This eases the role playing responsibility of the person chosen to be Gates.

Selected References

Books
Argyris, C. *Personality and Organization.* New York: Harper & Row, 1957.
Greenewalt, C. H. *The Uncommon Man: The Individual In the Organization.* New York: McGraw-Hill, 1959.

Anthologies
Huseman, R., Logue, C., and Freshley, D. *Readings in Interpersonal and Organizational Communication.* Boston, Massachusetts: Holbrook Press, Inc., 1969.
  Buchanan, P. C. "How Can 'We' Gain 'Their' Commitment?" p. 211.
  Galbraith, J. R. "Influencing the Decision to Produce," p. 219.
  Potter, C. J. "Persuasiveness—Powerful Tool," p. 252.
Leavitt, H. J., and Pondy, L. R. (Eds.). *Readings in Managerial Psychology.* Chicago, Illinois: University of Chicago Press. Hovland, C. I. "Studies in Persuasion," p. 179.

Articles
Genfan, H. "Managing Change," *Personnel Journal,* November 1969, p. 910.
Grote, R. C. "Effect of Leadership Changes On A Work Group," *Training and Development Journal,* July 1971, p. 18.
Miles, R. E. "Attitudes Toward Management Theory As A Factor In Managers' Relationships with Their Superiors," *Academy of Management Journal,* December 1964, pp. 308–314.

MANAGEMENT BY RUMOR

At precisely 7:30 p.m., William Jarvis called university extension class No. 431 to order. Titled, *Problems in Organizational Behavior,* the course was designed as a seminar to match organization theory with organizational realities.

The class had been very challenging for Jarvis, a management consultant who taught part time at the university, largely because of the student mix. Participants included both undergraduate and graduate students plus a number of industrial managers. The group was never content with theory alone. Instead, as Jarvis had hoped, the participants questioned and probed the validity of many management methods and techniques under diverse organizational climates. The result was typically lively and stimulating discussion.

"Last time," said Jarvis, "we were discussing how management decisions are accepted by individuals and groups.[1] We noted that there are some management decisions which will be enthusiastically accepted by the work group. Such popular decisions would include cost of living increases, your birthday as a paid holiday, or a personal parking place. Regardless of how management communicates the decision to you, your acceptance level and personal commitment to this decision will be quite high. The reason for a high degree of level of acceptance is obvious—*you can see only good things for yourself as a result of this management decision*. There appear to be few, if any, *unwanted consequences* which you must accept and live with as a result of the decision.

"Now," Jarvis continued, "we recognize that not all management decisions will be popular. Unpopular decisions include such items as budget cuts, personnel layoffs, and so forth. When a manager comes to a decision which he knows will be unpopular, he must deal positively with anticipated low acceptance levels.

"Assuming a manager feels he has made a proper or correct decision, he still has to 'sell' this idea to subordinates. Naturally, the more *unwanted consequences* seen by subordinates in a particular decision, the harder the manager will have to 'sell' in order to improve both individual and group acceptance."

"In real life though," asked one student, "can't a boss simply state his decision without selling it? I mean . . . *don't you have to do what he wants since he's the boss?*"

"Good point, Ted," Jarvis replied. "Indeed, many bosses do just that. On many decisions, particularly the trivial or routine, no selling is necessary. Also, by tradition, custom, or prior arrangement, some types of decisions are considered to be the sole prerogative of the boss. Here too, no selling may be necessary. Though often, the selling of a decision is ignored when it should be employed to build subordinate commitment.

"For example, autocratic managers typically ignore this decision 'selling' function and rely primarily on their power or rank within the organization to force compliance in lieu of gaining personal commitment from subordinates. While it is true that most decisions can be implemented through forced compliance alone, results are generally better when a high degree of acceptance to the decision exists among those concerned.

[1]*See, Caldwell's Hatchet Man*, p. 69.

"Individual and group acceptance of a particular decision can be improved through person-to-person discussion or by group meetings when a one-to-one approach is not practicable. Each of these techniques provides a vehicle for effective two-way communication in which most reasonable objections can be overcome by agreement or consensus rather than by direct order."

Wallace Helper raised his hand after Jarvis completed his summary.

"Yes, Wally?" asked Jarvis.

"Mr. Jarvis, what do you think about the idea of improving acceptance to decisions by using *rumors*?"

Jarvis laughed. "You're putting me on, of course."

"Not at all," said Helper, "and I don't mean to be facetious. I remember a situation in which management improved both individual and group commitment to a decision through the use of a rumor and wondered what you thought of this technique."

"I'm afraid I don't follow you, Wally."

"Well," said Helper, "last year my company was experiencing a rather severe financial squeeze. Product sales were very slow but our overhead and sales costs were excessively high. Most everyone realized we were having money problems but few understood the extent or how anyone of us might be affected."

"But," interrupted Jarvis, "how were rumors involved?"

Helper continued, "About the time most of us were getting pretty nervous about whether or not we would be laid off, a rumor began to circulate that there *would* be extensive personnel cutbacks. Rumor had it that as many as 30 percent of the staff would lose their jobs. We were stunned at the magnitude of the rumored cut!"

"Did management confirm the rumor?" asked Jarvis.

Helper said, "Now that's the interesting point," and continued, "Top management remained silent, refusing to confirm or deny the rumor. The official word was that the matter was under study. Morale really sank to the bottom in the next week while we waited for final word on the extensive cutbacks.

"Then, the announcement was made that a 5–7 percent personnel cut would be necessary. Needless to say we were all really happy that the number was so low. Most managers were able to fill their reduction quotas with voluntary terminations and by trimming a little 'deadwood' here and there. Very few really good people were let go."

"I'm afraid I'm still at a loss," said Jarvis. "Surely you're not saying that you had a high degree of acceptance to an unpopular decision to lay off personnel?"

75

"Exactly," replied Helper. "Because management refused to squelch the rumor about extensive layoffs we mentally adjusted our expectations to the worst possible situation. Then, when the actual 5–7 percent cut was announced, our acceptance was higher and our commitment better than if the rumor had not started in the first place.

"I think," Helper concluded, "that our management *purposely* started the rumor to improve acceptance of what they knew would be an unpopular decision!"

Discussion Questions

1. Discuss the concept of selling decisions to improve group commitment.
2. Is selling necessary if a decision has been made by group consensus? Explain.
3. What are the advantages of holding a meeting to sell a decision? What are the pitfalls?
4. Discuss the "rumor theory" suggested by Wally Helper. Is purposeful management by rumor workable? Should it be avoided?
5. Discuss the ethics of purposely starting a false rumor.

Special Project

Divide the class into groups of 4–5 each. Ask each group to assume it is the top management team faced with a layoff decision. You have also just heard the rumor that extensive (30 percent) cuts will be necessary although your preliminary analysis indicates that actual cuts will not be nearly as large.

Develop a group position on precisely what top management should do about the rumor. Allow 15–20 minutes for analysis and 5 minutes each for presentation.

Selected References

Books
Drucker, P. F. *Managing for Results*. New York: Harper & Row, 1964.
Simon, H. A. *The New Science of Management Decision*. New York: Harper & Row, 1960.

Anthologies
Effective Communication on the Job. New York: American Management Association, 1963. Halford, J. "Rumor Must Be Reckoned With," p. 116.
Huseman, R., Logue, C., and Freshley, D. *Readings in Interpersonal and Organizational Communication*. Boston, Massachusetts: Holbrook Press, Inc., 1969. Davis, K. "The Organization That's Not on the Chart," p. 156.
Leadership on the Job. New York: American Management Association, 1966. Halford, J. "The Care and Feeding of the Grapevine," p. 63.
Leavitt, H. J., and Pondy, L. R. (Eds.). *Readings in Managerial Psychology*. Chicago, Illinois: University of Chicago Press, 1964. Jackson, J. M. "The Organization and Its Communication Problems," p. 486.

Articles
Hershey, R. "The Grapevine—Here to Stay But Not Out of Control," *Personnel*, January–February 1966.

THE GREAT PIZZA FIASCO

Old West Food Corporation is a closely held family corporation which specializes in the processing of delicatessen type food items. These foods include pre-made sandwiches, potato salad, macaroni salad, cole slaw, and a small line of bachelor dinners. The bachelor dinners typically consist of assorted cold cuts, cheese, a tomato wedge, pickle, and noodle or potato salad.

These items are sold through several smaller chain stores and assorted small markets where customers make a selection from a refrigerated case.

For the most part, Old West was never known for innovation in product development. Product ideas came from two major sources:

1. Company officers would discuss (at regular meetings) the new delicatessen products being introduced at supermarkets by the big name brand food processors. Ideas which looked good were copied and introduced in Old West packaging. This was not considered unethical because only minor product differences were required to invalidate a product infringement claim by competition. Old West still had to make its product attractive, tasty, and fresh. Often Old West felt its copies were much better than the original versions.
2. Old West salesmen would often come up with ideas after visiting these retail outlets and talking to merchants. The merchants would discuss customer comments and preferences and make useful suggestions.

For ten years since it was founded, Old West had been run by Gerald Meyerson and his brother Roger. Gerald is President and handles Purchasing and Processing Operations. Roger is Vice-President and is in charge of Sales and Finance. The organization then had the following structure:

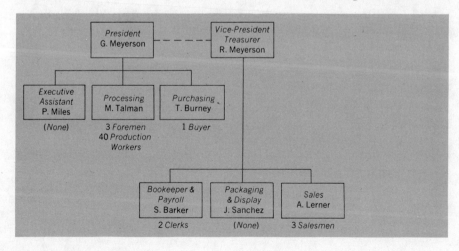

About two years ago, Phillip Miles was hired as an executive assistant to Gerald. Miles was a production expeditor with five years of experience at a large aerospace organization. Miles was also Gerald Meyerson's son-in-law. Gerald had always liked Miles and did not object too vigorously when his only child persuaded him to hire her husband. Phillip was just the man to add new blood to a tired, unimaginative organization.

In January of last year, Old West introduced an individual sized pre-baked frozen pizza. The idea again was not new, but it was a radical step for Old West in two ways:

1. Processing operations had to be expanded to include flash ovens and fast freeze cabinets.
2. Old West products were now in retail freezer cases as well as the cool delicatessen cases. New market potential existed.

The frozen pizza caught on quickly and production was brisk and profitable. Gerald Meyerson was elated. The pizza was Phillip Miles' idea. Phillip set up the operation and gave it the energy and drive it needed.

Gerald confided to Phillip that the organization needed more of the aggressiveness which Phillip demonstrated. It needed new ideas, incentives, and systems from modern industry. Gerald asked if Phillip could think of something else which would inspire the organization.

Miles reflected on the backgrounds of key people:

Marty Talman.   Age 43, 2 years of college, 15 years experience in food production, with Old West 7 years as Processing Manager. Talman hired his three foremen personally. They are very loyal. Production has, surprisingly, few major problems.

Tom Burney.   Age 37. Former assistant Bookkeeper at Old West. He became Purchasing Agent when that position was created 3 years ago. He is assisted by one buyer.

Sylvia Barker.   Age 32 and divorced. Five years experience in book-keeping prior to Old West. Six years with Old West. Moved up to her present spot in 1963. No formal education beyond high school, but a very hard worker. She arrives early and leaves late—a regular career girl.

Joe Sanchez.   Age 39. Art major in college, but did not finish. Great eye for design of boxes, trays, and plastic display packages. Works by himself and with vendors. A lot of sales success must be attributed to his package designs. Three years at Old West.

Al Lerner.   Age 51. Al has been selling food all his life. He looks like he enjoys his product, too. Not too hot at administration though. The salesmen seem to come and go. No incentives.

Incentives, thought Miles, were the key!

The following month Phillip Miles outlined his incentive plan to Gerald and Roger Meyerson. All people involved with new products were to be included in the *New Product Bonus Pool*. This would include Talman, his three foremen; Burney (but not the girl buyer), Sanchez, Lerner, his three salesmen; and, of course, Miles. Sylvia Barker was not involved in the development-production-sales cycle and was not to be included.

The plan would work like this:

New Products were to be emphasized. A product was considered new until its sales exceeded $100,000. One percent of the wholesale sales price of each of these new products (up to $100,000 in sales) would be set aside in a pool. This would be divided at the end of the year. The amount each person got would depend upon:

1. The amount of money in the pool
2. The number of pool members involved
3. Salary level of each. Pool shares would be weighted slightly based upon salary.

Gerald Meyerson bought the idea over the objections of his brother, Roger, who saw it as unwarranted salary increases in disguise. Gerald, however, felt that it would provide incentives for new ideas, better methods, greater sales, and increased profits. Above all, it would increase individual motivation through sharing in company success.

The formal announcement was made in March at a meeting with the key people. Gerald Meyerson gave the following illustration of possible bonus amounts:

"Assume ten new products this year with average sales of $75,000 each. At 1 percent of sales, this creates a new product pool of $7,500 ($75,000 × 10 × 1 percent). With 11 people in the pool the bonus would average almost $700 each."

Response to the plan was enthusiastic and a new spirit of togetherness seemed to prevail. Five new products were successfully introduced by August. Two others had been initiated, but taste and appearance problems sharply curtailed sales.

In October, several problems began to develop. Talman and Burney checked with Sylvia Barker to see how the pool size was growing. Sylvia snapped that she had no idea. She claimed she had only gross sales figures and suggested they see Roger Meyerson for the detailed new products sales information. When Talman asked Roger Meyerson, he was told the pool was coming along fine, but that he (Roger) was busy at the moment and could not provide the exact number.

By November, it appeared that seven new products would be involved, and that average sales would be nearer $50,000 than $75,000.

At the end of the year each person received his bonus with his regular paycheck. No announcement was made as to the amount each received, but when individuals started discussing the matter, it appeared that the bonuses varied from $150 to $300. The totals were much smaller than expected and the range was surprisingly large.

Tammy Brown, a payroll clerk, told her boyfried in Processing that Phil Miles got a check for almost $500. The word spread rapidly. Lerner asked Gerald Meyerson about it directly. Meyerson replied that Miles' check included some travel expense he had incurred. Lerner was hardly satisfied.

Everyone felt that they had been misled as to bonus amounts. The salary differential made it very vague. On top of that, there were too many people in the pool. Miles had hired a technician to assist him during the year. Had he been included? Miles had no comment.

Gerald Meyerson was disgusted. "Try to do something for your people and they get greedy," he complained to Miles. Early in January, he issued a curt memo which ended the new product bonus. In its place he substituted a one-time only flat salary increase of 5 percent for all persons who had been on the new products bonus.

"That should end that," he announced. It did not. Sylvia Barker and one of Al Lerner's salesmen quit the next week.

Discussion Questions

1. In what ways did the incentive plan produce *positive* or contributive employee behavior?
2. In what ways did the incentive plan produce *negative* employee behavior?
3. Was proper implementation and follow-up conducted? Explain.
4. How did Gerald Meyerson compound the problem?
5. Discuss this case in terms of:
   (a) Leadership style.
   (b) Effective communication.
6. How can sound behavioral elements be built into any incentive plan?

Special Project

Have the class develop new and effective groundrules for implementation of this management decision to establish a group incentive system which would enhance plan acceptance and create conditions for positive employee behavior.

Selected References

Books

Drucker, P. F. *The Practice of Management.* New York: Harper & Row, 1954.

Dubin, H. *et al. Leadership and Productivity.* San Francisco: Chandler Publishing Company, 1965.

Morrisey, G. L. *Management By Objectives and Results.* Reading, Massachusetts: Addison-Wesley, 1970.

Odiorne, G. S. *Management by Objectives.* New York: Pitman, 1965.

Anthologies

Hampton, D. R., Summer, C. E., and Webber, R. A. (Eds.). *Organizational Behavior and the Practice of Management.* Glenview, Illinois: Scott, Foresman and Company, 1968. Newman, W. H. "Strategic Considerations in Planning," p. 633.

Leadership on the Job. New York: American Management Association, 1966. Lazarus, S. "What to do When You've 'Goofed'," p. 262.

Leavitt, H. J., and Pondy, L. R., (Eds.). *Readings in Managerial Psychology.* Chicago, Illinois: University of Chicago Press, 1964. Dill, W. R. "Varieties of Administrative Decisions," p. 457.

Koontz, H., and O'Donnell, C. *Management: A Book of Readings.* New York: McGraw-Hill, 1968. Peck, G. A. "The Mechanics of Implementation," p. 156.
Wilson, C., and Alexis, M. "Basic Frameworks for Decisions," p. 98.

Articles

Argyris, C. "Resistance To Rational Management Systems," *Innovation,* Number Ten, 1970, p. 28.

Konrad, E. "Corporate Planning Shouldn't Be a One-Man Band," *Innovation,* Number Fifteen, 1970, p. 50.

Schmitt, R., and Roberts, R. "Creativity Versus Planning—You Can Have Both," *Innovation,* Number Nineteen, 1971, p. 52.

CASE STUDY CROSS REFERENCE

Although located elsewhere in this book, the following problem situations are also valuable in the study of Section 3:

Section 3

Acquiring and Keeping Talent

There was a long pause before Sikes replied. "That's the embarrassing part," he said at last. "We wouldn't dare admit this publicly, but *we didn't hire a single person* from that group! Management felt the applicants were too *far out* to fit in with our company."

PHILLIP SIKES
Show Us You're Really Creative!

INTRODUCTION

What techniques can be most effectively employed by commercial, industrial, and governmental organizations to screen and select qualified employment applicants? How honest should recruiters be with applicants? How can later job mis-match and job frustrations be avoided? What role should the job applicant play in the job match process? How can organizations avoid excessive turnover, particularly among their most capable and talented employees?

Cases in This Section

The Plight of Ralph Cummings

College graduate accepts a position with a growing company but the job does not meet his expectations . . . vague assignments . . . poor supervision . . . lack of communication . . . poor use of personnel . . . personal frustrations.

Show Us You're Really Creative!

An unusual view of personnel recruitment . . . a creativity campaign . . .

excellent response but a strange management dilemma results . . . what price creativity?

Where Do I Find a Black Cost Accountant?

Equal opportunity in employment . . . is it always possible? A personnel manager reviews some practical problems his organization faces.

The Rules Are Different for Women

An old problem re-examined . . . is business taking a more realistic view of female employees now? A professional woman offers her point of view.

At Home on the Range

A disturbing television broadcast shatters morale at a lonely government facility . . . increased employee turnover . . . inadequate personnel recruitment . . . poor image to the public . . . community relations with a nearby town . . . moral, social, and political overtones.

Dr. Shibata Has Resigned!

A key man suddenly resigns . . . where is the problem? Potential supervisory problems and poor communications . . . relations with co-workers . . . professionalism . . . team conflict . . . technical obsolescence.

THE PLIGHT OF RALPH CUMMINGS

In August five years ago, Ralph Cummings, an electronic technician, was discharged from the Navy. He immediately enrolled in the College of Engineering at the University of Maryland for the fall semester.

During the spring of his last semester, the University of Maryland, like other schools throughout the country, was invaded by an army of campus recruiters from companies representing many industries and organizations throughout the country.

Ralph was interviewed by fourteen companies but was most impressed by Lionel Baines from Marathon Systems. Baines spent considerable time with Ralph describing the activities of Marathon Systems, a company which had just been awarded a large government contract for major portions of the electronics guidance system for a Navy Surface-to-Air Missile System. This was the largest contract ever awarded to Marathon and its successful completion could guarantee a sound future for the company.

Baines described Marathon as a very dynamic company actively seeking promising personnel with management potential who were not afraid to tackle some large and challenging problems. He assured Ralph that advancement within the company would be rapid for those who showed promise and delivered results.

Lionel discussed Ralph's academic background and seemed quite impressed with his school record plus his electronics work in the Navy.

According to Baines, the company desperately needed personnel for the quality and reliability areas. Baines said that this was the hottest area of the whole company since the success of the entire project depended on coordinating the work of major parts subcontractors to ensure that Marathon could deliver a high quality, reliable, and "in-spec" product within estimated cost.

That evening Ralph reviewed the meeting with his wife, Sally. Ralph said that the position at Marathon sounded like just what he was looking for and hoped that he had made a good impression on Mr. Baines. The work sounded difficult and challenging but Ralph knew he would be successful if he received an offer.

The next morning as Ralph was preparing to leave for class, the phone rang. It was Lionel Baines who wondered if Ralph and his wife could meet him and other members of the interviewing team for dinner that evening.

Dinner that evening was a thrilling experience for the Cummingses. The conversation centered around how pleasant company-people were, what a fine area it was to live, the rosy future of the company, and other general aspects of Marathon. All three recruiters were most amiable and talked freely. They really seemed sold on Marathon and they overwhelmed Ralph and Sally with their enthusiasm.

Two weeks later, Ralph received an official offer from Marathon for the position of Reliability Engineer to commence the first Monday in July. Ralph was excited but decided not to accept until he had heard from the other companies with whom he had been talking.

He received five firm offers that spring. Monetarily, the offer from Marathon was third from the top. In late May he reviewed the offers with Sally and they both agreed that, based on what the interviewers had indicated, the job at Marathon offered the greatest opportunity. He mailed his formal acceptance the next day.

Ralph arose early on the morning of July 7 and reported to the Personnel

Office as the written offer of employment had instructed him. There he met Lionel Baines and renewed their short friendship.

As the two men walked from the Personnel Office to the Reliability Department, Ralph could not help but notice the almost frantic activity going on in all the areas they passed through.

"It certainly looks like things are jumping around here," Ralph commented.

"You'd better believe it," replied Lionel, "and you'll be in the middle of it in a few days."

Upon arrival in the Quality Assurance and Reliability area, they went straight to the Director's office. There were three other young men waiting in the outer office when they arrived. Ralph was introduced to Pam, the Director's secretary and asked to have a seat. Lionel left. Ralph introduced himself to the other recent college graduates who were also reporting to work, Tom Watkins, Bill Tomkins, and Ed Kololski.

After waiting for several minutes, the four men heard the intercom, "If they're all here, Pam, send 'em in."

"Good morning gents," said Ken Barlow, "have a seat." For the next hour or so, Ken outlined the responsibilities of the Quality Assurance and Reliability Department with particular emphasis on the current project. He pointed out that he had carefully reviewed the background and qualifications of the new employees and had already made assignments for each to specific jobs in which they would be well suited and could provide the best service for the company. Ralph was assigned to work for Ernest Lemon, Supervisor of Reliability for Subcontracts.

Lemon showed Ralph to his desk and introduced him around the area. In Lemon's office they reviewed Ralph's background and again discussed the importance of the new contract. Lemon concluded the meeting by telling Ralph that he should spend the next few days getting acquainted around the office and finding out what each person was doing.

After two weeks on the job, Ralph informed Lemon that he had met everyone in the office and was familiar with the general nature of the work. He asked if he might now be given a more specific task. Instead, Lemon asked Ralph to continue his orientation until he could come up with something specific. Lemon noted that he was tied up with a hot project at the present moment. They made an appointment to discuss it the following Friday.

Throughout the next week, Ralph kept busy by spending time with two men from a work group which was analyzing the characteristics of the inertial components of the missile guidance system. Ralph had done some work at school in the area of gyroscopic properties and already had some understanding of their work.

At the Friday meeting with Lemon, Ralph expressed his desire to be given an assignment in the inertial components group. Lemon said that this sounded like a good idea, but he felt that Ralph did not have enough experience in this area and required a somewhat firmer base. He suggested that Ralph spend the next few weeks reviewing work proposals submitted by various subcontractors for inertial subassemblies so that he would become more familiar with the operations of this area. A decision regarding permanent assignment could be made later.

During the next seven weeks, Ralph devoted his time to a careful review of all proposals submitted by potential subcontractors. He reported to Lemon when he had completed this review and again asked for an assignment. This time Lemon agreed and Ralph was told to report to Tim O'Connell, the inertial components group leader.

Tim O'Connell appeared pleased to have an assistant assigned to him; he had really been bogged down for the last couple of months and could use additional help. He handed Ralph a stack of rough proposal evaluations and asked him to review them.

Ralph spent the next three weeks reviewing Tim O'Connell's work. He found several areas in the proposal evaluations where his opinion differed from that expressed by Tim. In addition to this he corrected numerous grammatical errors in each evaluation. When he returned the evaluation to Tim, he anticipated being praised for his technical observations as well as his good job of editing.

"Well, what do you think?" asked O'Connell. "Do they read pretty well to you?"

"I found some minor errors and a few weak technical points," Ralph replied. He then summarized the areas of the evaluations which he considered weak. O'Connell was clearly upset.

"Look fella, I've been with this company for six years and on this project since it began. I don't need some college kid to come in here and tell me how to do my job! You were hired to assist me and what I want right now is a proof-reader. I appreciate the editorial comments but don't need the technical advice. From now on, when I give you a project, stay within the limits!"

In December, Ralph was called in to Ernest Lemon's office. This had been the first time he had talked to Lemon except for an occasional greeting in the hallway since he had been assigned to work with O'Connell.

"Well, Ralph, how have things been going?" Lemon asked.

"Pretty well, except . . ."

"As you undoubtedly know," Lemon interrupted, "this is semi-annual merit review time. I've reviewed your work and have talked to Tim O'Connell. Tim is pleased with your work and likes having you in the organization. Based upon his recommendations and my personal observations of you, I'm pleased to inform you that the company has granted you a seven and one-half percent increase in pay commencing the first of the year. Naturally, this is in addition to the four and a quarter cost-of-living increase we'll all be receiving. That's a pretty good jump, I'd say. What do you think?"

"I appreciate the raise and am glad you feel I'm doing a good job," Ralph replied, "but about all I've been doing is proof-reading. I sure would like an assignment where I could better apply my background and experience.

"Don't be too eager to get in over your head," replied Lemon. "It takes time to get used to this business. Look at Tim. He's one of the sharpest young guys we have and he was with us for three and a half years before he earned his own project. Be patient. You're doing a first-rate job. Stick with it."

Although Ralph was pleased with the raise, he was disappointed with the prospect of continuing in a position in which he could not apply his primary skills. He talked the problem over with Sally.

"This is your first experience in business. Maybe you're expecting too much," she said. "After all, the other men at the plant seem pleased with their progress. I don't see how we could do any better some place else."

By the end of March, the flow of paper over Ralph's desk had increased to the point where he could hardly proof-read it all. The inertial components proposals had been reviewed, revised, re-reviewed, and re-revised. It was time for the contract to be awarded. Ralph was again called into Ernest Lemon's office. During this interview he was informed that, because of his fine work on the inertial components program, he was being transferred to the printed circuits section to help them out. He was told that this promotion would carry a five percent raise and he would have the title of Assistant Project Leader. Ralph was pleased at the thought of finally getting a solid engineering job.

However, a month later Ralph felt that he was *still* a proof-reader. He asked his new project leader, Jim Saunders, if he could be assigned to some other tasks rather than simply reviewing the work of project engineers. "That's why they sent you over here," Saunders replied, somewhat surprised. "You're supposed to be good at it."

Ernest Lemon was shocked when he received Ralph's resignation in late April, less than a year after he was hired. Why, he wondered, would a young engineer who had been advanced so rapidly want to leave the company. He sighed as he filled out a new personnel requisition to replace Ralph Cummings.

Discussion Questions

1. Were Ralph's frustrations justified? Explain.
2. Do you feel that Ralph was misled during the employment interview? Explain.
3. How can a campus recruiter, challenged with the task of bidding for and obtaining skilled personnel, accurately represent existing job openings?
4. Discuss this case in terms of:
    (a) Recruitment policies.
    (b) First day orientation policies.
    (c) New employee motivation.
    (d) Employee expectations and job realities.
    (e) Employee coaching and counseling.
5. Evaluate the style and quality of supervision to which Ralph was exposed. What could Ralph's supervisors have done differently to prevent him from leaving in such a short time?
6. In what ways was Ralph Cummings to blame for this apparent man-job mismatch?
7. What is the proper role of the job applicant toward improving the man-job match?

Special Project

To portray the communications difficulties involved between job applicant and interviewer, have several members of the class role play a fictitious job interview. Have several "teams" of two (applicant and interviewer) prepare their 5 minute scripts prior to class and make their presentations in succession with comments from other class members who have acted as observers. Emphasize the role of the applicant as well as the interviewer.

Selected References

Books

Danielson, L. E. *Characteristics of Engineers and Scientists*. Ann Arbor, Michigan: Bureau of Industrial Relations, The University of Michigan, 1960.

Odiorne, G. S., and Hann, A. S. *Effective College Recruiting*. Ann Arbor, Michigan: Bureau of Industrial Relations, The University of Michigan, Report No. 13, 1961.

Anthologies

Effective Communication on the Job. New York: American Management Association, 1963. Schmidt, F. G. "Introducing the New Employee," p. 76.

Huseman, R., Logue, C., and Freshley, D. *Readings in Interpersonal and Organizational*

Communication. Boston, Massachusetts: Holbrook Press, Inc., 1969. Eisenstadt, A. "Interview Taking—A Neglected Skill," p. 263.

Leadership on the Job. New York: American Management Association, 1966. Ruchti, W. "When You Supervise Young Employees," p. 89.

Articles

Barker, R. "College Students Choose A Job: Inputs vs. Outputs," *Personnel Journal,* March 1970, p. 241.

Beak, J. R. "Where College Recruiting Goes Wrong," *Personnel,* September–October 1966, p. 22.

Carlson, R., Thayer, P., Mayfield, E., and Peterson, D. "Improvements in the Selection Interview," *Personnel Journal,* April 1971, p. 268.

Dempsey, F. K. (Jr.) "College Recruiting—A Reassessment," *Personnel Journal,* September 1970, p. 746.

Hackamack, L. C., and Iannone, C. R. "Selecting, Recruiting, Retaining Today's College Graduate," *Personnel Journal,* December 1969, p. 988.

Lee, S. M. "Job Selection by College Graduates," *Personnel Journal,* May 1970, p. 392.

Marion, B. W., and Trieb, S. E. "Job Orientation—A Factor In Employee Performance and Turnover," *Personnel Journal,* October 1969, p. 799.

Salemi, E. C., and Monahan, J. B. "The Psychological Contract of Employment: Do Recruiters and Students Agree?" *Personnel Journal,* December 1970, p. 986.

Seiler, D. A. "Job Needs of the Newly Hired Professional," *Personnel Journal,* November 1970, p. 923.

SHOW US YOU'RE REALLY CREATIVE!

At the conclusion of the monthly *Greater St. Louis Personnel Managers Association* meeting, Del Condon worked his way through the crowd toward Phillip Sikes. Condon had heard of an unusual approach being used by Allen Pharmaceutical Corporation to screen potential applicants and was anxious to get more information from their Personnel Manager. Fortunately, Condon caught up to Sikes just as he was leaving and invited him to coffee.

"How are things over at National Photocopy?" asked Sikes after the two men were seated in a nearby coffee shop. "It's been about three months since I last saw you at a meeting."

"Pretty good," replied Condon. "Our regular line of photocopy equipment has been selling well and we have two advanced products which will be introduced in the next six months. Frankly, I've been too busy to get to many professional meetings because we're involved in a large personnel recruitment effort."

"Sounds good," said Sikes smiling broadly, "I like to hear that my fellow personnel managers work as hard as I do." He sipped his coffee and, sensing that there was more than idle talk on Condon's mind added, "Is there something I can do for you?"

"As a matter of fact there is," replied Condon. "Our personnel recruitment effort has been going slower than top management would like and I thought you might have some good ideas to share with me since we're not competitors."

"Happy to help out an associate if I can," said Sikes. "What seems to be the problem?"

"Well, as you know, this is currently a tight labor market for professional people. At National Photocopy we offer good working conditions, salary, and the usual benefits package. We've even written some glowing advertisements for the newspaper want ads about the exciting and challenging career opportunities available at our company. But, we still can't seem to attract the talent we're after."

"Are you possibly too selective in the initial interviews?" asked Sikes.

"Not really. We're selective, of course, but our problem is not as much a case of weeding out the applicants as it is getting enough people to apply in the first case. We're simply getting too few applicants for the positions we have available. I'm concerned that some of the more talented people around are simply not being stimulated by our ads to send in a resumé or come in for an interview."

Condon continued, "Two months ago I saw an employment advertisement from Allen Pharmaceutical which really looked interesting and I wanted to ask you about the response you got."

"I suppose you're referring to our *creativity campaign*?" asked Sikes.

"Yes. As I recall, the bold title on the advertisement read, *Show Us You're Really Creative*."

"That's the one," said Sikes. He leaned back and recited the ad from memory.

> Allen Pharmaceutical Corporation, the nation's foremost manufacturer of sophisticated laboratory and hospital equipment, needs qualified professionals in a broad range of technical and management disciplines for new openings in both the United States and European operations.
>
> These are career positions with a dynamic growth oriented organization. We expect outstanding contributions from all our personnel and, therefore, hire only the most promising. If you *really* are talented and have specific skills which you feel will help us achieve our growth goals, we want to hear from you.
>
> But, please, no tired or routine resumés. *If you're really creative it should be apparent from your inquiry alone.* Please respond to . . . etc., etc. . . .

Condon laughed. "You know that advertisement by heart."

"I ought to," replied Sikes, "I wrote it! We were facing the same tight labor market, and top management wanted Industrial Relations to try a fresh, inventive approach to personnel recruitment."

"Well," asked Condon, "if it's not confidential, I'd like to know what response you received."

"Fantastic! Nothing less than fantastic! We typically receive twenty to thirty replies which can be traced directly to a general employment advertisement in which we call out no specific job requirements. In this case, within two weeks, we had well *over a hundred replies* which could only have been prompted by the creativity advertisement."

Sikes continued, "You wouldn't believe the wild responses we received. No one sent in his resumé . . . on plain paper, I mean. We received numerous replies with personal history and achievements information recorded on tape and cassette cartridges. One fellow sent us a videotape of himself describing his background. Three sent short filmstrips with each film frame describing some facet of his background.

"Some responses were even more unusual. One man sent us a punched paper tape which printed out his background when inserted into an automatic typewriter. Another submitted a series of computer punch cards which we processed and obtained a printout of his experience. One lazy guy simply jotted his experience out in pencil on a large brown paper bag and sent it on to us with the notation that he considered himself 'practical as well as inventive.'"

Condon shook his head in amazement. "It's hard to believe that your request to demonstrate creativity would be so enthusiastically received."

"We only ran the ad once so there's no way of knowing in advance if it would work as well the second time . . . or whether another company such as yours could adopt a similar gimmick."

"We have no intention of copying your approach," said Condon. "I'm merely after fresh ideas and wanted to find out what the response would be to such an unusual personnel recruitment approach."

Condon hesitated and then decided to ask a more confidential question. "Tell me," he said, "of those hundred or more professionals who responded, how many did you actually hire?"

There was a long pause before Sikes replied. "That's the embarrassing part," he said at last. "We wouldn't dare admit this publicly, but *we didn't hire a single person* from that group! Management felt the applicants were too *far out* to fit in with our company."

Discussion Questions

1. What do you think of the personnel recruitment campaign used by Allen Pharmaceutical?
2. Allen Pharmaceutical asked for creative responses but felt the people were "too far out." Explain this management dilemma.

3. What possible approaches might Del Condon of National Photocopy use to attract professional talent to his company?

Special Project

Review the job opportunities section of local newspapers. Clip out advertisements which are particularly appealing to you.

Classify them in terms of:

1. Eye catching appeal.
2. Approach, style, or technique.
3. Credibility.

Present in class.

Selected References

Books

Mandell, M. M. *The Selection Process: Choosing The Right Man For the Job.* New York: American Management Association, 1964.

Anthologies

Huseman, R., Logue, C., and Freshley, D. *Readings in Interpersonal and Organizational Communication.* Boston, Massachusetts: Holbrook Press, Inc., 1969. Downs, C. W. "What Does the Selection Interview Accomplish?" p. 287.

Leavitt, H. J., and Pondy, L. R. (Eds.). *Readings in Managerial Psychology.* Chicago, Illinois: University of Chicago Press, 1964. Haire, M. "Use of Tests in Employee Selection," p. 157.

Articles

Bierman, J. "Taking Down the 'Inventor Keep Out' Sign," *Innovation*, Number Thirteen, 1970, p. 51.

Fielder, F. E. "Engineer the Job to Fit the Manager," *Harvard Business Review*, September–October 1965.

"Fitting the Job to the Man," *Time*, November 9, 1970, p. 74.

Gallagher, W., and Phelps, E. D. "Integrated Approach to Technical Staffing," *Harvard Business Review*, July–August 1963, p. 122.

Ginsburg, S., and Neuhoff, R. C. "Selection of A Superior Group," *Personnel Journal*, October 1969, p. 813.

Jantsch, E. "To Help Students More Help Society More," *Innovation*, Number Four, 1969, p. 18.

Johnson, G. R. "Building A Staff-Hire or Train?" *Personnel Journal*, March 1970, p. 222.

Martin, R. A. "Toward More Productive Interviewing," *Personnel Journal*, May 1971, p. 359.

WHERE DO I FIND A BLACK COST ACCOUNTANT?

Paul Collier, personnel manager at Farmingdale Valve Company, has had over twenty years experience in industrial relations activities. He offers his views on some practical problems he has encountered in equal opportunity for employment:

"Equal opportunity in employment is now the law for all organizations doing business with the federal government ... and I can say with pride that our company has always had an official policy of no discrimination based upon race, religion, sex, age, or physical disability.

"Unfortunately we all have biases, sometimes unconscious ones, which affect hiring, promotion, job assignment, and layoff decisions. No doubt some employees or applicants may have felt discriminated against throughout the years. Most of the situations I personally reviewed were complaints without foundation, but I'm sure a small number were true.

"Philosophy or biases aside, we do have some practical problems relative to equal opportunity. Our plant is quite old and located in one of the poorer city neighborhoods. We also have two contracts for special military aircraft valves and have just received another.

"We're having no trouble staffing for increased manufacturing operations but are having a devil of a time filling professional positions both in terms of available candidates and government pressures. Some people, particularly women, are reluctant to drive and work in this part of the city. I tell them that our company has excellent community relationships and our experience with robbery and vandalism is no worse than anywhere else ... but I'm sure location is a negative hiring factor.

"Our biggest problem though is with government pressures for hiring larger percentages of minority workers more in line with the local population mix. So far we have been unable to fully comply. Our intent is good and many manufacturing positions filled recently have been from minority groups. But, tell me, where do I find a black cost accountant?"

Discussion Questions

1. Evaluate and discuss Paul Collier's position on finding professional employees from various minority groups.
2. How might Collier remedy this problem?
3. The unconscious biases mentioned by Collier often are in the form of *institutional discrimination* such as seniority and referral systems. Discuss the problem of institutional forms of discrimination.

For Industrial Groups in Particular
4. What are the "unofficial" attitudes of your organization relative to employment and personnel practices?
5. Paul Collier raises some practical problems about equal employment opportunity. Discuss these and others which may be applicable for your organization.
6. Is your company covered under Department of Labor Order No. 4? Discuss the implications of this and any later similar orders.

Special Projects

1. Develop a positive and workable promotional or advertising campaign which would be effective in attracting professionals from various minority groups. Prepare as an out-of-class assignment and present details to the entire group.
2. How does local industry meet this challenge? Conduct a survey of local firms. Initial contacts should be made in writing to Personnel Manager, Personnel Director, or Director of Industrial Relations if you do not have a named individual.
3. Many organizations in the United States are now involved in improving equal opportunity in hiring and upgrading through the U.S. Government Executive Order 11246 (specific sections). This order has created the concept of Affirmative Action Programs. The following excerpts from the Federal Register[1] explain the meaning of Affirmative Action Programs:

SUBPART A—GENERAL

§60-2.1 Title, purpose and scope.

This part shall also be known as "Order No. 4," and shall cover nonconstruction contractors. Section 60-1.40 of this chapter, Affirmative Action Compliance Programs, requires that within 120 days from the commencement of a contract each prime contractor or subcontractor with 50 or more employees and a contract of $50,000 or more develop a written affirmative action compliance program for each of its establishments. A review of agency compliance surveys indicates that many contractors do not have affirmative action programs on file at the time an establishment is visited by a compliance investigator. This part details the agency review procedure and the results of a contractor's failure to develop and maintain an affirmative action program and then sets forth detailed guidelines to be used by contractors and Government agencies in developing and judging these programs as well as the good faith effort required to transform the programs from paper commitments to equal employment opportunity.

SUBPART B—REQUIRED CONTENTS OF AFFIRMATIVE ACTION PROGRAMS

§60-2.11 Required utilization analysis and goals.

Affirmative action programs must contain the following information:
(a) An analysis of all major job categories at the facility, with explanations if minorities are currently being underutilized in any one or more job categories (job "category" herein meaning one or a group of jobs having similar content, wage rates and opportunities. "Underutilization" is defined as having fewer minorities in a particular job category than would reasonably be expected by their availability. In determining whether minorities are being underutilized in any job category, the contractor will consider at least all of the following factors:

(1) The minority population of the labor area surrounding the facility;
(2) The size of the minority unemployment force in the labor area surrounding the facility;
(3) The percentage of minority work force as compared with the total work force in the immediate labor area;

[1]*Federal Register*, Volume 35, Number 25, Thursday, February 5, 1970, Washington, D.C.

(4) The general availability of minorities having requisite skills in the immediate labor area:

(5) The availability of minorities having requisite skills in an area in which the contractor can reasonably recruit;

(6) The availability of promotable minority employees within the contractor's organization;

(7) The anticipated expansion, contraction and turnover of and in the work force;

(8) The existence of training institutions capable of training minorities in the requisite skills; and

(9) The degree of training which the contractor is reasonably able to undertake as a means of making all job classes available to minorities.

What impact has Order No. 4 had on one or more firms in your area? What has been their progress and problems? Have a select committee discuss Order No. 4 with qualified representation of local firms and report their findings in class.

Note. Order No. 4 referenced in this case study was revised on December 4, 1971 to include women as well as minorities. (*Federal Register*, Volume 36, Number 234). Most sections are identical to the original issue with most paragraphs now reading . . . with respect to minorities *and women*.

Selected References

Articles

Barrett, R. S. "Grey Areas in Black and White Testing," *Harvard Business Review*, January–February 1968, p. 92.

Bramwell, J. "A Black View of White Management," *Innovation*, Number Nine, 1970, p. 36.

Foss, L. "The Corporate Search for Soul," *Personnel Journal*, December 1970, p. 1021.

Haynes, U. (Jr.) "Equal Job Opportunity: The Credibility Gap," *Harvard Business Review*, May–June 1968, p. 113.

Jaffe, C. L., Cohen, S. L., and Cherry, R. "Supervisory Selection Program for Disadvantaged or Minority Employees," *Training and Development Journal*, January 1972, p. 22.

Johnson, F. R. "Recruiting, Retaining, and Advancing Minority Employees," *Training and Development Journal*, January 1972, p. 28.

Kidder, A. E., and Adams, P. "The Black MBA—Not Qualified?—Or Misunderstood?" *Personnel Journal*, October 1969, p. 818.

Lawrie, J. W. "Making it—the Hardest Way," *Psychology Today*, November 1969, p. 29.

Purcell, T. V. "Break Down Your Employment Barriers," *Harvard Business Review*, July–August 1968, p. 65.

Weymar, C. S., and Goekaed, J. R. "Barriers to Hiring the Blacks," *Harvard Business Review*, September–October 1969, p. 144.

THE RULES ARE DIFFERENT FOR WOMEN

"The roles we have played as minorities, the roles we have played as women, and the roles we have played as majority males have all got to be reconciled."

JOHN L. WILKS
Deputy Assistant Secretary of Labor
From a speech to members of the
Merchants and Manufacturers Association
Los Angeles, December 2, 1971

Marcia Osborn is attractive and articulate, a housewife in her mid-thirties, and married to a government contract administrator with the Army in Silver Spring, Maryland. The Osborns have one child in elementary school and two others of pre-school age. They own a modest home near Bethesda, have a large circle of friends, and enjoy numerous community activities.

Marcia has a B.A. in Business Administration with a major in Finance. She has not been employed since her marriage eight years ago. Recently, Marcia has considered seeking work in her field when all of her children are in school but has doubts based upon her job experience just after college.

"All this talk today about equal rights for women simply will not change the basic attitudes that men have about the work environment. Whatever they say about accepting women as equals is just that . . . a lot of talk.

"There are, of course, traditional fields for women such as teaching, nursing, or airline stewardess, all largely dead end vocations with little opportunity for career development. Within industry women are accepted for assembly work, reception, secretarial and clerical work, but little else. The professional and executive level is closed to us!

"When I was in college the system was fair for men and women. I worked hard and was able to graduate in the top ten percent of my class. After graduation I took an accounting job with a small company and soon found that the rules were completely different.

"First, I was paid less than any other professional in the office. I expected an entry level salary having no prior accounting experience but later found that all white-collar males, even non-professionals, were earning more.

"The job was never very difficult. I found myself finishing early each day and asking for additional assignments. I was given more work but it was always routine paperwork which any clerk-typist could handle.

"Over a period of months I made several procedural and work simplification suggestions which were politely acknowledged and ignored. There was a prevailing attitude that if it wasn't a man's idea it couldn't be any good. At the time I really wanted a career and planned to continue working after I married Phillip, but I quit on the day I was asked to fill in as substitute PBX operator."

Discussion Questions

1. How typical is Marcia Osborn's story?
2. Would she find business and industry more fair today than 10 years ago?
3. What, in your opinion, are the more common forms of discrimination against women?

4. Some state and local laws long held to be "in the best interest of women" are now being challenged as being discriminatory. What is their general nature? Discuss.

Special Projects

1. Plan and conduct a 30 minute class debate on *Equal Opportunity for Women: Fact or Fantasy?* Allow time for teams to organize, plan, and collect necessary data.
2. U.S. Department of Labor Order No. 4 has recently been revised to include women as well as minorities in the establishment of equal opportunity in employment programs.[1] Have a select committee discuss the impact of Order No. 4 (Revised) with local employers and present their findings in class.

Selected References

Books
DuBrin, A. J. *Women in Transition*. Springfield, Illinois: Charles C. Thomas, 1972.
Levinson, H. *Executive Stress*. New York: Harper & Row, 1970, Chapter 4: "Why Women Work."

Articles
Bird, C. "Women in Business: The Invisible Bar," *Personnel*, May–June 1968, p. 29.
Horner, M. S. "Fail: Bright Women," *Psychology Today*, November 1969, p. 36.
Lunardi, V. "Sex Discrimination in Industry," *Management Review*, July 1966.
Pogrebin, L. C. "What to Do If Your Boss Discriminates Against Women," *Ladies Home Journal*, January 1972, p. 46.

Literature
Job Discrimination Handbook, Human Rights For Women, 1128 National Press Building, Washington, D.C., 20004, $0.50 each.
Laws In Sex Discrimination In Employment, Women's Bureau, U.S. Department of Labor, Washington, D.C., $0.30 each.

AT HOME ON THE RANGE

VIDEO: We follow a single automobile as it moves along a two lane asphalt road through a relatively barren high desert area.

ANNOUNCER: "North of the sleepy desert town of Mojave, California, the highway suddenly veers to the right and knifes its way along the desert floor. To the left are the bleak eastern slopes of the great Sierra Nevada mountain range; to the right are fields of craggy sagebrush dotted here and there by lonely joshua trees . . .

[1]Order No. 4 (Revised), *Federal Register*, Volume 36. Number 234, December 4, 1971. *See also, Where Do I Find a Black Cost Accountant?* page 93.

their arms reaching mournfully upward as if begging for rain.
Now and then the road cuts through a small dry lake where blowing yellow sand is all that remains of a once fertile valley. Ahead?
Ahead there appears to be nothing but the same emptiness for any
casual visitor to this part of the vast Mojave Desert."

VIDEO: In the distance at nearly the center of a long low valley,
evidence of life is quite apparent. Two distinct towns can be
seen, one separated from the other by less than a mile and
both fifteen miles off the main highway.

ANNOUNCER: "It is no surprise then that most drivers on their way
to the beautiful ski areas of the Sierra Nevada pay little attention
to the dual oasis fifteen miles to the right and down at the bottom
of the desert floor. Those who do know that this is the location of
Fort Arnold Burkett and its companion town of Richline are
still probably unimpressed, or, perhaps, indifferent. Who cares
about a lonely Army Proving Ground, especially when there is
skiing ahead?"

VIDEO: Long shot of a tall barbed wire fence with sign:

FORT ARNOLD BURKETT
DESERT PROVING STATION

Camera cuts to sentries at main gate checking pass cards and ad-
mitting vehicles.

ANNOUNCER: "Relatively obscure and certainly remote geographically,
Fort Arnold Burkett is not even widely known among the military . . . much less the general public. Yet a small but extremely
significant part of military research and development takes place
here. Here is where the ADAM-204 tactical field weapon was
developed and tested. ADAM-204 is the weapon which can be
fitted with an atomic device although it has never as yet been so
employed . . ."

So began a television network documentary a year ago called, *The Many
Faces of Our Federal Government*; a presentation which was destined to have
long lasting effects on Fort Arnold Burkett and the town of Richline
over and above its planned shock value for the public. The program went
on to portray Fort Burkett as a super secret center for development and
testing of various unspecified doomsday devices and hinted that its isolated
inhabitants (the majority well educated civilian professionals and technicians) were right-leaning reactionaries, out of touch with the real world.

99

In the weeks that followed the broadcast, the following events transpired:

1. Public furor was aroused against the continued existence of Fort Burkett.

2. A prominent senator and three members of the House of Representatives drafted bills for abandonment of Fort Burkett activities. All bills were quietly dropped after discussions with a high ranking White House official.

3. Colonel J. Clayton Morse, military commander of Fort Burkett, held several press conferences in which he angrily denied all allegations made by the network and called the broadcast "a case of pure fabrication in the worst traditions of journalism." All major networks carried his rebuttal statements.

4. Colonel Morse was quietly reassigned to a largely ceremonial position at Fort Leonard Wood in Missouri.

5. Technical direction of Fort Arnold Burkett was temporarily transferred to Dr. Stephen Brill, civilian director of test operations until a new commander could be named. (It is common practice for a civilian to head actual technical operations with administration handled largely through a staff of military officers and men. Officially the Fort is headed by a military officer although 80 percent of the staff is civilian.)

6. Many key civilian personnel quit during the next three months.

7. Differences of opinion flared into outbursts of anger and resentment between workers and residents of Fort Burkett and civilians in and around the town of Richline.

8. Morale dropped sharply and several critical program milestones were not achieved on schedule.

9. Two months ago Colonel Willis T. Acone was named to direct operations at Fort Burkett. Acone was particularly noted for his work in developing a new image for the Army with particular emphasis on recruitment and re-enlistments.

10. Dr. Stephen Brill was permanently appointed to the post of Director of Technical operations. This created a civil counterpart to the ranking military officer and a dual leadership for Fort Burkett. It was widely hinted that these moves would free the civilian work force from military dictates to a greater degree and place technical direction in the hands of a more qualified person. The appointment of Acone was clearly seen as an attempt to improve morale, improve civilian recruitment, and reduce civilian turnover.

In his first two weeks on the job, Colonel Acone was briefed on the status of existing programs. Convinced that no unusual technical obstacles existed, he advised Brill to continue operations with the intent of meeting previously established target dates and project objectives.

The next task for Colonel Acone was to attack the problems of morale, poor recruitment, and high turnover. He reviewed general data about Fort Burkett, its personnel, and the general community.

Data

Fort Burkett Employment

1175	Civilian — All Skills
250	Military
1425	Total

Population

3200	Military and Civilian (including Dependents) within Fort Burkett
2700	Richline and surrounding area
5900	Total

Population Affected by Fort Burkett

3200	Fort Burkett Personnel and Dependents
1200	From Richline wholly dependent on Burkett (personnel living in Richline but working at Burkett)
700	From Richline partially affected by Burkett (merchants, truckers, teachers, etc.)
5100	Totally or partially dependent on Burkett

Fort Burkett Projects (Last 5 years)

	(percent)
Military — unclassified	47
Military — minimal security	18
Military — secret	5
Non-military programs*	27
Not categorized	3
Total	100

*Non-military programs included:
  Sea Rescue Systems Development
  Commercial Aircraft Escape Procedures
  Commercial Aircraft Safety Studies
  Jet engine testing
  Automobile Crash Safety Studies
  NASA Space Vehicle Testing

Personnel Turnover (Percent per year)

Traditional "average"	7.0	
Fifteen months ago	6.2	(Prior to T.V. broadcast)
Six months ago	18.7	
Current	14.2	

Number of Job Positions Open

Traditional "average"	40
Fifteen months ago	33 (Prior to T.V. broadcast)
Six months ago	85
Current	72

Ratio of Job Acceptances to Offers Made

	To Government Employees Now At Other Locations	To College Graduates And Other Non-Government Employees
	(percent)	(percent)
Traditional "average"	17	12
Fifteen months ago	18	15
Six months ago	8	4
Current	9	4

Average Age of Fort Burkett Employee

	(years)
Ten years ago	37.0
Five years ago	35.9
Two years ago	37.1
One year ago	39.9
Current	42.7

Political Registration (Last Election)

	Fort Burkett	Richline
	(percent)	(percent)
Democrat	47	43
Republican	41	45
Other	4	5
Decline to State	8	7
Total	100	100

Note. The Burkett–Richline community has voted for the winning candidate in the last four presidential races and the last three California senatorial races.

A private survey poll taken three months ago asked: What is your opinion about the activities at Fort Burkett? Should they be continued?

	Burkett Personnel	Richline Personnel	General Public
	(percent)	(percent)	(percent)
Definitely in national and public interest—continue	74	62	39
Mostly in national and public interest	18	15	15
Much work worthwhile but should stop some activities	5	14	15
Abandon	2	4	12
No opinion	1	5	19
Total	100	100	100

Colonel Acone then requested the Personnel Management Branch to:

1. Review files of all persons who voluntarily terminated employment in the last twelve months with particular emphasis on statements they may have made during termination and to list the most typical reasons for leaving Burkett.
2. Conduct an attitude survey within Fort Burkett and Richline to determine prevailing attitudes about the Fort, the work, the community, etc.

One week ago the following information was submitted to Colonel Acone as being representative of prevailing attitudes:

1. *Of those who voluntarily terminated their employment*

"My wife was sick and tired of seeing the same people every day. She complained about lack of shopping and the things only a city can offer. So, I finally gave in."

"There's something artificial about Burkett. I mean, living behind a barbed wire fence like a prisoner of some kind."

"The work itself was interesting, but waiting in line for good family housing was too much. I have four children and the best I could get was a three bedroom bungalow at $275 a month. That's no bargain, and prices in Richline are even more expensive."[1]

"When I was told about the quiet peaceful high desert, no one mentioned the winter winds and sandstorms. We lived in dust up to our ankles!"

"Too much of a military atmosphere. You know, M.P.s as patrolmen and street traffic controllers."

"My project was cancelled and I couldn't find a suitable alternative."

"Couldn't stand going into Richline for any reason. That town is a parasite."

"My wife and I began to have personal problems! She admitted becoming romantically involved with one of the non-coms."

"The place is deadsville (a young bachelor)."

---

[1]Government rental housing on Fort Burkett property is available to all employees on a first-come-first-served basis as available. Higher service ranks can usually qualify for better housing. Seniority is also used as a basis for moving to better housing.

2. *Attitudes of Fort Burkett personnel who expressed no desire to leave*

"No matter what people say, this is great country! No smog, no congestion, no freeways, no city pressures. I had an ulcer for five years while working in L.A. but it's about gone now!"

"It's very peaceful here. You feel you're a part of nature."

"I'm far more creative at Burkett than any place else I've ever worked. I like the environment and the caliber of people they hire—real professionals."

"I wish more people knew about the civilian test programs going on up here. All they get on television is that small part which hardly involves any of us."

"You can advance faster here through the G.S.[2] ratings than anywhere else in government work and you have far more decision-making freedom too."

"Tell me one other place you can live in the United States where culture is brought to you at a drastically subsidized price. Last week there were four presentations by the San Francisco Ballet Company at the Fort auditorium. We get the best up here, *the best*."

Some second thoughts by those who plan to stay:

"Wish they'd clean up the company (Fort) store."

"Every time we get a cost of living increase, prices magically go up the same amount all over Richline. They have us coming and going."

"I do worry about the children. How can they develop a realistic picture of the world living in an unreal man-made utopia?"

3. *Attitudes expressed by several persons in Richline*

WAITRESS: "They (Fort personnel) always act like they're better than we are."

DOCTOR: "I'm quite comfortable here. However, we do treat more psychosomatic problems than the average, particularly among women and teenagers.

MOTEL OPERATOR: "The Army practically forced me to add on rooms to my motel on the promise of new programs which would bring frequent visitors. So far, the opposite has been true!"

[2]G.S.—Government Service Ratings.

TRUCK DRIVER: "Hell, I was drifting from job to job until I settled in Richline. If the government wasn't here, there wouldn't be jobs like mine."

HIGH SCHOOL PRINCIPAL: "Fort Burkett has two elementary schools behind the gates but the junior high and high school are in Richline and serve students of both. We've had no special problems here but the Fort kids are a little brighter on the average and more career oriented. Luckily no significant drug problems to date. I like it here."

AUTO DEALER: If it weren't for Fort Burkett I wouldn't have a business.

Colonel Acone carefully analyzed all material submitted to him and made an announcement to his staff at the next regular meeting.

"Gentlemen, we have had and continue to have several complex behavioral and environmental problems on our hands. Fortunately, I believe we can do a great deal to improve the situation and I suggest we start right now."

Discussion Questions

1. How might government recruiters better approach the problem of personnel recruitment to avoid later frustration and disappointment?
2. What steps can realistically be taken to reduce turnover?
3. What can be done to improve the image of Fort Burkett to the public as well as prospective employees?
4. What can be done to improve local community relations?
5. What role should be played by community leaders in Richline?

Special Project

Prepare a detailed analysis and set of recommendations for this case on an individual basis and submit as a formal paper.

Selected References

Books

Bennis, W. G. *Changing Organizations: Essays on the development and evolution of human organizations.* New York: McGraw-Hill, 1966.

Drucker, P. F. *The Age of Discontinuity:* Guidelines To Our Changing Society. New York: Harper & Row, 1969.

Likert, R. *The Human Organization:* Its Management and Value. New York: McGraw-Hill, 1967.

Anthologies

Hampton, D. R., Summer, C. E., and Webber, R. A. (Eds.). *Organizational Behavior and the Practice of Management*. Glenview, Illinois: Scott, Foresman and Company, 1968.
   Dearborn, C., and Simon, H. "Selective Perception," p. 162.
   Leavitt, H. J. "Perception: From The Inside Looking Out," p. 155.
Huseman, R., Logue, C., and Freshley, D. *Readings in Interpersonal and Organizational Communication*. Boston, Massachussets: Holbrook Press, Inc., 1969.
   Schultz, R. S. "How to Handle Grievances," p. 310.
   Timbers, E. "Strengthening Motivation Through Communication," p. 203.
Leavitt, H. J., and Pondy, L. R. (Eds.). *Readings in Managerial Psychology*. Chicago, Illinois: University of Chicago Press, 1964. Schelling, T. C. "Bargaining, Communication, and Limited War," p. 422.
Koontz, H., and O'Donnell, C. *Management: A Book of Readings*. New York: McGraw-Hill, 1968. Koontz, H. "Challenges for Intellectual Leadership in Management," p. 674.

Articles

Miller, T. F. "How to Slow the Turnover Flow," *Personnel Journal*, May 1968.
Nadler, L. "The Organization as a Micro-Culture," *Personnel Journal*, December 1969, p. 949.
Sheldon, D. "Building More-Effective Teams," *Innovation*, Number Fifteen, 1970, p. 32.
Zaleznik, A. "Management of Disappointment," *Harvard Business Review*, November–December 1967, p. 59.

DR. SHIBATA HAS RESIGNED!

Todd Daniels was stunned when he read the short interoffice memorandum:

August 7

To: Todd Daniels
From: I. O. Shibata
Subject: Resignation

Please accept my resignation effective August 31.
   Although I do not have another position at the moment, I cannot continue working in a climate which is not conducive to creativity. It is very unfortunate that this company equates ability in direct proportion to seniority.

With regret,
I. O. SHIBATA

cc R. Moore

It was 6:30 p.m. Friday evening. Todd Daniels had just arrived back at the office after being away at a four day conference in *Computer Assisted Product Design* in New York. Daniels, the Associate Director of Research, had planned to stop by the office for only a few minutes to pick up his mail which he knew would have accumulated over the past several days and then drive home. If anything looked urgent he would then have the weekend to give it some thought.

Well, *this* certainly was urgent. *Dr. Shibata has resigned!* That thought refused to leave his mind as he continued to sort through the many routine pieces of correspondence which were on his desk. Why? Why should Shibata quit so suddenly? What did he mean about ability and seniority?

Normally, Daniels would be far less concerned over a resignation, but Shibata would be a significant loss. The thirty-nine year old researcher had only been with the company for fourteen months but already had made several major technical contributions. Two of his concepts were already incorporated in new product designs being readied for production.

Shibata, with a Ph.D. in Electronic Engineering, was respected nationally for his theoretical papers and presentations to the American Society of Electronic Physics and other professional organizations. He had two patents to his credit and a stable, creative work background.

Daniels himself had originally approved hiring Shibata. It was just over a year ago when the company was attempting to move into the design and manufacture of a new line of sophisticated computer peripheral equipment. Shibata was hired to provide the extra bit of talent to ensure that these new products would be technically superior to all existing competition. Until now, Shibata had been doing just that . . . and, apparently, from outward appearances at least, happy with his work and the company.

Damn!, thought Daniels. If a problem was developing, why hadn't Moore taken care of it before? Why do these things end up on my desk when it's often too late for corrective action?

Daniels thought a moment about Roger Moore, head of the Peripheral Products Research group. Although Moore reported to Daniels, the two did not meet frequently. For one thing, most of the research projects were of longer duration and weekly reports were unnecessary. Moore, generally cool headed, tended to solve his own problems and later tell Daniels what he had done. Another reason for their infrequent meetings was that Daniels spent most of his time fighting fires in other design groups. Daniels hated to admit the truth of the last point, but it was true, nevertheless.

Most of the mail was routine and Daniels was down to the last few pieces. Then a closed envelope marked *Confidential* caught his eye and he opened it.

August 5

To: Todd Daniels
From: Roger Moore
Subject: Sam Fischer

Sam Fischer continues to cause problems for me. I respect the fact that he is one of our most senior employees in terms of length of employment. He is certainly one of our most loyal employees. But, he is having constant blowups with Dr. Shibata and Dr. Mason on technical matters.

Sam is a fair technical man, but no match for those two. Both Shibata and Mason are annoyed with his antiquated ideas and methodologies, and I could lose one or both of them because of it.

Under other circumstances I would transfer the man. But, you know how highly Martin Masters regards him. Martin still thinks of him as "Mr. Research" in this company, even though he hasn't come up with anything significant in years.

Could you please inform Martin of the seriousness of the problem, in a diplomatic way of course, before I take some kind of action?

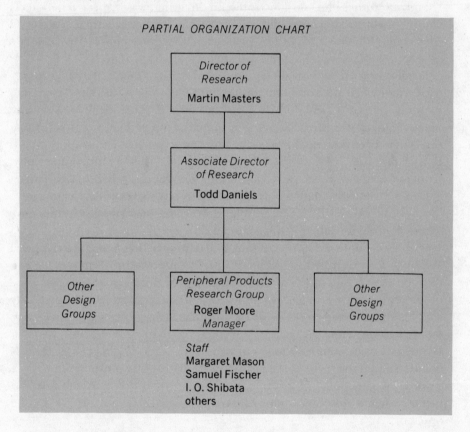

PARTIAL ORGANIZATION CHART

Discussion Questions

1. What can (should) be done about Shibata's resignation?
2. How would you handle the Sam Fischer situation?
3. To what degree should Martin Masters be involved?
4. Can this work team be effectively rebuilt?
5. What factors should be weighed when organizing a work team?

6. One school of thought says the optimum life of any work team (without significant personnel changes) is two to three years. Agree or disagree? Why?
7. What is meant by technical obsolescence?

Special Project

Prepare and submit a well researched paper titled, "Technical Obsolescence— What Can Be Done?"

Selected References

Books
Danielson, L. E. *Characteristics of Engineers and Scientists*. Ann Arbor, Michigan: Bureau of Industrial Relations, The University of Michigan, 1960.
Evans, C. G. *Supervising R & D Personnel*. New York: American Management Association, Inc., 1969.
Pelz, D. C., and Andrews, F. M. *Scientists in Organizations*. New York: Wiley, 1966.

Anthologies
Preparing Tomorrow's Business Leaders Today. Drucker, P. F. (Ed.). Englewood Cliffs, New Jersey: Prentice-Hall, 1969. Zand, D. E. "Managing the Knowledge Organization," p. 112.

Articles
Badawy, M. K. "Understanding The Role Orientations of Scientists and Engineers," *Personnel Journal*, June 1971, p. 449.
Breton, E. J. "Caution: Fragile Inventive Talent; Handle With Care," *Innovation*, Number Nineteen, 1971, p. 44.
Chartier, R. "Managing the Knowledge Employee," *Personnel Journal*, August 1968, p. 558.
Dalton, G. W., and Thompson, P. H. "Accelerating Obsolescence of Older Engineers," *Harvard Business Review*, September–October 1971, p. 57.
"How to Handle Prima Donnas," *Industry Week*, April 27, 1970, p. 28.
Hughes, E. C. "Preserving Individualism on the R & D Team," *Harvard Business Review*, January–February 1968, p. 72.
Lee, S. M. "Organizational Identification of Scientists," *Academy of Management Journal*, September 1969, p. 327.
Pelz, D. "What It Takes to Make a Problem Solver Productive," *Innovation*, Number Nine, 1970, p. 2.
Roberts, E. "What it Takes to be an Entrepreneur . . . and to Hang on to One," *Innovation*, Number Seven, 1969, p. 46.
Walton, R. "The Inventor and The Company," *Innovation*, Number Four, 1969, p. 36.
Young, R. "No Room for the Searcher," *Innovation*, Number Eleven, 1970, p. 51.

CASE STUDY CROSS REFERENCE

Although located elsewhere in this book, the following problem situations are also valuable in the study of Section 4:

Achievement, Growth, and Recognition

"Ferris, I just don't understand what you're asking me to do. You're a man with unquestioned talent in a field which needs and fully recognizes your talent! You're a specialist, Ferris . . . a specialist! One of the best! Why in heaven's name do you want to get into consumer advertising? It's a big sea full of big fish. You'll be lost there, man . . . lost!"

ARMSTEAD
The Specialist

INTRODUCTION

What is the nature of achievement? How is it different from recognition? How can individual and group contributions to organizational progress and goals be identified? What forms should recognition take to maintain individual motivation and group morale? Can achievement and frustration occur together? How can individual and team growth be fostered through appropriate forms of recognition? Why is continued personal growth so necessary? What is the role of money in personal recognition?

Cases in This Section

The Specialist

An executive questions the thinking of an employee who wishes to change specialty fields . . . why tamper with obvious success? . . . the employee yearns for yet another challenge . . . what consequences must be faced?

Can I Find Happiness with a Pump?

Promotion for successful effort may not be a just reward . . . a field representative examines his feelings about his work as he considers a new assignment.

The Marginal Purchasing Agent

The dilemma of low motivation on the job and high motivation off the job . . . some interesting aspects of the problem . . . should the job be altered or is fault rightly with the employee? . . . the concept of self-actualization.

Employee of the Month

One form of individual recognition has adverse morale effects on others . . . fair or unfair system? . . . the value of it all.

Big Bash at Bergmann's

An unusual form of group recognition comes under critical review . . . is it working? . . . does it motivate after all? . . . some potentially dangerous situations . . . a high price to pay.

Recognition Won't Buy Bread

Job satisfaction and job dissatisfaction . . . money is not that important . . . or is it? . . . a confused supervisor sorts out a common dilemma . . . what needs are being satisfied?

THE SPECIALIST

Author's note. Years ago I heard a story about the composer George Gershwin who was apparently then at the zenith of his career. Americans everywhere were singing and humming those catchy tunes which had made him famous and his output of pop music seemed limitless. Oddly, Gershwin himself was unhappy. He longed to make a contribution in a more serious vein and, against the advice of friends, went to Europe to study classical composition and to consider his future role in music.

While in Europe, Gershwin approached the great composer, Maurice Ravel, and asked if the master would consider having him as a pupil. But Ravel declined and is reported to have said, "Why do you wish to be a second rate Ravel when you can be a first rate Gershwin?" Still determined, Gershwin was later to produce such works as a piano concerto, *An American in Paris* suite, and the great American blues-opera, *Porgy and Bess*.

"Ferris, it seems to me that we've been over this entire thing . . . and not too long ago as I recall." Armstead was visibly bothered by the repetition of a discussion which he thought he had previously resolved.

"I'm sorry, Mr. Armstead. I really don't mean to be pushy. I realize you're quite busy on the new Imperial Coffee account . . . but I feel I could make a definite contribution on *that very job*! Perhaps it might even relieve you of some of the burden you're carrying."

"But it's a consumer account, Ferris!" Armstead's voice was louder now as he tried to keep himself from "bellowing" as the staff liked to call it. "Consumer accounts are entirely different from industrial accounts. It takes a completely different set of skills."

"Mr. Armstead," Ferris responded, "I know that my request is out of the ordinary . . . I feel I can make a switch from industrial advertising to consumer advertising . . . and that I'll do even better there . . ."

Armstead was silent for a moment. He reached across the top of his desk to the silver pitcher filled with ice water and poured a glass for himself. He gestured with the pitcher toward Ferris but Ferris declined. Armstead slowly drank the entire glass of water, obviously buying several seconds of time to think.

"Ferris," Armstead said at last, "You're a young man with most of your career ahead of you. This is no time to get side tracked. Stay with what you're doing now. Quite frankly, industrial accounts are still the backbone of our business. That's where we have to concentrate our big guns."

"Mr. Armstead . . .," interrupted Ferris, "I'm not unhappy with my work, but I feel there are so many more creative possibilities on the consumer side . . ."

"The grass is always greener, Ferris," replied Armstead. "In a few years you'll begin to appreciate that jumping from impulse to impulse is no way to build a meaningful career. Take our firm for example. Crutchfield and I were both industrial sales representatives before we got into advertising. We knew the tool and machine business inside out. In no time we cornered several large accounts from other advertising agencies and we still have most of them too! We specialized . . . and we were successful!"

"Armstead, Crutchfield, and Associates is also in consumer advertising," countered Ferris."

"Ah, but that's a different situation and can't be compared to what you're asking. We were in a healthy cash position at the time and my partner, Crutchfield, wanted to acquire a creative but financially strapped consumer agency to round out our services. So, we bought Ralph Briggs and Associates and got our consumer accounts in the process."

113

Ferris started to respond but Armstead politely cut him off.

"Look, Ferris, why do you suppose Armstead, Crutchfield, and Associates hired you two years ago?"

"As I recall, it was largely because of my display advertisement for medical diagnostic equipment which won the Industrial Advertising Award of Excellence in the Medical Equipment category that year."

"Exactly, Ferris. We needed another sharp creative writer with the ability to cope with the most difficult technology . . . one who could relate to the needs and interests of the hospital or clinic. That's not an easy skill to come by. We hired you because you were a proven quantity and we had plenty of creative work for you to do. You can't complain about that, can you?"

"Not at all, Mr. Armstead. This is a good place to work . . . free of the phonies and deadbeats which can infiltrate an agency. And I have to admit I've had plenty of work to do."

"And don't forget, Ferris, that the firm had you nominated for this year's Industrial Advertising Award for your brilliant work on the Bio-Vid Electronic Scanner. You'll probably win it hands down, too!"

"You know I appreciate that, Mr. Armstead."

"And we pay you well too, don't we?"

"Yes, you do. I certainly have no complaint on that score."

"Ferris, I just don't understand what you're asking me to do. You're a man with unquestioned talent in a field which needs and fully recognizes your talent! You're a specialist, Ferris . . . a specialist! One of the best! Why in heaven's name do you want to get into consumer advertising? It's a big sea full of big fish. You'll be lost there, man . . . lost!"

"I don't think so," replied Ferris patiently. "I realize I'd be competing in a more difficult field, but I feel some ideas I learned in industrial work might be applied to consumer accounts." Ferris paused and took a deep breath. "I don't know quite how to explain it Mr. Armstead . . . it's like I've climbed up the foothills from a valley and I'm now on some type of plateau. I can see the valley below so I know I've made a lot of progress. I should be happy I know, but up ahead I see a mountain . . . and I have to climb it!"

Discussion Questions

1. Is Ferris a motivated employee by most general definitions of the word? Explain.
2. Why is Armstead so reluctant to move Ferris to a consumer account?
3. What *positive* motivational effects can exist for an employee who becomes a highly respected expert or specialist within his organization, industry, or field of work?

4. What *negative* motivational effects can exist for a specialist within his organization, industry, or field of work?
5. How is job specialization related to the concept of technical and managerial obsolescence?

Special Project

Class discussion or out-of-class written assignment: A paradox often exists between the need for specialists and generalists in any organization. What are the *realistic limits* to individual specialization within organizations to satisfy these somewhat contradictory requirements:
  (a) Personal growth and development for the individual.
  (b) Realistic breakdown of work between individuals and departments.
  (c) Short term economic realities for the organization.
  (d) Long term economic realities for the organization.
  (e) Creativity and innovation.
  (f) etc.

Selected References

Books
Dubrin, A. J. *The Practice of Managerial Psychology.* New York: Pergamon Press Inc., 1971, Chapters 6, 12.
Herzberg, F. *Work and the Nature of Man.* Cleveland: World, 1966.
Nadler, L. *Developing Human Resources.* Houston, Texas: Gulf Publishing, 1970.

Anthologies
Effective Communication on the Job. New York: American Management Association, 1963.
    Pigors, P. "What is Meaning and How Can We Share It?" p. 35.
Leavitt, H. J., and Pondy, L. R. (Eds.). *Readings in Managerial Psychology.* Chicago, Illinois: University of Chicago Press, 1964.
    MacKinnon, D. W. "The Nature and Nurture of Creative Talent," p. 90.
    McClelland, D. C. "Business Drive and National Achievement," p. 122.

Articles
Breton, E. J. "Caution: Fragile Inventive Talent; Handle With Care," *Innovation*, Number Nineteen, 1971, p. 44.
Delbecq, A. L., and Elfner, E. S. "Low Cosmopolitan Orientations and Career Strategies for Specialists," *Academy of Management Journal*, December 1970, p. 373.
Myers, D. W. "A Quantitative Analysis of Employee Creativity," *Personnel Journal*, November 1969, p. 873.

CAN I FIND HAPPINESS WITH A PUMP?

The term, Field Representative, covers a broad spectrum of activity which varies with every company and industry. In general, the Field Representative is a liaison man between company and customer. He is expected to be an extension of the home office—a goodwill ambassador, trouble shooter, equipment repairman, and complaint department rolled into one.

The Field Representative may drive a company car and call routinely on metropolitan accounts, or he may be located in some remote geographic area for months on end. He has more freedom than most professionals and, typically, a greater sense of personal satisfaction and accomplishment from his work. But, he too has his frustrations.

Vincent Margolin is a structural engineer employed by the Cleveland Nuclear Engineering Corporation of Cleveland, Ohio. Cleveland Nuclear designs and builds nuclear powered electric generating stations under contract to private regional power companies. These plants are built to basic specifications established by the United States Atomic Energy Commission and modified to meet local geographic conditions. They are usually located somewhat away from major metropolitan centers.

Margolin is one of two key project representatives at a construction site in central Arkansas. He is the focal point through which all mechanical design changes are made, whether originated at corporate headquarters in Cleveland for customer acceptance, or, by the customer for review by Cleveland Nuclear corporate engineering. Russell Stover is his counterpart for electronic and electrical hardware design changes. Actual construction work is performed by approved heavy plant construction firms under contract to Cleveland Nuclear.

Margolin tells an interesting story about his work and a decision which he will soon have to make:

"Most fellows wouldn't care for this type of work which, I guess, means you have to be an 'odd-ball' to be a good field representative.

"First of all, getting a nuclear plant constructed and on-line (operational) takes several years and most field men stay on from start to finish unless hardship conditions develop. This means that you have to move your entire family to some community near the site and make it your home until the job is over. Then you pack up, move on to the next site, and start over.

"Field work does have a 20 percent pay differential over equivalent corporate engineering but that just barely covers the extra real expenses. Most people have the idea that living costs are dirt cheap out here in the 'boonies' but that's hardly the case. Housing is the biggest problem. There just aren't that many homes available and, when the local folks hear that Cleveland Nuclear is moving in a group of workers, the rents shoot up astronomically.

"We work a regular six day week and, when a plant is going 'critical,' we work Sundays too. It's pretty hard on both men and their families. Sometimes nerves get frayed after several straight weeks of 10–12 hours per day. I've even been told to go to hell by one man's wife when I phoned and asked him to report for an emergency Saturday night shift!

"Yet with all the complaining we do, I for one wouldn't have it any other way. I love the challenge, variety, and responsibility which goes with the job. I have to be a jack-of-all-trades so the job is never dull. Each new day brings new problems and I enjoy having the authority to make major decisions without the help of a bunch of staff guys.

"Several months ago, I was asked to return to corporate engineering in Cleveland after this plant is on-line. I haven't given them an answer as yet but I'll probably turn the job down.

"Here's my dilemma. Promotions are few and far between out here in the field. Everyone knows that the way upward in this company is through corporate engineering. But, at the same time, if I go back to Corporate they'll turn me into a specialist . . . probably on hydraulic pumps because I'm strongest in that area. Then all I'll ever do is handle pump problems as they develop. It might be all right for some, but I just don't see how I can ever find happiness with a pump in Cleveland."

Discussion Questions

1. What fundamental motivational problem is involved in this case?
2. Is specialization of work at "home office" inevitable as envisioned by Margolin?
3. How might Margolin help advance his own career and still retain the job satisfactions he currently enjoys?

Of Particular Interest to Industrial Groups

4. How typical is Vincent Margolin compared to field personnel with whom you are familiar?
5. If your organization employs field personnel, discuss:
   (a) Field personnel selection procedures.
   (b) Field communication problems.
   (c) Field promotion, transfer, and training problems.

Special Project

Many unwanted and undesirable promotions or assignments often occur within organizations resulting in less than optimal use of existing personnel. One way to avoid such mistakes is through the effective use of a long term *Employee Career Development* program.

Research recent literature on Employee Career Development or Manager Development programs and submit a paper on your findings which shows how such a program typically works in practice to help both employee and employer.

Caution. Do not confuse this *long term career planning* with shorter management training courses and programs. Literature on both is extensive, overlapping, and often misleading.

Selected References

Books
Foulkes, F. K. *Creating More Meaningful Work*. New York: American Management Association, 1969.
Hinrichs, J. R. *High-Talent Personnel: Managing a Critical Resource*. New York: American Management Association, 1966.
Hower, R. M., and Orth, C. D. (III). *Managers and Scientists*. Boston, Massachusetts: Division of Research, Harvard Business School, 1963.

Anthologies
Hampton, D. R., Summer, C. E., and Webber, R. A. (Eds.). *Organization Behavior and the Practice of Management*. Glenview, Illinois: Scott, Foresman and Company, 1968. McClelland, D. C. "The Achievement Motive," p. 122.

Articles
Dewhirst, H. D. "Impact of Organizational Climate On The Desire To Manage Among Engineers and Scientists," *Personnel Journal*, March 1971, p. 196.
Ferguson, L. L. "Better Management of Managers' Careers," *Harvard Business Review*, 1966, No. 44, p. 139.
Harsha, K. K. "Can Creativity and Management Coexist?" *Personnel Journal*, May 1971, p. 396.

THE MARGINAL PURCHASING AGENT

Dale Sumner was rarely asked for his professional advice at a Sunday afternoon backyard barbecue, but this was the exception. Having recently moved to San Diego, Sumner and his wife were pleased to have a get-acquainted neighborhood party held in their honor at a nearby home.

About mid-afternoon Sumner found himself engaged in an interesting conversation with Lloyd and Natalie James, host and hostess of the party. James was the Director of Material Procurement for the privately financed Phipps Institute for Ocean Research, and Sumner asked numerous questions about the Institute and its work.

"I don't think I caught your speciality," asked James.

"Human behavior in organizations," replied Sumner. "I recently accepted a position in the Business Department at California State University, San

Diego, which is what brought me to this part of the country. I also had a small management consulting practice in Indianapolis, which I hope to re-establish here."

"That sounds very interesting," said Natalie, "What might you consult with a company about?"

Sumner smiled. "I work primarily in the areas of personnel morale and motivation."

"You're the expert who knows how to 'turn people on' toward their work?" asked James.

"I wish motivation were as simple as a mechanical turning on or off. Unfortunately, it is a very complex set of overlapping variables. Behavioral scientists have found some of the answers but in many areas we still know very little."

"You know," offered James, "I've been thinking as you were talking. I have a man working for me who is absolutely *impossible* to motivate. Maybe you can give me some ideas on what I can do to . . ."

Natalie broke in and attempted to change the subject. "Lloyd darling, this is a party. Don't bother Mr. Sumner with your office problems now."

"That's quite all right, Mrs. James," replied Sumner. "I don't know if I can be of any help, but I'd be very interested in hearing more about your problem employee."

Lloyd James needed no further prompting to tell Sumner about Allen Whitney, the marginal purchasing agent.

"It's not that he doesn't know his job," said James. "Allen Whitney has been in the procurement business for years and knows someone in every sales and order department between Santa Barbara and Tijuana, Mexico. But, somehow, he can't seem to concentrate on his work and even the routine procurements usually take him longer than any of my other purchasing agents."

"If it's not lack of training, perhaps it's a low energy or ability level?" asked Sumner. "We must admit to quantitative differences between individuals relative to innate abilities and energy."

"That's not it either," replied James. "Whitney is a friendly, enthusiastic, high-energy guy. Everyone likes him, including the people he works with by phone as well as others in the office. The problem is that his enthusiasm and energies seem to be all directed outward toward other activities and he has little left for the job."

"Could you give me an example?" asked Sumner.

"Actually several," replied James. "For one thing, Allen is president of the San Diego County Association of Purchasing Agents, an organization he has been active in for years. Phipps Institute supports and encourages employees to be active in outside professional societies and associations. We even cover his small out-of-pocket expenses associated with the non-salaried association presidency.

"I see," said Sumner. "While the Phipps Institute unofficially supports Whitney in this professional society, his efforts in carrying out the duties it entails takes away from his productive time as a purchasing agent."

"Exactly!" said James. "Whitney spends excessive amounts of time on the telephone organizing association meetings and conducting its other business, and he constantly falls behind in his schedule of procurements."

"You mentioned numerous examples. Can you cite others?" asked Sumner.

"Professional activities mostly," replied James. "But Allen Whitney is also very active in the Boy Scouts of America and a local Republican organization."

The two men were interrupted by Jill Sumner who steered them to the pot-luck table for a second helping of food. Still eating, Sumner then followed his wife around the large yard and garden area as she introduced him to other neighbors she had met that afternoon.

Later, when most of the guests had left and their two wives had gone into the house, Dale Sumner joined Lloyd James poolside with a can of beer and suggested they continue their earlier conversation.

"Have you spoken to Whitney about the interference of outside activities with his work at the Institute?" asked Sumner.

"On numerous occasions but, regrettably, I don't get very far. Whitney's attendance record is very good and he does get his job done and so I can't get him to see the problem."

"Please continue," said Sumner.

"Last week, for instance, I spoke with him about some procurement which had been delayed. I hoped to show him he was just doing marginal work. But, in each instance, he had a plausible excuse as to the reason for the delay . . . some logjam beyond his control."

Sumner broke in. "And you feel that if Whitney expended even part of the energy he does on his outside activities toward his regular job he could break those logjams he spoke of?"

"Yes, that's it," said James. "It's a matter of priorities. If he were constantly calling his stockbroker or handling other personal business on the job I could have him stop it or face termination. As it is, however, these outside activities are tacitly approved by the Institute and Whitney has a perfect alibi."

"So you want to get Whitney to see the need to reverse his personal set of job priorities and increase his motivation toward his procurement work?" asked Sumner.

"Right! But how do I do it?" asked James in return.

"It may not be possible," replied Sumner after some thought. "Without knowing the man personally and hearing his side of the story it is not possible to be sure. Offhand, it appears that Allen Whitney no longer finds challenge and growth in his daily work as a purchasing agent. He does what is absolutely necessary and then turns his efforts outward to those activities in which he can further grow, achieve, and be recognized for his personal contributions. Like the majority of employees, Allen Whitney self-actualizes in outside activities and hobbies."

Discussion Questions

1. What did Sumner mean by his last statement? Discuss.
2. What steps might James take to alter Allen Whitney's set of priorities?
3. Can a re-structuring of priorities take place without the full consent and support of Allen Whitney? Why?
4. James said that Whitney does marginally acceptable work. Should James have a technique or method to determine what exactly determines or establishes marginally acceptable from unacceptable performance? How is this done on jobs which cannot be easily measured?

Special Project

Large numbers of employed persons in organizations find greater self-actualization in their off-the-job activities than in the daily performance of their regular work assignments. Much has been written recently about the numerous ways in which work can be re-structured to provide greater personal satisfaction and the more efficient and motivated use of human resources.

Prepare a well-documented research paper titled, *Achieving Job Satisfaction* which illustrates the theoretical and practical bases for self-actualization in the work environment.

Selected References

Anthologies
Koontz, H., and O'Donnell, C. *Management: A Book of Readings*. New York: McGraw-Hill, 1968.
Brown, W. "What Is Work?" p. 290.

Articles
Fielder, F. E. "Engineer the Job to Fit the Manager," *Harvard Business Review*, September–October 1965.
Kuhn, D. G., Slocum, J. W. Jr., and Chase, R. B. "Does Job Performance Affect Employee Satisfaction?" *Personnel Journal*, June 1971, p. 455.

Meyer, H. "If People Fear to Fail, Can Organizations Ever Succeed?" *Innovation*, Number Eight, 1969, p. 56.

Porter, L. W., and Lawler, E. E. "What Job Attitudes Tell About Motivation," *Harvard Business Review*, January–February 1968, p. 118.

Slocum, J. W. Jr., Miller, J. D., and Misshauk, M. J. "Needs, Environmental Work Satisfaction and Job Performance," *Training and Development Journal*, February 1970, p. 12.

Steinmetz, L. "The Unsatisfactory Performer: Salvage or Discharge," *Personnel*, May–June 1968, p. 46.

EMPLOYEE OF THE MONTH

Nate Silver and Herb Wallace stopped to read the recently posted notice on a company bulletin board:

EDWIN TROWBRIDGE—EMPLOYEE OF THE MONTH

Edwin Trowbridge of Department A-14, Senior Cost Analyst, has been named by the Employee Achievements Committee as *Employee of the Month* for his many contributions in the areas of product cost reduction and value analysis. In particular, Ed Trowbridge is credited with submitting three proposals for materials and methods changes which are estimated to save the company a total of $107,000 in a twelve month period.

Mr. Trowbridge joined the company two years ago in our Purchasing Department and moved to his current assignment early this year.

Congratulations, Ed Trowbridge!

(*signed*)

JUSTIN DUFRESNE
President

Nate Silver winced. "What a deal," he mumbled.

"How's that?" asked Wallace.

"The award . . . Eddy Trowbridge is going to pocket a hundred bucks for being named Employee of the Month," replied Silver.

Wallace was puzzled. "I don't see what you're getting at," he replied. "There's always a one hundred dollar award for being named Employee of the Month."

"Yeah," said Silver, "but it's ridiculous! Have you noticed that it always goes to a person who's working in some area of cost or production . . . you know, where it's easy to count dollars."

"That's not too surprising," Wallace countered. "Some job performances are easier to measure than others. A fellow in production or cost . . . or even engineering has an advantage in this type of program because his work can be equated more readily to dollars spent or dollars saved."

Wallace smiled and continued, "You really don't expect that a graphic illustrator like me would ever get that award do you?"

"Well, why the hell not?" Silver asked. "It seems to me that *everyone* should have an equal chance!"

"In theory everyone does," said Wallace. "My supervisor explained to me that any employee on his particular job for a minimum of three months and with the company for a minimum of six months is eligible. If the supervisor feels that the person has made an outstanding contribution, he can nominate the employee. The Employee Achievements Committee takes it from there."

"But that's not how it works in practice," Silver complained. "It's nearly impossible to get nominated unless you can prove you've saved the company a bundle of bucks. That's the way supervisors play the game because they know that's what the committee is looking for."

"I'm sure," said Wallace, "just as it is with so many laws, rules, and systems . . . that some persons are more equal than others. I don't let it bother me."

"I think it's a rotten system and hurts morale instead of helping it."

"Nate Silver, I believe you're *jealous* of Trowbridge."

"No," grumbled Silver, "actually I like Eddy Trowbridge. It's just this dumb system of honoring only one employee each month as if they're the only ones who contribute anything. How about the rest of us who work our fool tails off and never receive any recognition? I tell you, it's a dumb system!"

Discussion Questions

1. Is Nate Silver fair in his criticism of the Employee of the Month award system? Explain.
2. What types of *positive* employee behavior can this form of recognition system tend to develop.
3. What types of *negative* employee behavior can this form of recognition system tend to develop?
4. If this recognition system failed to work well (as Silver claimed) would you say that the difficulty is:
   (a) Because any recognition system which names specific individuals is unworkable in practice? Explain.
   (b) Because the groundrules and/or procedural aspects of the recognition system are unfair? Explain.
5. Name and discuss other approaches this organization might use to positively honor specific employee contributions without lowering the morale of other employees.

Special Project

Assume that the individual recognition system described in this case is not working well primarily due to procedural reasons. Break the class into groups of 4–6 persons and give them 30 minutes to develop and list a reasonable set of rules or guidelines for an Employee of the Month award system which would:

(a) Be workable in most organizations without being administratively cumbersome.

(b) Be reasonably fair to all employees.

(c) Offer built-in behavioral aspects to improve individual motivation, group morale, and overall productivity.

Have each group, in turn, describe their proposed Employee of the Month system with emphasis on the positive behavioral aspects they have built in. Compare similarities and discuss any unusual "rules and regulations" suggested.

Note. Flip chart paper and felt-tip pens are particularly handy for small group work and for presentation of results to the entire class.

Selected References

Books

Gellerman, S. W. *Motivation and Productivity*. New York: American Management Association, 1963.

Sayles, L., and Strauss, G. *Human Behavior in Organizations*. Englewood Cliffs, New Jersey: Prentice-Hall, 1966.

Anthologies

Leavitt, H. J., and Pondy, L. R. (Eds.). *Readings in Managerial Psychology*. Chicago, Illinois: The University of Chicago Press, 1964.

   Maslow, A. H. "A Theory of Human Motivation: The Basic Needs," p. 6.

   Zalkind, S. S., and Costello, T. W. "Perception: Implications for Administration," p. 32.

Articles

Marcus, E. E. "What Do You Mean, 'Evaluation?'," *Personnel Journal*, May 1971, p. 354.

Myers, M. S. "Every Employee A Manager," *California Management Review*, Spring 1968.

BIG BASH AT BERGMANN'S

Frank Wales, General Manager of Pride-Air Corporation, quickly glanced at the food and beverage invoice from Bergmann's Restaurant which had been submitted to him along with several others from Accounts Payable for his signature approval. Wales tried to spend as little time as possible on the less important or trivial aspects of his job and initialing routine invoices was one task he usually did quite rapidly and in batches when possible.

Wales almost initialed the Bergmann invoice before the impact of the bill struck him.

"Good grief!" he bellowed. "One thousand and thirty-seven dollars for lousy drinks and hors d'oeuvres?" He slapped the paper down on his desk, shook his head in disbelief, and punched the office intercom button on his phone.

Moments later, Wales' administrative assistant, Dale Mitchell, appeared and reviewed the invoice with his boss.

"It appears to be in order," Mitchell said. Then smiling broadly added, "I'd sure hate to pay for it out of my own pocket though."

"I ought to make Hector Gonzales pay for it out of *his* own pocket," Wales replied. "That might keep future project party bills in line." He paused and added, "Mitch, are you sure this invoice is okay? I realize I approved the Landmark Project party, but I had the impression it would be in the neighborhood of six hundred dollars or six fifty tops."

"No, I'm sure it's correct," said Mitchell. "Bergmann's restaurant has never gouged us in the past for company activities, retirement parties, and our other catered affairs. I don't see why they would do so now."

Mitchell took out a pen and made some rapid computations on the reverse side of Bergmann's invoice.

"Let's see," he said. "Approximately 140 persons at an estimated seven dollars each would be . . . nine hundred eighty dollars. Add tax and gratuities and the one thousand and thirty-seven dollar figure is about right."

"One hundred and forty persons!" Wales shouted. "I never authorized that many attendees. Gonzales had better have a good explanation for this!" Frank Wales reluctantly initialed the Bergmann invoice for payment.

"I'm sure he will," said Mitchell. "Gonzales invited me to attend, which I did incidentally . . . even though I'm not a part of the Landmark Project Team. So, my costs are part of the total bill. And, I saw several other members of general management there. In fact, I remarked to Gonzales at the time that the party was larger than I expected and he said that *you* had approved the attendance of certain categories of management and support personnel not specifically on the Landmark team."

Wales rubbed his chin and reflected on his last meeting with Gonzales. "Come to think of it, I guess I did . . . but I wasn't thinking about the number of people involved. Gonzales' suggestion to have top management people attend for reasons of group morale and motivation made sense at the time. Perhaps I'm to blame for not counting heads before I approved the request."

Mitchell nodded.

"Mitch," said Wales, "You know I'm 100 percent behind any management technique which will improve communication, morale, and productivity, but I'm sure beginning to doubt the validity of group recognition through the project party approach."

Wales continued, "Last year when Gonzales first suggested the idea of holding a group recognition party for those persons working on Project Delta it sounded like an excellent idea. The Delta team had completed design and construction of prototype hardware on schedule and below target costs. And, in doing so, had provided our company with a technological breakthrough in this particular marketing area. Since so many people had worked so hard and so long to achieve success it seemed only fair for the company to visibly demonstrate its appreciation and recognition for everyone's effort.

"Gonzales argued that the project manager and several key project personnel were already widely credited and would continue to be recognized for their efforts through photos in the company paper, company news releases and the like. He wanted the 'little guy,' as he called him, to be recognized as well. A big Saturday evening party at Bergmann's where everyone could rub shoulders as equals appeared to be a great way to do it."

Mitchell sat back in his chair and smiled. "I have to admit that the hoped for motivational effects did occur," he said. "People let their hair down and had one hell of a good time. Morale remained high through the remainder of the project activity as well."

"Seems to me," replied Wales, "that you were against the original idea for the Project Delta party."

"I was. I saw several inherent problems in that particular form of group recognition. But, at the time, Hector Gonzales was the Personnel Department's bright young man with all that training in the behavioral sciences. He was very convincing and finally won me over. That's when I suggested that you approve the party even though I had some reservations."

Mitchell continued, "While it appeared that Gonzales was right about group recognition after the Project Delta party, I doubted that the same effect would be created if the technique was later repeated."

"You'll recall," said Mitchell, "the problems which developed at the second party for Project Delta, after final product shipments were made?"

"You mean Carl Kopek's rude comments to both a waitress and Mr. Bergmann, the owner?"

"Yes, that primarily, plus the general overexuberance of the group."

"Well," replied Wales, "I was upset at the time. Kopek always was a loudmouth and his voluntary resignation the next Monday saved me the trouble of having to let him go. In fact, I seriously considered canceling all future project parties, except that the feedback from the participants was that they all had a great time! Most apparently felt that Kopek's behavior in no way reflected on the company and its employees. I guess that's why I went along with Gonzales for the Landmark Project party last Saturday."

"Frank," said Mitchell, "with all due respect to Gonzales and the behavioral scientists, I think we should drop this group recognition party from now on. There are far too many potential problems in it for the motivational mileage we get in return. Let me list my personal reservations about the concept."

The following is the list of objections that Dale Mitchell put on the office blackboard:

1. **Group recognition parties are expensive.**
2. **Recognition is equal for unequal contributions.**
3. **Too many guests make it a company party.**
4. **When repeated, parties lose their motivational effect. Soon it will be an expected thing.**
5. **Drinking and general behavior is often socially excessive and reflects on the company as a whole.**
6. **It can be as morally dangerous as an uncontrolled Christmas party.**

Discussion Questions

1. Is Dale Mitchell fair in his criticism of the project party approach to group recognition? Explain.
2. What types of *positive* employee behavior can this form of group recognition system tend to develop?
3. What types of *negative* employee behavior can this form of group recognition system tend to develop?
4. If this recognition system failed to work well (as Mitchell claimed) would you say the difficulty is:
   (a) Because any system for group recognition is unworkable in practice?
   (b) Because the groundrules and/or procedural aspects of the recognition system are unfair?
5. Suppose Frank Wales decided to retain the project party approach over Dale Mitchell's objections. How might he reduce the potential effects of Mitchell's specific objections?
6. Are group recognition techniques compatible with the concept of individual recognition for specific contribution? Explain.
7. What type of employee is most likely to obtain the greatest motivational impact from the party?

Special Project

Have the entire class act as a body of one to brainstorm *alternative approaches* this company might use to retain group recognition. Have one or two participants list ideas on the blackboard the moment they are suggested.

For example

(a)   Have a formal dinner.

(b)   Address by president.

(c)   Small bonus to all.

(d)   etc.

(Get at least 20–30 ideas listed before stopping.)

Then.   Conduct a *critical analysis* of each technique as an out-of-class assignment. Some ideas can be categorized for convenience of analysis.

Note.   Proper brainstorming technique prohibits *negative* or *judicial* statements while ideas are being generated. The ideation phase is characterized by a constant flow of ideas . . . the wilder the better! Unusable ideas can be sorted out during later analysis.

Selected References

Books

Gellerman, S. W. *Management by Motivation.* New York: American Management Association, 1968, Chapter 2.

Anthologies

Huseman, R., Logue, C., and Freshley, D. *Readings in Interpersonal and Organizational Communication.* Boston, Massachusetts: Holbrook Press, Inc., 1969. Nirenberg, J. S. "Communicating for Greater Insight and Persuasiveness," p. 239.

Leavitt, H. J., and Pondy, L. R. (Eds.). *Readings in Managerial Psychology.* Chicago, Illinois: University of Chicago Press, 1964.
Crutchfield, R. S. "Conformity and Character," p. 315.
Lewin, K. "The Psychology of Success and Failure," p. 25.

Booklets

What's Wrong With Work? Organization Development Program Group, Industrial Relations Committee, National Association of Manufacturers, 277 Park Avenue, New York, N.Y. 10017, ($2.50 per copy).

RECOGNITION WON'T BUY BREAD

Steve Marks does not particularly like the performance appraisal and merit increase system his company uses but he has to live with it. Not much better nor worse than most others, it works on the pool of money available concept. For example:

If the total payroll for this fiscal year is one million dollars (and if business is stable and cash available) a fixed percentage is established for promotions and merit increases for the coming period. If this fixed percentage is 5 percent, a pool of money is set aside for salary increases amounting to $50,000.

Although usually not official policy, the effect of this pool of money concept is to force each supervisor to increase wages (give raises) in his work area to the point which on the average will not exceed 5 percent of his current direct payroll.

In theory the supervisor is to reward the better producer with a large increase and give the average worker only a nominal increase. The marginal employee should receive no merit increase whatsoever.[1]

However, in practice, the situation is often quite different. Faced with the 5 percent rule, a supervisor such as Steve Marks finds that he cannot use his merit pool in a way which will fully reward the most competent performers. In practice, *almost everyone* gets some merit increase to keep the complaints to a minimum.

Steve Marks describes the inequities of the merit review system as it operates in his organization and tells of other recent experiences:

"Most everyone has to get some kind of increase or you have a near rebellion on your hands. I hate to admit it, but the average performer ends up getting the average (5 percent) merit increase. If the guy is a cut below average he gets 2–3 percent. Anything less than that and the man is insulted. So . . . that leaves 7–8 percent for the top contributors. As a raise it's not bad, but it's only 2–3 percent more than Mr. Average, hardly an incentive for extra output!

"The system really bothered me until I attended a short management seminar which our company sponsored. Seventeen supervisors attended the program which was conducted by some big name management consultant from New York.

"This consultant made a big issue out of the fact that we place far too much emphasis on money and raises. *He said that money doesn't motivate people!* Then he went on to list his findings on what *did* motivate people. I don't remember the order exactly, but it was something like this:

> Challenging Work
> Interesting Work
> Variety of Work
> Freedom of Action
> Responsibility
> Sense of Accomplishment

[1]Cost of living increases are usually handled separately from merit increases based on work performance and are given to *all* employees as a fixed percentage (e.g. 0.7 percent) regardless of actual performance on the job.

Personal Growth and Development
Recognition
Friendly co-workers
Good Working Conditions
Salary

"Imagine! *Salary was at the bottom of the list!* At first it was hard to believe, but when I thought about it I could see that all of those other things were pretty important too. Somehow I felt a little less concerned about merit review limitations for better employees at the conclusion of the seminar.

"The week after the seminar I reviewed the performance of one of my top people. We use an anniversary date (from date of employment) to stagger reviews, and this man had completed his first full year with the company.

"Remembering what I had learned at the management seminar, I stressed the man's contributions and made a special point of recognizing his individual achievements since he had been hired. Then we spoke of ways to enrich his job, to make it more interesting and challenging. We even set objectives for the coming months and yardsticks for measuring goal achievement. I was pretty proud of myself until we got around to the specific amount of his merit increase.

"He was really upset. 'Five percent?' he said. 'Is that all I'm worth after all those words about what a great job I've done? Save those fancy words for some other guy . . . recognition won't buy bread at my store!'"

Discussion Questions

1. Analyze and discuss Steve Marks' dilemma.
2. Analyze this case from the viewpoint of:
   (a) Job dissatisfaction (hygiene factors).
   (b) Job satisfaction (motivators).
3. Does *company policy and procedure* most affect employee job satisfaction or dissatisfaction? Explain.
4. Does the *supervisor or manager* most affect employee job satisfaction or dissatisfaction? Explain.
5. One prominent industrial psychologist has said that money (in the form of wages and wage increases) must be considered in *two* distinct ways:
   (a) Money for membership.
   (b) Money for motivation.
   Can you explain the difference between the two?
6. Discuss this case in terms of Maslow's *Hierarchy of Human Needs*.

Special Project

If participants are versed in recent motivational theory, have the entire class develop two lists:

(a) Job factors which have a strong correlation to *job dissatisfaction*.
(b) Job factors which have a strong correlation to *job satisfaction*.

List items for easy view of all on blackboard or flip chart and discuss them individually and by common groupings.

Selected References

Books
Gellerman, S. W. *Management by Motivation*. New York: American Management Association, 1968, Chapters 9, 10.

Articles
Bolt, R. H. "Money Isn't the Only Objective For An Innovative Organization," *Innovation*, Number Six, 1969, p. 26.
Broad, B. M. "Not By Bread Alone," *Personnel Journal*, November 1970, p. 913.
Evans, W. A. "Pay for Performance: Fact or Fable," *Personnel Journal*, September 1970, p. 726.
Herzberg F. "One More Time: How Do You Motivate Employees?" *Harvard Business Review*, January–February 1968, p. 53.
Kaplan, H., Tausky, C., and Bolaria, B. "Job Enrichment," *Personnel Journal*, October 1969, p. 791.
Lawler, E. E. "The Paycheck as an (Expensive) Communication Device," *Innovation*, Number Three, 1969, p. 48.
Lawson, T. R. "How Much Is A Job Worth?" *Personnel*, September–October 1966, p. 16.
McClelland, D. C. "Money as a Motivator: Some Research Insights," *Management Review*, February 1968, p. 23.
Meyer, H. "Is Your Pay Plan Full of Cobwebs?" *Innovation*, Number Fourteen, 1970, p. 56.

CASE STUDY CROSS REFERENCE

Although located elsewhere in this book, the following problem situations are also valuable in the study of Section 5:

- Eureka, I'll Call It the Wheel!   page 11
- Dear Home Office: Do You Read Me?   page 17
- The Secret of Bradford's Warehouse   page 36
- The Plight of Ralph Cummings   page 84
- The Rules Are Different for Women   page 96
- Dr. Shibata Has Resigned!   page 106
- A Highly Motivated "Kook"   page 134

Section 5

Problems in Motivation

6

"Look, Brad, I know you get all those aeronautical design theory courses in college and you expect to design planes your first week out of college. Face it, there's a certain amount of routine work in any job. Everyday can't be a learning experience like it was in college."

"I don't see why not," replied Kirkeby. "If I was hired to eventually design planes, shouldn't I be working next to designers instead of piddling around with trivia?"

ANTHONY CARBONI
BRAD KIRKEBY
A Talk with Kirkeby's Son

INTRODUCTION

How does an effective supervisor work with persons who fail or defy accepted levels of productivity? What forces cause people to exhibit unusual motivational patterns? How do external or System imposed forces influence individual motivation? Can technology or employee age be motivational factors?

Cases in This Section

A Highly Motivated "Kook"

A long term supervisor hires a bright, young talent . . . and gets more than he bargained for . . . unusual dress and work patterns . . . high degree of motivation . . . some counterproductive behavior . . . a real talent or a "kook"?

The Legion of Dead Men

A middle aged employee is transferred to a new work group and the supervisor vows to make him productive again ... a personal story of frustration ... one final chance to perform ... the question of managerial and technical obsolescence.

A Matter of Accommodation

An interesting telephone conversation between two doctors illustrates how "innocent" outsiders can affect an individual's job motivation ... health and age ... or just laziness?

No Room at the Top

The frustrations of several employees who cannot move to higher salaried levels ... two solutions are offered ... problems with each ... can group morale and effectiveness be maintained?

A Talk with Kirkeby's Son

The apprentice is unhappy ... when will the meaningful work begin? ... waiting in line for the good jobs ... knowing when someone is ready for advancement ... best effort on all jobs ... effective use of talent.

A HIGHLY MOTIVATED "KOOK"

Fred Pierce is an administrative manager with an interesting story to tell about motivation and conformity:

"A year or so ago I read in the paper about the university administrator who told a conference of businessmen that the university's problem would soon be industry's problem. He was talking, of course, about the graduates who held different ideas about dress, behavior, politics ... you know, the whole gap thing.

"Our company was cautious. We're a small organization and consider ourselves to be a family of sorts. People who work here know each other quite well and enjoy working together. And you have to be careful who you add to the team. The old story about one bad apple spoiling the lot is really true when a small group is involved.

"No one said, avoid hiring persons with unusual hair styles or clothes but I'm sure that when there was a choice between two job applicants, the one who appeared 'straight' had the edge. You may call it discrimination, but I call it reality. You have to hire people you can be comfortable with. How can you have a team if people are too . . . well, different . . . if they don't hold certain basic values?

"The first cases of unusual dress and appearance showed up out in the shop areas, in shipping and receiving, and other unskilled and semi-skilled work areas. Charlie in Personnel told me that these fellows were qualified for the work and that he made every effort not to be biased when interviewing applicants. Charlie also said it was a trend . . . that more and more young applicants displayed a 'mod' or 'hip' appearance and so we'd have to get used to having them as co-workers. As Charlie put it, 'When you have one job opening and ten beards apply, you hire a beard.'

"For the most part we've had no problems. Some of the kids were duds on the job . . . no motivation at all. We had to get rid of them. But we've *always had that problem*! Some of us were expecting bigger problems like drug use on the job but, cross your fingers, no problems so far. Oddly enough, some of our older employees began to alter their dress patterns to some degree. Not too much . . . brighter shirts, less conservative ties, and somewhat fuller hair cuts. The older women resisted change a little more. I don't really know why.

"Well, I really should get to my point. I needed a business administration graduate with a couple of year's experience on computer operations. We were computerizing a number of our accounting and operational information systems. I had an employee requisition prepared and started interviewing applicants.

"There were a number of applicants, but my choice was an easy one. I hired Steve Springer, a tall, clean cut lad, about twenty-six years old. Steve had a good college record and a clean bill of health from his one post-college employer. He had a full cut of bright red hair and sported a medium, but well manicured, mustache. His dress was straight and slightly conservative. He was articulate, eager, and obviously confident although not overbearing.

"The first few weeks I had no particular problems with Steve. I had him on an individual assignment where he reported directly to me. He was well grounded in the computer sciences and quickly grasped the nature of our particular computer applications. He worked smoothly, often rapidly, but seldom carelessly. It looked like a good man-job match until . . .

"One day I noticed a change. Steve had been wearing suits to work each day, all somewhat sportier than the conservative one he wore during the interview. I had expected that . . . there's an old saying that you always wear your most 'sincere suit' when you apply for a job. Suddenly though, the suits were gone and Steve showed up in casual slacks and sport shirts.

"I thought about challenging him on this because shirts and ties are pretty standard dress for men in office and administrative areas, but decided to drop it. After all, I reasoned, he is on an individual assignment and I also received no negative reactions from other managers or employees.

"On one particular Tuesday morning after a long four day holiday weekend, Steve came to work in sandals (no socks!) and was sporting the beginning of a full red beard. At this point we had a long talk about his rights, company expectations, and the attitudes of other employees. It was quite amiable. Steve kept the beard, but I got him to wear socks.

"For a month or two nothing in particular happened. Then, at the request of Mel Lopshire in Cost Accounting, I loaned Steve to Mel for a complex programming assignment. It was then that Steve began working late each night and coming in at one or two o'clock the next afternoon. This frustrated a number of people he had been working closely with on prior assignments and I ended up getting plenty of static from other managers.

"I was just about to read the riot act to him when Lopshire announced that Steve had completed the programming, a task which had been twice started and stalled under other programmers. How could I be upset with Steve when Lopshire was extolling his virtues all over the company?

"Well, it's been that way ever since. Springer struts around this place like he owns it and he's won over enough managers so that he can get away with it. I'll admit that he's motivated and very talented, but he bends (never breaks) most company rules whenever it suits his purpose. Often enough to anger and frustrate me but never enough to get fired.

"He came close to being terminated once though. As a joke, one morning he defaced his security badge by pasting a picture of a Disney cartoon character over his own picture. The guards at the gate were quite busy and waved him on through. Seems he wore the badge that way all day before he was noticed by anyone other than a giggly secretary. By the time I found out about it the picture was gone and Springer had avoided a security violation.

"In the research and engineering areas they often speak of such unusual talented persons as 'prima donnas' but he's just a 'kook' as far as I'm concerned! And I'll be damned if I know what to do with him now that he's been here almost a whole year!"

Discussion Questions

1. What, if anything, should Fred Pierce do now?
2. Would you answer (1) differently if Springer were not so talented? Explain.
3. Separate, define, and discuss the issues involved in this case.
4. How far should an organization bend its own rules for one (or a few) talented persons?
5. What are the implications to an organization of bending the rules too much?
6. What are the implications to an organization of bending the rules too little?
7. What is a rational approach to this dilemma:
   (a) In the Springer case?
   (b) In general?

Special Projects

1. Read the case study, "*Show Us You're Really Creative*" and correlate the issues defined there with those presented in this case.
2. Obtain the services of a qualified outside person to offer current business attitudes on these issues in class (personal appearance) or on tape (interviewed by a select committee). Remember to give plenty of lead time, make your purposes clear, and never keep the person beyond the time requested.
2. (*Alternate*) One or more members of the business, psychology, or sociology staff may frequently consult with local business and industrial leaders on issues such as these. Their views may be very useful. Other similar speaker suggestions are:
   (a) College study placement director.
   (b) City, county, or state employment counselors.

Selected References

Books

Bassett, G. A. *Management Styles in Transition.* New York: American Management Association, 1966.

Guilford, J. S., and Gray, D. E. *Motivation and Modern Management.* Reading, Massachusetts: Addison-Wesley, 1970.

Mandell, M. M. *The Selection Process: Choosing The Right Man For The Job.* New York: American Management Association, 1964.

Nadler, D. *The New Employee.* Houston, Texas: Gulf Publishing, 1971.

Anthologies

Hampton, D. R., Summer, C. E., and Webber, R. A. (Eds.). *Organizational Behavior and the Practice of Management.* Glenview, Illinois: Scott, Foresman and Company, 1968.
Argyris, C. "Personality and Organization," p. 138.
Barnard, C. I. "The Theory of Authority," p. 451.

Huseman, R., Logue, C., and Freshley, D. *Readings in Interpersonal and Organizational Communication.* Boston, Massachusetts: Holbrook Press, Inc., 1969. Wiksell, M. J. "Talking It Over *Is* Important," p. 236.

Articles

Ford, R. N. "The Obstinate Employee," *Psychology Today*, November 1969, p. 32.

Haynes, M. E. "Improving Performance Through Employee Discussions," *Personnel Journal*, February 1970, p. 138.

Myers, M. S. "Who Are Your Motivated Workers?" *Harvard Business Review*, January–February 1964, p. 73.

Nouri, C. J., and Fridl, J. J. "The Relevance of Motivational Concepts To Individual and Corporate Objectives," *Personnel Journal*, November 1970, p. 900.

Penzer, W. N. "Managing Motivated Employees," *Personnel Journal*, May 1971, p. 367.

Zeitlein, L. R. "Planning for a Successful Performance Review Program," *Personnel Journal*, December 1969, p. 957.

THE LEGION OF DEAD MEN

"Managerial obsolescence is that situation where a once capable manager is no longer up to date in terms of present organizational needs and expectations and has lost his capacity for adapting to change, and where this situation seriously restricts his effectiveness."

L. M. CONE JR.
Toward a Theory of Managerial Obsolescence
p. 72

No one seems to know for certain when Henderson died. Some say it was two years ago when he was assigned to supervise the Data Input (key-punch) Center. Still others say it happened much earlier, that J. B. Henderson died five or six years ago when he was passed over for the position of Assistant to the General Manager. One old timer in the organization swears that Henderson died over eight years ago when he (Henderson) was unfortunately assigned to work for several months under the dictatorial Harry Flick (now retired — bless him!).

For most, the question is an academic one. The fact remains that, for whatever reason or set of reasons in the recent or distant past, Henderson is unproductive ... ineffective ... obsolete ... dead!

Curiously, Henderson is not alone in the organization. A Personnel Department spokesman recently admitted, somewhat reluctantly, that scattered instances of managerial obsolescence exist within the organization but quickly added that the number and percentage of cases was insignificant.

One less cautious young manager suggested privately to a friend that, *although he had no obsolete persons in his department*, their number in the organization was legion ... perhaps in the range of 5–10 percent! The friend, an organizational wag, couldn't resist a pun and tagged the obsolete ones, "The Legion of Dead Men." And this rather grotesque title was to remain thereafter as part of the organizational jargon, usually spoken only at unofficial executive gatherings and never committed to meeting minutes.

What happened to the obsolete employees like J. B. Henderson? Some retired. That was the painless way to go. With gold watch and a hearty handshake from the President, he would bid farewell to his many friends and recount tidbits of his thirty-two loyal years in a short, often choked, retirement dinner speech...totally unaware that his departure was welcomed!

Unfortunately, and contrary to a popular conception of managerial and technical obsolescence, not many were near or at retirement age. A very large number of retirees were active and productive employees right up to their last day on the job. Indeed, the majority of the now obsolete managers were in the 40–55 age range and many still in their thirties.

What happened to these non-performers? For most it was an endless string of relatively insignificant assignments designed to keep them occupied and out of the way. Cruel? Yes. Talent wasting? Certainly. But listen to the lament of J. B. Henderson's current manager, a man who feels he has tried to solve the problem and failed:

"I didn't ask for Henderson and I certainly never would have hired him. He came to me through Surplus[1] and I had no choice except to take him, since the job requirements of the position I had open were close enough to his background. With seventeen years experience with this organization, Henderson's personnel file was so stuffed that, *on paper*, he could qualify for most any general supervisory or staff position as long as it wasn't too technical!

"Like most managers, I'm wary of the Surplus System. I know that it has been effectively employed for years as a procedural vehicle for balanc-

[1]A system (known by a variety of names) used in some large organizations to balance interdepartmental manpower requirements and minimize employee layoffs. In theory, Department A cannot hire from the outside to fill a vacancy until the *Surplus List* has been checked. Department B can place a man on the Surplus List when they are reducing their manpower requirements. If the person in surplus is not taken by another department in thirty days, he is terminated for lack of work. Conversely, if Department A needs a man with basic skills of the person on the Surplus List, then Department A is obliged to take that person rather than hire from the outside. In practice the system is both good and poor at the same time, emphasizing employee security on one hand and yet sometimes shunting non-performers from one work area to another. Such a system does not *create* managerial obsolescence, but tolerates it and highlights it in its procedural operation.

ing manpower requirements. It certainly wouldn't make sense to have me laying off good people for lack of work, while some guy in the next building is hiring people off the street. But the system works just as well in keeping the deadwood around.

"I needed a man and Personnel suggested Henderson who had just been placed on the Surplus List. Not knowing the man personally, I immediately requested his personnel file for review. His recent semi-annual performance ratings were fair-to-good, nothing on which to reject him. His current boss said his job performance was good, that he was a productive supervisor who got along well with his people. But I heard some contrary remarks from several people who used to work for him. The consensus among these employees was that Henderson hindered production because they had to keep briefing him on their technical approaches to the job, things a man keeping up with his business should really know.

"I should have known better. Even when I talked to Henderson about the work in our area, I could almost catch a glint of fear in his eyes at possibly getting in over his head. However, he did express background skills and interest in the job. At the time I thought to myself, *so what* if Henderson's personnel file has probably been doctored.[2] The chances are very good, I convinced myself, that if he has not been performing well it was probably due to the kind of supervision he had or the type of non-challenging assignments he had been given. In other words, I thought myself to be a better than average manager who could motivate Henderson where others had failed.

"In his new job Henderson was essentially my assistant. He supervised no one directly and was to handle special assignments with particular emphasis on coordinating the activities of my group with others in the organization. It looked like a good job match for Henderson. He apparently knew his way around the organization and his role would be supportive rather than creative.

"The first assignment I gave Henderson was to collect product data

---

[2] A questionable technique used by some managers in which a marginal or poorly performing employee is appraised *officially for the record* as somewhat better than he actually is. For both manager and man it avoids direct confrontation with the problem of having to justify termination proceedings. Should the supervisor decide to terminate the man, someone in a higher managerial position inevitably asks the embarrassing question, "Why do you want to terminate him *now* after eight years? If he's *that bad* he should have been fired years ago!" Thus the natural tendency exists to get rid of a problem employee via interdepartmental transfer or voluntary termination.

which was being developed by several operating units and compile it into one, more meaningful source document.[3]

"To make sure I wasn't giving Henderson too much rope, I asked him to report weekly on his progress which, I felt, would take four to six weeks.

"The first two weekly coaching sessions were uneventful. Henderson said he was making the necessary contacts and obtaining information without difficulty. I asked if there were any obstacles to his progress with which I could help, but his reaction was negative.

"At our third weekly meeting I asked Henderson to show me what he had put together to date. He hedged, indicating that his notes were still in loose form. I consented to wait another week, but decided to watch him more closely as he worked.

"Using an informal and somewhat random observation technique, I noted his activities during the next week. Henderson was never purposely wasting time or 'goofing off' during any of my casual observations. However, I did notice several behavioral patterns to exist:

1. *Low energy level*—He always appeared busy but essentially 'plodded' through the day.
2. *Poor work habits*—Showed a definite tendency to repeat steps such as going back to ask more questions in a department he had just visited. Other habits noted were long telephone calls on routine topics and lengthy coffee breaks. Desk and work area were unusually cluttered with notes, half written sheets, and related materials.
3. *Motivation*—There was no outward interest in the work itself. Henderson appeared to be approaching it from a mechanistic point of view. Many times I saw him staring at the wall for minutes on end, pencil in hand and a blank sheet of paper on his desk. Was he in deep thought or merely staring into space?

"At our fourth meeting I reviewed Henderson's notes. Even a cursory glance showed several errors and obvious omissions. When I showed them to Henderson, he appeared pleased that I had caught 'a couple of slips' on his part but appeared confident that the bulk of his work was technically sound.

[3]Data retrieval is a difficult problem for many organizations. Information or data of any type developed by one operating unit is often of interest to other such groups but this need may not be apparent to the originating group, which discards data (or merely does not bother to catalog or organize the data) after it completes its work. To eliminate unnecessary work duplications, many organizations establish Data Centers or Information Control Centers into which all data by-products are transferred, edited, organized, indexed, and redistributed to probable user areas in a much easier to use format or computer printout.

"At the fifth coaching session he had corrected the prior errors, but there was little additional progress. On the possibility that some outside factors were bothering Henderson, I asked him to tell me more of himself, his family, and his outside interests and activities. I learned little that might create work related problems:

1. Henderson was 48 years old and in good health, a slightly overweight, non-drinker, who puffed regularly at one of three pipes he kept in a rack on his desk. (The work time lost due to the continual ritual of pipe stuffing, lighting, re-lighting, and cleaning is another subject in itself, but I considered it to be a work habits problem only incidental to his overall effectiveness.)
2. His wife was an elementary school teacher who had recently won a school district award for the experimental use of Programmed Instructional techniques for fifth grade mathematics.
3. Henderson had two daughters, both in high school. He expressed pleasure with his children in both their academic and social development. I caught no trace of special problems with the girls in any of his comments.
4. Henderson owned his own home and the family traveled frequently, often camping out with the pick-up truck camper which he owned.

"I concluded that external forces were not at the root of Henderson's problem. More likely it was the result of past poor supervision, narrow work assignments, or a promotion without adequate preparation. I talked at length with Henderson about his prior assignments but could not dig out any specific past situations, persons, or assignments which might have progressively reduced his effectiveness. (At no time in my conversation did I give Henderson the feeling that we were discussing his job effectiveness. It was, at all times, a general counseling session in which an interested manager was merely trying to learn more about a specific employee.)

"At meeting eight I asked Henderson why the data collection project was not yet complete. He insisted that the project would be in my hands within a week, that he had been held up in two critical areas by unco-operative supervisors. I became angry and demanded to know why he had not informed me of this before! I explained that it was my job to work out this type of problem. Henderson countered by saying that he preferred not to bother me with 'people problems' and had already worked through the conflicts in question.

"Late yesterday afternoon on my way to a meeting I ran into a very distressed manager, Barry Talbot. Talbot had several unpleasant words to say about J. B. Henderson. According to Talbot, it appeared that Henderson was interfering with their work in the process of his data collection. Talbot made it clear that he was happy to cooperate in the data collection process but he had no time to spend training my personnel who, in his words were, 'marking time until retirement.'

"This morning I intended to discuss the Talbot problem with Henderson at length but he called in sick. On my desk was his completed report, apparently placed there yesterday when I was in the meeting. I read it through and was shocked at the low quality, poor organization, and inept writing! For all practical purposes, ten man-weeks of effort was wasted, and I may have lost the respect of Barry Talbot and others in the process!

"I guess I'll just have to figure out some way to get rid of Henderson through the Surplus System."

Discussion Questions

1. What is the next step this supervisor should take with Henderson?
2. Do you think Henderson will acknowledge the overall low quality of the report? Explain.
3. Could this problem have been prevented? How?
4. What are the factors which contribute to managerial and technical obsolescence?
5. How is each of the following involved in the problem of managerial or technical obsolescence? That is, how is each often at fault for helping create the problem and how might each help prevent the problem:
    (a) The Individual?
    (b) The Supervisor?
    (c) The Company or Organization?
    (d) Selection and Promotion Systems?
    (e) Colleges and Universities?
6. What are the managerial dilemmas (pros and cons) of terminating Henderson at this point?

Special Projects

1. Have one or more class participants read the recent business satire titled, *The Peter Principle* by Dr. Lawrence J. Peter. Have them report to the class on:
    (a) The essential principles in the book.
    (b) How organizations can refute these principles with effective personnel selection, training, and development programs.

2. Prepare and submit a well-researched paper titled, *Technical and Managerial Obsolescence — What Can Be Done?*

Selected References

Books

Gellerman, S. W. *Motivation and Productivity*. New York: American Management Association, 1963.

Gellerman, S. W. *Management by Motivation*. New York: American Management Association, 1968, Chapters 6, 8.

Anthologies

Koontz, H., and O'Donnell, C. *Management: A Book of Readings*. New York: McGraw-Hill, 1968. Huber, G. "Motivation and Competence," p. 435.

Leadership on the Job. New York: American Management Association, 1966. Ruchti, W. "How Old Is Old?" p. 99.

Articles

Burack, E. H., and Pati, G. C. "Technology and Managerial Obsolescence," *MSU Business Topics*, Spring 1970, p. 49.

Cone, L. M. Jr. *"Toward a Theory of Managerial Obsolescence: An empirical and theoretical study."* Unpublished doctoral dissertation, New York University, 1968. (Also University Microfilms, Ann Arbor, Michigan, No. 68-13, 224, 1968.)

Gardner, J. W. "Can Organization Dry Rot Be Prevented," *Personnel Administration*, May–June 1966.

Levinson, H. "On Being a Middle Aged Manager," *Harvard Business Review*, July–August 1969, p. 51.

Meyers, M. S. "Conditions For Manager Motivation," *Harvard Business Review*, January–February 1966.

Schwartz, S. J. "A Cure for the 'I don't Care' Syndrome," *Personnel Journal*, July 1971, p. 528.

Steinmetz, L. "The Unsatisfactory Performer: Salvage or Discharge," *Personnel*, May–June 1968, p. 46.

A MATTER OF ACCOMMODATION

NURSE: (*answering phone*) Good morning, Dr. Haskell's office. How may we help you?

GUERERRA: I'd like to speak to Dr. Haskell please.

NURSE: I'm sorry, but Dr. Haskell is in with a patient and can't be disturbed. Perhaps if you'll give me your name and phone number the doctor can call you back?

GUERERRA: Nurse, this is Dr. Ernest Guererra at Pittman-Webber Manufacturing. I'd like to speak with Dr. Haskell about one of his patients.

NURSE: Oh, excuse me Dr. Guererra. If you'll hold on I'll see if Dr. Haskell can come to the phone.

HASKELL: (*after some delay*) Hello, George Haskell here.

GUERERRA: Dr. Haskell, this is Ernest Guererra, staff physician at Pittman-Webber Manufacturing. I'd like to talk to you for a moment about a patient of yours . . . a Mrs. Lucille Pennwalt.

HASKELL: Pennwalt? I'm sorry doctor but you caught me in the middle of a diagnosis. I'm afraid I don't recall offhand . . .

GUERERRA: Lucille Pennwalt. Widowed, 52 or 53 years old, red hair and somewhat overweight?

HASKELL: Oh, yes. Now I recall. Comes to me periodically on routine matters. Saw her last about a week or two ago.

GUERERRA: May I inquire as to the nature of the visit?

HASKELL: As I recall it was either headaches or insomnia. I believe I prescribed something or other. If you're treating her for something I can get her file.

GUERERRA: That probably won't be necessary, Dr. Haskell. Let me explain my interest. In addition to being on staff at St. Anthony's Hospital, I serve part time as house physician at Pittman-Webber Manufacturing, mostly employment physicals but also a range of industrial accident and health activities. I also do some counseling on job related problems which stem wholly or in part from physical disabilities or handicaps.

HASKELL: I see. And how is Mrs. Pennwalt involved?

GUERERRA: Mrs. Pennwalt has been with the company for twelve years, ever since her husband died. She has had a good to better-than-average attendance and job performance record over the years but recently her work has begun to fall off sharply.

HASKELL: Any particular medical problem?

GUERERRA: That's why I'm calling you. Mrs. Pennwalt has been in to see my nurse on and off complaining that she can't handle the heavy work . . . that her muscles get stiff . . . back hurts . . . a whole range of complaints.

HASKELL: You examined her?

GUERERRA: Last week. Mrs. Pennwalt wanted to be placed on an "easier" job but none was available in her pay range. I certified that she was medically healthy to continue unless she preferred to enter the hospital for more extensive testing . . . which she refused.

HASKELL: And you want to know if I found anything which might prevent her from doing her job?

GUERERRA: Yes.

HASKELL: One moment, I'll get her file.

HASKELL: (*two minutes later*) Nothing here. Very routine.

GUERERRA: Then, Dr. Haskell, why did you certify that Lucille Pennwalt should not lift any heavy objects? Her supervisor brought your note to me last Monday.

HASKELL: (*temporary silence*) Yes, come to think of it, I did have my nurse prepare a note to that effect which I later signed. Never really read it though.

GUERERRA: And your reason, Dr. Haskell?

HASKELL: (*clears throat*) For the same reason you would help one of your regular patients. Quite frankly, Mrs. Pennwalt asked me to prepare the note. She said she wasn't as young as she used to be and was tired of picking up heavy boxes at work which, she said, men should be hired to do. It was merely a matter of accommodation for a regular patient.

GUERERRA: You place me in a somewhat difficult position . . .

HASKELL: Look, Guererra, what's the problem?

GUERERRA: Personal motivation . . . Mrs. Pennwalt is apparently getting a little lazy and wants to get by doing as little as possible. They have an expression in industry for a long-termer who does less and less with little or no fear of reprisal . . . they call it, "owning the job." Such behavior is not only counterproductive but perplexing to supervisors who have known the employee for a long period of time and very irritating to co-workers who *are* expected to follow the rules.

HASKELL: I see. Exactly what does Mrs. Pennwalt do?

GUERERRA: Drill press operator.

HASKELL: *UGH!* Haven't you people automated out those mind-deadening jobs yet?

GUERERRA: Unfortunately not. But that's up to the engineers and tool designers. I'm only the company doctor.

HASKELL: What about those heavy weights?

GUERERRA: Work in small boxes is moved by hand trucks to each work station. Each box of parts weighs about 35–40 pounds and must be picked up and moved several times. Not excessive by state standards.

HASKELL: And now you have an unmotivated employee who is doing less and less, some confused supervisors, and unhappy co-workers?

GUERERRA: That's it.

HASKELL: Doctor, I'm sorry . . . really I am. But as you can tell from my office address, I am hardly in the country club circuit. My practice is composed of middle to low income patients . . . blue collar and Medicare. I can't afford to alienate them. I need the Mrs. Pennwalts who come back regularly for me to check for throat viruses and hypertension.

GUERERRA: So you won't change your mind on the lifting?

HASKELL: If I do I betray a trust she has with me. Then, I lose a patient and who knows how many of her friends. Maybe the work *is* too heavy for her. It isn't for me to say. No, Dr. Guererra, you'll have to work out the problem some other way.

Discussion Questions

1. What action should Dr. Guererra recommend to company management at this time?
2. Assuming no special medical problem exists, what steps could be taken to improve Mrs. Pennwalt's attitude and performance at work?
3. Assuming Mrs. Pennwalt is relieved of lifting boxes (and other female operators are not), how can the motivation of others to produce be maintained?
4. How might this type problem be prevented in the future?

Special Project

What laws, union contracts, company rules, and informal agreements affect employee safety, health, working conditions, and disability in your state.? Prepare a thorough list of these with brief descriptions and prepare an analysis of how such laws and agreements:

(a) *Positively* affect employee motivation, morale, and productivity.
(b) *Negatively* affect employee motivation, morale, and productivity.

Recent court rulings have invalidated certain state laws for women concerning hours of work, rest periods, and lifting of weights. These actions further the rights of women for equal opportunity in employment. Weight limitations, for example, established by state laws have, at times, had the net effect of legally excluding women from higher job and pay categories. Also see, *The Rules Are Different For Women*, p. 96.

The federal government is also actively involved in employee health and safety. Obtain a copy of the reference guide booklet to *The Williams-Steiger Occupational Safety and Health Act of 1970* (address in references). What are the organizational implications of this Act?

Selected References

Books
Levinson, P. *et al. Men, Management and Mental Health.* Cambridge, Massachusetts: Harvard University Press, 1963.
Maslow, A. H. *Motivation and Personality.* New York: Harper & Brothers, 1954.
Roethlisberger, F. J. *Management and the Worker.* Cambridge, Massachusetts: Harvard University Press, 1956.

Anthologies
Hampton, D. R., Summer, C. E., and Webber, R. A. (Eds.). *Organizational Behavior and the Practice of Management.* Glenview, Illinois: Scott, Foresman and Company, 1968.
  Maslow, A. H. "A Theory of Human Motivation: The Basic Needs," p. 27.

Simon, H., Smithburg, D., and Thompson, V. "Authority: Its Nature and Motives," p. 461.

Leadership on the Job. New York: American Management Association, 1966. Ruchti, W. "How Old Is Old?" p. 99.

Articles

MacMillan, M. H. "The Threshold of Tolerance," *Personnel Journal*, February 1970, p. 98.

Maier, N. R. F. "How to Get Rid of an Unwanted Employee," *Personnel Administration*, November–December 1965.

Schwartz, S. J. "A Cure for the 'I Don't Care' Syndrome," *Personnel Journal*, July 1971, p. 528.

Steinmetz, L. "The Unsatisfactory Performer: Salvage or Discharge," *Personnel*, May–June 1968, p. 46.

Wollenberger, J. B. "Acceptable Work Rules and Penalties," *Personnel*, July–August 1963, p. 23.

Booklets

Reference guide to *The Williams-Steiger Occupational Safety and Health Act of 1970*. U.S. Department of Labor. Order from, Superintendent of Documents, U.S. Government Printing Office, Washington, D.C. 20402, Stock number 2915-0001 (Price $0.20 each).

NO ROOM AT THE TOP

Lewis Latimer, Supervisor of Special Test Operations, has a motivational problem created by organizational structure and work rules. The problem is a familiar one to many managers in business and industry even if the titles here are different. Let Lew Latimer explain:

"My problem is easy to explain but beyond me in terms of solution. I'm a supervisor at an electronics company which manufactures desk top electronic calculators. I head a group of about twenty special electrical test technicians. These men don't test parts on the assembly line but conduct special electrical tests on completed units as directed by management. We do such things as:

1. Conduct systems tests on field failure units.
2. Conduct on-going reliability testing.
3. Conduct experimental testing for engineering.
4. Conduct special customer product testing (e.g. units for special applications).

"My men are electronics specialists typically, with military electronics background or are graduates of electronic trade schools. Some have certificates of completion from junior colleges which specialize in the sciences. We train the men we hire on the use of our test equipment and procedures but require practical electronic test experience as an employment prerequisite.

"The company currently has three technician classifications. They are:

Technician C   *Trainee*. (Six months maximum.)

Technician B   *Equipment Test Technician*. Familiar with all usual systems tests. Can perform all tests without assistance other than use of test manuals. (Up to four years.)

Technician A   *Senior Equipment Test Technician*. Must perform all functions of Technician B plus be able to calibrate test equipment and write test specifications. (No limit.)

"Most men are hired as Technician C, which is considered an entry level position. If they learn their job well, they are promoted to Technician B at the end of six months. Technician B carries a higher pay scale and a limit of four years that the classification can be maintained. The purpose of this is to force a man to qualify for a broader range of responsibility. The same is true for Technician A. Most men qualify for Technician A in about three years.

"So, in my department, the majority of men are now in the top pay classification. It breaks out like this:

Technician C	1 man
Technician B	5 men
Technician A	14 men
Total	20 men

"We're a young company in a fast moving industry. We make a good, reliable line of calculators, and most of our employees are proud of their products and the company. This has certainly been true of my technicians. You couldn't find a more highly motivated bunch of guys anywhere in the company.

"In recent months attitudes have begun to change. Several of the men have soured on the company and their jobs, after they reached the top of the pay scale for Technician A. For them, there's no place to go in the company and they know it.

"It's beginning to show up in their work too. A few of the men are taking a much more casual attitude toward their work than they used to . . . the old team spirit is really gone. When five o'clock comes the whole area is deserted. And these are guys that I used to have to chase home each evening.

"I talked to Frank Duncan about the problem. Frank is my boss and the Director of Operations at our facility. I suggested that the most promising persons in the Technician A category should be allowed to move to the

Junior Engineer classification. But Frank didn't care much for this solution. He said that all engineering classifications should be used only for professionals (he means college graduates), and that if we opened this classification to non-professionals (he means my technicians), morale problems will develop in other areas.

"Duncan said he would consider a Super-Grade classification for outstanding men in the Technician A category, and asked me to write a new job description for this classification.

"For the moment I'm going along with that approach for lack of anything better, but I feel it is a short-range solution and the problem will be back with us in a year or so."

Discussion Questions

1. What is the fundamental issue(s) involved in this case?
2. What are the implications of the Super-Grade technician classification from the viewpoint of employee performance, job attitudes, and morale?
3. What are the implications of allowing technicians to move to a "professional" classification?
4. How else might this problem be effectively resolved.

Special Project

Assign the following topics as research papers to several class members:
(a) The Case *For* Job Classifications.
(b) The Case *Against* Job Classifications.
Have reports read and discussed at a later session.

Selected References

Books
Myers, M. S. *Every Employee A Manager*. New York: McGraw-Hill, 1970.

Articles
Brianas, J. G. "Between Employees and Supervisors: Three Cases In Point," *Personnel Journal*, November 1970, p. 892.
Guyton, T. "The Identification of Executive Potential," *Personnel Journal*, November 1969, p. 866.
Herzberg, F. "One More Time: How Do You Motivate Employees?" *Harvard Business Review*, January–February 1968, p. 53.
Maugham, I. "Building An Effective Work Team," *Training and Development Journal*, January 1971, p. 20.
Paul, W. E., Robertson, K. B., and Herzberg, F. "Job Enrichment Pays Off," *Harvard Business Review*, March–April 1969, p. 61.
Pyle, W. "Accounting For Your People," *Innovation*, Number Ten, 1970, p. 46.

Walker, J., Luthans, F., and Hodgetts, R., "Who Really Are The Promotables?" *Personnel Journal*, February 1970, p. 123.

Wernimont, P. F. "What Supervisors and Subordinates Expect Of Each Other," *Personnel Journal*, March 1971, p. 204.

Wright, R. "Managing Man As A Capital Asset," *Personnel Journal*, April 1970, p. 290.

A TALK WITH KIRKEBY'S SON

"Now a similar kind of mechanism (inability to express hostility towards its real source) has traditionally operated in most American companies. The boss says in effect, 'Look, if you work for me, I'm going to have to frustrate you sometimes—over salaries, job conditions, company rules, whatever. And if you get frustrated you'll be hostile. But don't express this hostility to me because I'm the boss. Displace your hostilities. Go home and beat your wife. Or go home and join some kook organization. That or just eat your heart out.'"

FREDERICK HERZBERG
"The New Kid in The Company,"
Innovation, Number Eight, 1969, p. 41

"Did you want to see me?" Brad Kirkeby poked his head into the open doorway of his boss' office.

"Sure did, Brad. Come on in. I'll be finished with these overtime authorizations in a minute." Anthony Carboni continued initialing time cards while Kirkeby came in and sat down. Putting the cards in a neat stack to one side of his desk, Carboni looked up and smiled.

"Well Brad, how's it going?"

"Boring as hell!"

Carboni retained his composure. He cared little for the disrespectfulness of so many young people and their total lack of tact. But Carboni had two reasons for restraint in this case. First, Brad Kirkeby was recently out of college and on an eighteen-month company rotational training program. He would only be in Carboni's section for another forty-five days. Secondly, Brad was the son of Lawrence Kirkeby, one of Lockport Aircraft's most capable designers.

"I'm sorry to hear that," replied Carboni. "What seems to be the problem?"

"I'm going out of my mind with print check."[1] Kirkeby's response was emphatic but not hostile.

"Well," said Carboni, "someone has to check prints."

[1]Print check—a review of blueprints or engineering drawings and specifications prepared by others.

151

"But why me?" replied Kirkeby. "Can't a draftsman or a clerk do it?"

"Oh, I suppose he could," said Carboni, "but this is the way we've always developed potential structure designers . . . by having them learn all phases of the business from the bottom up."

"No disrespect intended, Mr. Carboni, but that argument escapes me. It's like saying that if you want to be an actor you have to have experience as a stagehand. I joined Lockport Aircraft to design airplanes not check prints."

"And so you will, Brad . . . eventually."

Kirkeby laughed. "Eventually . . . in time, Brad . . . wait your turn, Brad. In the long run it will all work out. Mr. Carboni, do you know what Lord Keynes, the famous British economist, said about the long run?"

"No," replied Carboni growing less patient each moment.

"Lord Keynes said, 'In the long run we'll all be dead!'"

"Meaning?"

"Meaning that I don't want to die or retire before I'm given a meaningful job to do."

Carboni lit a small cigar and puffed several times while looking directly at Kirkeby.

"I'm trying to understand you, Brad," he replied at last. "But you are simply going to have to adjust to the fact that you are out of college and in the real world now. It takes years of experience before you assume major structural design responsibility."

"That's because what they call experience in the Lockport Aircraft training program is merely a succession of routine tasks which could be done as well by a moron. Experience is learning and I'm not learning anything!"

"Look, Brad. I know you get all those aeronautical design theory courses in college and you expect to design planes your first week out of college. Face it, there's a certain amount of routine work in any job. Everyday can't be a learning experience like it was in college."

"I don't see why not," replied Kirkeby. "If I was hired to eventually design planes, shouldn't I be working next to designers instead of piddling around with trivia."

"The work in this section is hardly trivia!" Carboni was angry now but forced himself to keep from shouting. "But the work in this section is not the issue. You want to design airplanes like your father . . . right?"

"Right."

"Well," said Carboni, "your father has been with Lockport Aircraft for twenty-five years . . . eight years longer than I have. He started at the bottom and worked himself up step by step until, now, he's one of the most respected designers in the industry."

"My father is living proof of how ridiculous the System is. He had models at home when I was a boy . . . models he built in his spare time of wing and fuselage structures for as yet undreamed of mach 1 and mach 1.5 power-plants."

"Lawrence Kirkeby was always considered to be a very talented person," replied Carboni calmly.

Brad Kirkeby continued, "He was way ahead of his time. And what did this company have him doing for most of those years? Did they use his creative talents to design planes, or on research to advance the state-of-the-art? No. That would have been too obvious. They made him waste nearly twenty potentially creative years on trivial assignments before he became a designer with the authority to control technical considerations."

"How naive can you be, Brad Kirkeby? Do you really believe that your father alone came upon this advanced design information and was frustrated for years by a repressive and unresponsive management?" Carboni was angry now and let it show as he continued.

"Sure your father was talented. That's how he got to be Chief Designer at Lockport Aircraft. But he was and is still a mortal like the rest of us. Lawrence Kirkeby made his share of mistakes along the line. It was only after years of detailing and understudy with our top designers that his own ideas began to evolve and his real talents began to show. That's when he was moved to a responsible design position."

Brad Kirkeby started to reply, but Carboni cut him off.

"That's the trouble with you kids nowadays. You want everything in life without having to pay the price for it. You tell me you're bored with your job and ought to be designing planes instead. For your information, there are at least thirty bright young men currently in the company who have already passed this apprenticeship which you consider so useless and are now on detailing and limited design activity. Do you suggest I pass them up and promote you to the head of the class simply because you're bored with your present assignment?"

"Of course not, but . . ." Brad Kirkeby made an attempt to intervene.

"You're damned right I won't," shouted Carboni, answering his own question. "You've been in my section two months now and have turned in only mediocre work at best. You probably can justify that to yourself on the grounds that the work doesn't turn you on. Well, let me tell you something, Brad Kirkeby, talent is one hell of a lot more than just saying you have it. Talent is proving it in the work you do *now* . . . not the work you say you'll do next year or the year after! For all of your big talk about how great you are and how dull the work is, you have yet to prove to me you're anything but a phony!''

Discussion Questions

1. What issues are involved in this case?
2. To what extent do you agree with the basic position(s) taken by Brad Kirkeby?
3. To what extent do you agree with the basic position(s) taken by Anthony Carboni?
4. Can these two viewpoints be reconciled? Discuss.
5. It has been said that there is a great difference between ten years of experience and one year of experience repeated ten times. Discuss.
6. What is relevant job experience as you see it?

Special Projects

1. Prepare a study of two to six companies in your area which have entry level formal training programs for college graduates. What do such programs include? How long do they take? What are their strong and weak points? How might they be improved?
2. Correlate this case with the issues developed in, *"The Plight of Ralph Cummings."*

Selected References

Books

Knowles, H. P., and Saxberg, B. O. *Personality and Leadership Behavior*. Reading, Massachusetts: Addison-Wesley, 1971.

Maier, N. R. F., and Hayes, J. J. *Creative Management*. New York: Wiley, 1962.

Nadler, D. *The New Employee*. Houston, Texas: Gulf Publishing, 1971.

Anthologies

Effective Communication on the Job. New York: American Management Association, 1963. Gray, R. D. "What Your Boss Wants to Know," p. 125.

Hampton, D. R., Summer, C. E., and Webber, R. A. (Eds.). *Organizational Behavior and the Practice of Management*. Glenview, Illinois: Scott, Foresman and Company, 1968.
Dearborn, D., and Simon, H. "Selective Perception," p. 162.
Mechanic, D. "Sources of Power of Lower Participants in Complex Organizations," p. 425.

Huseman, R., Logue, C., and Freshley, D. *Readings in Interpersonal and Organizational Communication*. Boston, Massachusetts: Holbrook Press, Inc., 1969. Lee, I. J. "They Talk Past Each Other," p. 24.

Leadership on the Job. New York: American Management Association, 1966. Ruchti, W. "When You Supervise Young Employees," p. 89.

Articles

Fielden, J. S. "The Right Young People for Business," *Harvard Business Review*, March–April 1966, p. 76.

Gaddis, P. O. "Winning Over Indifferent Youth," *Harvard Business Review*, July–August 1969, p. 154.

Gomersall, E. R., and Meyers, M. S. "Breakthrough In On-The-Job Training," *Harvard Business Review*, July–August 1966, p. 62.

Haynes, M. E. "Improving Performance Through Employee Discussions," *Personnel Journal*, February 1970, p. 138.

Herzberg, F. "The New Kid in the Company," *Innovation*, Number Eight, 1969, p. 41.

"How to Handle Prima Donnas," *Industry Week*, April 27, 1970, p. 28.

Nouri, C. J., and Fridl, J. J. "The Relevance of Motivational Concepts To Individual and Corporate Objectives," *Personnel Journal*, November 1970, p. 900.

Pelz, D. "What It Takes To Make A Problem Solver Productive," *Innovation*, Number Nine, 1970, p. 2.

Repp, W. "Motivating the NOW Generation," *Personnel Journal*, July 1971, p. 540.

Roche, W. J., and MacKinnon, N. L. "Motivating People With Meaningful Work," *Harvard Business Review*, May–June 1970, p. 97.

Seiler, D. A. "Job Needs of the Newly Hired Professional," *Personnel Journal*, November 1970, p. 923.

Wheelen, T. L. "Executives Can Agree on Student Training," *Personnel Journal*, May 1971, p. 405.

CASE STUDY CROSS REFERENCE

Although located elsewhere in this book, the following problem situations are also valuable in the study of Section 6:

Personal Problems and Job Effectiveness

"Keller completed the reporting sequence for checkpoint I minus thirty, took one long last drag on his cigarette, and squashed it out in the crowded ashtray. Utopia? Hell! It was one big rat-race and getting bigger all the time. Keller recalled how he once naively felt that his problems with Naomi would disappear after they left Minneapolis and came to the Cape with the space program. Now, ten thousand arguments later, Keller knew there was no escape..."

No Response from Monitor
Twenty-three

INTRODUCTION

What is the proper role of the manager when employee personal problems arise and interfere with effective production? What can be done if the problem is undiagnosed or if the employee refuses to discuss it? When should the manager enlist the aid of qualified professional assistance? Is counseling and advice a good course of action? Can problems be ignored?

Cases in This Section

What Makes Fawcett Late?

Violation of work rules... work stoppages... morale of other workers ...counseling...a hidden problem...unknown motives and a lack of frankness.

Time to Buy More Chemistry

A young supervisor, new to the job, finds himself in a drug scene beyond his control . . . no fear of recrimination . . . covering up for others . . . the real toll in effectivity.

No Response from Monitor Twenty-three

A difficult and mentally demanding job runs counter to problems at home . . . no one to talk to about the problems . . . the pressure builds to an understandable conclusion. Can the problem be predicted and treated in advance?

No More Coddling . . . No More Pleas

Another messed up sales contact and the Director of Marketing decides to act . . . a confrontation on alcoholism . . . replay of an old record . . . a clear decision . . . but a wise one?

Department Chaplain

A department manager finds herself unable to remain out of the home problems of one of her employees . . . patience at first but later a series of demands . . . the employee begs for help if he is to succeed in the future . . . does he really want to be helped . . . or is it a game?

WHAT MAKES FAWCETT LATE?

A supervisor, who recently dealt with a difficult attendance and late arrival problem with one of his key subordinates, carefully documented his case for possible later disciplinary action. This is his story:

"Leon Fawcett has had an intolerable tardy record. He is late every day and sometimes as late as four hours or more. I have counseled with him three times in a period of four months to no avail. Since he has been tight-lipped about his reasons or excuses for his excessive tardiness, it has been difficult to diagnose or prescribe a remedy. I have followed four successive plans of action:

1. At the suggestion of the division manager, I increased his work load hoping that he would rise up to the occasion and put in an eight-hour day. It didn't work.
2. I arranged for Industrial Relations to counsel with him, since I suspected his tardiness might be due to a deep-seated resentment that he had never been promoted to supervisor. He refused to cooperate or even discuss the situation with Industrial Relations personnel.

3. I arranged for the medical department to give him a medical examination, since I suspected that a physical problem might be the root of the problem. Fawcett refused to take the examination.
4. I warned him that continued tardiness would result in disciplinary action and placed a written criticism in his personal file."

Problem Background

"Leon Fawcett is a test engineer in the Avionics Laboratory. He performs prototype and developmental functional and systems tests on electronics equipment. Often he has to improvise and develop his own test procedures and techniques. Leon has three hourly paid technicians assigned to him who assist him. Leon's problem is that he reports to work late *every day*! He is late from fifteen minutes to five hours each day. Some days he doesn't report to work at all, nor does he bother to call in. I have counseled with him, in private, three times in the last four months. He admits that he is late but sees nothing wrong in it. He claims it's the privilege of being a professional man.

"Leon is a very knowledgeable person and a very clever improviser. I would hate to lose him, but I can't tolerate his excessive tardiness either. I've come to the point where I must do something—fast!"

Pertinent Data

A. Personal information about Leon Fawcett:

1. Leon is 55 years old.
2. Has 15 years seniority.
3. His personnel folder is clean.
4. He's a likable person.

B. I inherited the problem when I was appointed manager six months ago.
C. The previous manager had counseled with Fawcett several times and then had decided to disregard his tardiness.
D. Fawcett acknowledges that his habits may be different from those of others but offers no explanations or alibis. He says I'm making a big thing out of it. The previous manager didn't make a major issue of it.
E. He claims that he is a professional person, and insisting he be in on time would be the same as forcing him to punch a time clock.
F. He disowns any responsibility to the three hourly paid technicians because they do not report to him, but to a manufacturing supervisor who is not in the same building.

G. He shrugs his shoulders when told he is setting a bad example and that he is acquiring a poor image and a poor record.

H. In addition to his lateness, Leon has a poor attendance record. He reports sick at least two or three times each month.

I. Leon never works late. He only arrives late.

J. At various times Leon has expressed resentment that he has not been promoted to supervisor in the past.

Secondary Problems Caused by Fawcett's Tardiness

A. The three hourly paid technicians, who have been assigned to help Leon, take advantage of his tardiness. They don't go to work until he shows up, claiming they are at a point where they need instructions.

B. This puts an additional burden on me because now I have to do Leon's job as well as my own.

C. Another professional has started to emulate Leon recently. Obviously he figures that, if Leon can get away with it, why can't he?

D. As this situation becomes common knowledge it reflects on Leon, the laboratory and me.

E. Leon can't see it but he is short-changing the job, the laboratory, and himself.

What Makes Fawcett Late?

A. If we knew this, then the cure might be more apparent.

B. If Leon has a deep-seated resentment in that he has never been promoted to supervisor, then:

　1. His tardiness may be his way of getting even.

　2. It gives him a sense of importance that he can break the rules and get away with it.

C. Physical and emotional problems may be involved.

　1. I suspect Leon may have an ulcer. I notice he is very selective about what he eats when we go to lunch together.

　2. He has commented at times that, when he eats the wrong foods, he can't sleep at night.

　3. In addition he is very emotional and worries excessively. Undoubtedly when he is worried he has trouble falling to sleep at night.

　4. When he does fall asleep, it is in the wee hours of the morning and so he sleeps late and thus reports to work late.

　5. I do not believe that he has an alcohol problem.

Possible Solutions

A. When I discussed the problem with my immediate superior he recommended the following:

  1. "Obviously Leon is careless about his attendance record because he is bored; he doesn't have enough to do.

  2. So, double his work load, and when he sees he can't do it all during his present working habits, he will start coming to work earlier."

B. To arrange for Industrial Relations to again counsel with Leon as to how he can make supervisor.

C. To set up a medical examination for Leon with the medical department and get Leon to take the exam.

  1. Brief the examining doctor with the facts concerning Leon's attendance and my suspicions.

  2. If his problem is physical, the doctor should be able to help.

  3. If his problem is emotional, maybe he can recommend a good psychiatrist.

D. To give Leon three written criticisms and then fire him.

Discussion Questions

1. What would you do about Fawcett? Why?
2. What other alternative should be explored?
3. Is there a policy problem here? Explain.
4. Could a third person be effectively used here? Explain.

Special Projects

Problems of this type are particularly distressing to managers because the employee often refuses to discuss the nature of the problem. Often it is because he does not sufficiently trust his supervisor to "level" or have an honest discussion without fear of recrimination.

1. Assume a communications problem exists in this case. Divide the class into groups of 4–5 to discuss methods or approaches which the supervisor might use to get Fawcett to talk honestly about the problem. Have groups go beyond the usual superficial, "Come on Leon, you can tell ol' George about it," and have them discuss specific techniques for breaking down person-to-person communications barriers.

  Allow 30 minutes discussion and 10 minutes for each report.

2. Assume that the supervisor was finally able to get Fawcett to discuss his problem and the problem turned out to be alcoholism, drugs, or a mental disorder. What should the supervisor's proper role be at this point?

  Use group discussion and reports as above.

Selected References

Books
Berne, E. *Games People Play*. New York: Grove Press, Inc., 1964.
Harris, T. A. *I'm OK — You're OK*. New York: Harper & Row, 1969.
James, M., and Jongeward, D. *Born To Win*. Reading, Massachusetts: Addison-Wesley, 1972.

Anthologies
Huseman, R., Logue, C., and Freshley, D. *Readings in Interpersonal and Organizational Communication*. Boston, Massachusetts: Holbrook Press, Inc., 1969.
   Walton, E. "Motivation to Communicate," p. 247.
   Wiksell, M. J. "Talking It Over *Is* Important," p. 236.
Leadership on the Job. New York: American Management Association, 1966. (Ed.). "Why Are They Late For Work?" p. 196.
Leavitt, H. J., and Pondy, L. R. (Eds.). *Readings in Managerial Psychology*. Chicago, Illinois: University of Chicago Press, 1964. Gibb, J. R. "Defensive Communication," p. 191.

Articles
Bennett, C. C. "Secrets Are For Sharing," *Psychology Today*, February 1969, p. 30.
Gary, A. L. "Industrial Absenteeism: An Evaluation of Three Methods of Treatment," *Personnel Journal*, May 1971, p. 352.
Hartman, R. I., and Gibson, J. J. "The Persistent Problem of Employee Absenteeism," *Personnel Journal*, July 1971, p. 535.

Literature
Recognizing and Supervising Troubled Employees, (Personnel Management Series Number 18), Bureau of Policies and Standards, U.S. Civil Service Commission, Obtain booklet by writing: Superintendent of Documents, U.S. Government Printing Office, Washington, D.C. 20402 (Price 15¢).

TIME TO BUY MORE CHEMISTRY

A young supervisor was recently interviewed by a reporter for a local newspaper regarding his experiences with employees using drugs while at work. The supervisor is not an expert in narcotics use, or in individual behavior patterns while under the influence of drugs. Most of what he does know about the subject has been a result of a recent assignment in which he observed drug use among certain persons reporting to him. Some were quite outspoken about their activities. Many of the following statements are based on information supplied by users and are presumed to be true.

While not a user of drugs himself, the supervisor prefers to remain anonymous in order to avoid any complications in his new job. Referred to here as Jeff Stevens, this is not his real name.

REPORTER: Jeff, the shocking thing throughout our discussion so far is not that drugs are used in business and industry but, in many cases, drugs are used openly with little or no fear of disciplinary action or job loss.

STEVENS: I certainly can't speak for industry as a whole, but from what I observed this was certainly true at Omega Microfilm Services.[1] And, from the individual relationships and systems established to facilitate drug use at Omega, I would suspect that this is also true in many other organizations.

REPORTER: Would you say that there was something different about Omega operations which made it particularly susceptible to drug infiltration?

STEVENS: I'd have to answer that both yes and no. Relative to microfilming operations as an industry I'd say no . . . I've worked in several repro and photo shops and never experienced the problem before. However there were certain aspects of the highly repetitive work and very poor company management which made Omega particularly vulnerable.

REPORTER: Perhaps we ought to put all of this in sequence. How did you happen to be in this unusual situation?

STEVENS: About six months ago I responded to a blind ad in a help wanted column for a night supervisor with strong microfilming experience. I had no supervisory experience at the time but had acted in a lead man capacity with my present employer for several months. All of my work experience had been in either microfilming operations or production photo shops.

REPORTER: And you received an answer?

STEVENS: Yes. About a week later I received a phone call from a Mr. Matt Boyle, who introduced himself as the General Manager of Omega Microfilm Services. He indicated that O.M.S. had just received a substantial contract from a major manufacturer to convert all that company's records to microfilm. This required the addition of a night shift and a night shift supervisor.

REPORTER: Is this a common type of service?

STEVENS: Oh, yes. Many large organizations recognize the need for document size reduction and information retrieval systems. But the microfilm cameras are quite expensive and so this work is usually contracted out to a document services firm such as Omega. Documents are usually picked up at the customer's office, microfilmed, coded, and later returned for a flat fee or contract price.

REPORTER: So Omega operations consisted primarily of microfilming equipment and camera operators.

[1]Not the real name of the company. All names of persons affiliated with Omega as later referenced are also fictitious.

STEVENS: Correct. It was a small shop in an industrial section of the city. Except for a few offices up front, the entire area was devoted to microfilm operations and storage.

REPORTER: Everything appeared to be in order?

STEVENS: I thought so at the time. I really wanted to get into supervision so I gambled on an unknown firm. My biggest concern was that when the "big job" was completed, I and the rest of the night shift would be terminated. Mr. Boyle assured me that my job was secure. Actually, he indicated that he was grooming me to replace the day shift supervisor with whom he was experiencing problems.

REPORTER: Did Boyle define the problems?

STEVENS: No. I was to find out later that the man was a chronic alcoholic who even drank heavily on the job. This was part of the drug problem actually. He was afraid to turn anyone in for drug use when they might just as easily fink on him.

REPORTER: So you took the job?

STEVENS: I showed up on Monday afternoon somewhat early, but no Matt Boyle. He was away on a sales call according to Tina Wells, a combination secretary and bookkeeper. So, I just walked out back and introduced myself.

REPORTER: What did you find?

STEVENS: The day shift foreman, Al Chambers, was in his office apparently reviewing records but clearly feeling no pain. He greeted me somewhat apprehensively but did give me a quick tour of the place including cursory introductions.

REPORTER: How many people were there in the shop?

STEVENS: About twenty on days and thirteen or fourteen at night. It seems small but, because of equipment limitations, two work shifts were required.

REPORTER: Go on.

STEVENS: Chambers left about five o'clock after introducing me to the incoming night shift group. Incredible as it seems, it appears that the night shift had been operating with little or no supervision for two weeks!

REPORTER: And the night shift crew?

STEVENS: An unusual group to say the least. Four were young black gals supporting themselves or their families. They were sharp, and turned out the bulk of the work. The others were transients mostly . . . college kids and drifters. Two or three had a very irregular attendance pattern. Except for the women I mentioned, none of the others cared very much about their job or the quality of work they turned in.

REPORTER: Is this typical for such an operation?

STEVENS: I don't think so. I later learned that Omega was in financial trouble. They were paying lowest scale for operators and were, in some cases, forced to accept the dregs from the bottom of the labor barrel.

REPORTER: When did you first suspect drug problems?

STEVENS: The very first night. A radio back in the shop blared continuous solid soul and rock music hour after hour and the operators worked methodically . . . almost in time to the beat. The music appeared to be a hypnotic pacer. I tried to turn it down once but was advised that music was the custom at night. I dropped the subject and decided to discuss it later with Boyle.

REPORTER: You say that the music paced the employees. Then, apparently, work was being produced?

STEVENS: Oh, yes. But there were quality problems as well.

REPORTER: When did you first actually witness drug use on the job?

STEVENS: About 8:30 p.m. A catering truck arrived at the back door of the shop at precisely our break time. I went out to the truck with the group and bought a cup of coffee. Many, however, preferred orange juice.

REPORTER: Orange juice?

STEVENS: Yes. I saw two or three openly pop several small pills into their mouths and wash them down with orange juice. One fellow smiled broadly, winked at me and said, "Energy, man, energy."

REPORTER: What did you do?

STEVENS: Nothing. I was too shook. I went back to the small office that Chambers and I shared and sorted through orders and other paperwork. Not only was it obviously in a total mess but there were possible signs of time card changes and incorrect time charges. When everyone left that evening I walked slowly through the shop past each camera. The air reeked of marijuana. I cursed myself for being so stupid to take the job and nearly vomited from the lingering stale odor.

REPORTER: Did you confront Mr. Boyle with this drug information?

STEVENS: I couldn't. It was Wednesday and Boyle had still not shown up at Omega. So, I just carried on as best I could.

REPORTER: Was there no one else you could talk to?

STEVENS: Not really. Chambers had his own problem and I didn't trust the front office secretary. A Mr. Hewitt had come in on Tuesday and introduced himself as an Omega financial partner but I hesitated breaking the information to him. I decided to wait for Boyle to return.

REPORTER: And, in the meantime?

STEVENS: I began to see the real work problems induced by drug use.

After continuous runs of good film from one operator I found an entire series of rejects. When I checked the camera I found that the proper reduction setting had not been made for the new work. The film processor (operator) had failed to make the correct set-up[2] for photographing the new series of documents and the batch was unusable. In other words, an operator could repeat identical and routine steps while under the influence but often forgot to make even the simplest changes . . . couldn't handle any deviation from the normal situation.

REPORTER: Was this behavior typical of any one particular drug?

STEVENS: Eddy Bass, one of the college boys who smoked grass but claimed to be clean of drugs, said these guys were on L.S.D. I never asked them directly.

REPORTER: And their behavior on the job other than the errors you noted?

STEVENS: Very placid . . . almost docile. Followed work instructions in a mechanical sort of way. One appeared to be afraid every time I came close to him. I had to make most set-ups myself to reduce the high reject rate.

REPORTER: Any other drugs?

STEVENS: Probably a whole range of pills and on and off use of marijuana. If heroin or other hard narcotics were being used, I saw no evidence of it while I was there. However, Bass hinted that a good fix before work could last all evening.

REPORTER: Any other erratic behavior?

STEVENS: I almost forgot. On Thursday evening I had my most frightening experience. I stopped to talk to Little Poe (as the group called him) about his work and he went to pieces right before my eyes! Although my questions were routine, he was so nervous he couldn't sit still . . . even for an instant. Up and down he went, his arms flailing the air all over the place and his speech largely unintelligible. He darted back and forth behind his camera, first confronting me and then hiding in a grotesquely nervous way. Bass and one of the gals walked Little Poe out the back door for fresh air. He didn't return.

REPORTER: Speed?

STEVENS: That's what Bass told me. I really don't know. It was a crazy nightmare that whole first week . . . just one crazy, incredible nightmare!

REPORTER: Then what happened?

STEVENS: Over the weekend I received a phone call from Matt Boyle.

[2]A set-up for example would be a change from 24X reduction to 50X reduction.

He apologized for being away all week but said he had been busy negotiating contract cutbacks. I told Boyle I was quitting and told him why.

REPORTER: Was he shocked?

STEVENS: No, I got the impression he was aware of the drug problem but was ignoring it for one reason or another. He begged me to stay. Boyle said that contract reductions would eliminate the night shift but that he was terminating Chambers and I was to be day shift supervisor.

REPORTER: And you agreed?

STEVENS: Temporarily . . . I didn't have another job. Besides, Boyle allowed me to make several layoff choices and I got rid of several problems that way.

REPORTER: Wasn't one of these a "pusher"?

STEVENS: We laid him off before we could prove it for sure. Apparently, he was doctoring employee time cards for more overtime pay (ignored totally by Chambers). He then skimmed off these excess wages by supplying most of the stuff. He allowed credit buying each day and took his cut from paychecks at the end of the week.

REPORTER: Were all of the night shift employees on drugs?

STEVENS: No, about half were clean.

REPORTER: Why didn't the persons not on drugs either quit or tell management of the problem?

STEVENS: I don't know for sure . . . possibly fear or possibly concern about losing their jobs as well.

REPORTER: Did the personnel cutback eliminate the drug problem at Omega?

STEVENS: Partially. We got rid of the worst offenders but kept those we needed to get the job done. Boyle finally realized that the combination of low productivity, high rejects, and inept supervision had brought Omega to the brink of bankruptcy.

REPORTER: That bad?

STEVENS: Yes. Early my second week we were running low on supplies and I asked Boyle to buy more chemistry.[3] He refused and asked us to cut solutions with water to save money.

REPORTER: Does that work?

STEVENS: Only temporarily. After a while the photos become grainy and later worthless and it costs you more money in the end. It was academic anyhow. On Friday of the second week Boyle announced suspension of all activities. I never did get paid.

[3]Chemistry—film developer, hypo, stop fix; the photographic materials and supplies necessary to continue operations.

Discussion Questions

1. Why had this problem not been uncovered and resolved before Stevens arrived?
2. Did Stevens behave correctly the first week? Discuss. What would you have done?
3. Stevens describes two conditions which make an organization particularly vulnerable to drug infiltration. Discuss these and other possible conditions.
4. Could this drug problem have occurred in a "well managed" organization as opposed to Omega? Discuss.
5. How should business and industrial organizations react to similar drug problems. (Separate this question into meaningful sub-sections to make answers possible.)

Special Projects

1. Prepare a research paper as an outside assignment on the topic, *Drug Use, Industry's Latest Personnel Problem*. As with question (5) above, this special project may have to be subdivided and given to several study groups as assignments.
2. Several major insurance companies now have extensive literature available on this subject, much of it geared to the practical needs of the manager and supervisor faced with the problem. With reasonable notice through your instructor, copies may be obtained for classroom discussion. A few insurance companies also have 16 mm. films on free loan which deal with drugs and alcohol in the work environment. Be sure to check well in advance to need as these films are tightly scheduled and sent only to groups upon formal request with specified need dates.

Selected References

Books

Willig, S. H. *Legal Considerations: Drug Abuse in Industry and Business*. From the Symposium on Drug Abuse in Industry, Philadelphia, 1970. Symposium Enterprises, P.O. Box 356, North Miami, Florida 33161, 1971.

Literature

Common Sense Lives Here, Coordinating Council on Drug Abuse Education and Information, Drug Abuse, P.O. Box 2000, Washington, D.C. (Price $2.00)

National Clearing House for Drug Abuse Information, 5454 Wisconsin Avenue, Chevy Chase, Maryland 20015 (Single courtesy copies of materials on drugs.)

What About Drugs And Employees?, Public Relations Department, Kemper Insurance Group, 4750 North Sheridan Road, Chicago, Illinois 60640 (No charge for single copies.)

NO RESPONSE FROM MONITOR TWENTY-THREE

Loudspeaker: IGNITION MINUS FORTY-FIVE MINUTES...

Paul Keller tripped the sequence switches at control monitor 23 in accordance with the countdown instruction book just to his left. All hydraulic systems were functioning normally in the second stage of the spacecraft booster at checkpoint I minus forty-five. Keller automatically snapped his master control switch to GREEN and knew that his electronic impulse along with hundreds of others from similar consoles within the Cape Kennedy complex signalled continuation of the countdown.

Free momentarily from data input, Keller leaned back in his chair, stretched his arms above his head and then rubbed the back of his neck. The monitor lights on console 23 glowed routinely.

It used to be an incredible challenge, fantastically interesting work at the very fringe of man's knowledge about himself and his universe. Keller recalled his first day in Brevard County, Florida, with his wife and young daughter. How happy they were that day. Here was the future, the good life . . . forever. And Keller was going to be part of that fantastic, utopian future . . .

Loudspeaker: IGNITION MINUS THIRTY-FIVE MINUTES . . .

Keller panicked! His mind had wandered momentarily and he lost his place in the countdown instructions. Seconds later he found the correct place and tripped the proper sequence of switches for checkpoint I minus thirty-five. No problem. Keller snapped master control to GREEN and wiped his brow. He knew he was late reporting and would hear about it later.

Damn!, he thought, I used to know countdown cold for seven systems monitors without countdown instructions. But now . . . you're slipping Keller . . . you're slipping, he thought. Shaking his head, Keller reassured himself that he was overly tired today . . . just tired.

Loudspeaker: IGNITION MINUS THIRTY MINUTES . . .

Keller completed the reporting sequence for checkpoint I minus thirty, took one long last drag on his cigarette, and squashed it out in the crowded ashtray. Utopia? Hell! It was one big rat-race and getting bigger all the time. Keller recalled how he once naively felt that his problems with Naomi would disappear after they left Minneapolis and came to the Cape with the space program. Now, ten thousand arguments later, Keller knew there was no escape . . .

> "Only one can of beer left, Naomi? One stinking lousy can of beer, cold lunchmeat and potato salad? Is that all a man gets after twelve hours of mental exhaustion?"
>
> "Oh, shut up, Paul! I'm so sick of you playing Mr. Important. You get leftovers because I never know when you're coming home . . . your daughter hardly knows you . . . and you treat us like nobodies . . . incidental to your great personal contribution to the Space Age."

169

"Don't knock it, Naomi. That job is plenty important to me, to the Team, and it gets you everything you've ever wanted . . . more! Between this house and the boat, we're up to our ears in debt."

"Now don't try to pin our money problems on me, Paul Keller. You're the one who has to have all the same goodies as the scientists earning twice your salary. Face it, Paul. You're just a button-pushing technician regardless of how fancy a title they give you. You can be replaced Paul. You can be replaced by any S.O.B. who can read and punch buttons!"

Loudspeaker: IGNITION MINUS TWENTY-FIVE MINUTES . . .

A red light blinked ominously indicating a potential hydraulic fluid leak in subsystem seven of stage two. Keller felt his heartbeat and pulse rate increase. Rule 1 . . . report malfunction immediately and stop the count. Keller punched POTENTIAL ABORT on the master control.

Loudspeaker: THE COUNT IS STOPPED AT IGNITION MINUS TWENTY-FOUR MINUTES SEVENTEEN SECONDS.

Keller fumbled with the countdown instructions. Any POTENTIAL ABORT required a cross check to separate an actual malfunction from sporadic signal error. Keller began to perspire nervously as he initiated standard cross check procedures.

"Monitor 23, this is Control. Have you got an actual abort, Paul?" The voice in the headset was cool, but impatient. "Decision required in thirty seconds."

"I know, I know," Keller mumbled. "I'm cross checking right now."

Keller felt the silence closing in around him. Cross check one proved inconclusive. Keller automatically followed detailed instructions for cross check two.

"Do you need help, Keller?" asked the voice in the headset.

"No, I'm O.K."

Keller continued cross check two.

"Decision required," demanded the voice in the headset. "Dependent systems must be deactivated in fifteen seconds."

Keller read and re-read the console data. It looked like a sporadic error signal . . . the system appeared to be in order . . .

"Decision required," demanded the voice in the headset.

"Continue count," blurted Keller at last. "Subsystem seven fully operational." Keller slumped back in his chair.

Loudspeaker: THE COUNT IS RESUMED AT IGNITION MINUS TWENTY-FOUR MINUTES SEVENTEEN SECONDS.

Keller knew that within an hour after lift off, Barksdale would call him in for a personal conference. "What's wrong lately, Paul?" he would say. "Is there anything I can help with? You seem so tense lately." But he wouldn't really want to listen. Barksdale was the kind of person who read weakness into any personal problems and demanded that they be purged from the mind the moment his men checked out their consoles.

More likely Barksdale would demand that Keller make endless practice runs on cross check procedures while he stood nearby . . . watching and noting any errors . . . while the pressure grew and grew . . .

Today's performance was surely the kiss of death for any wage increase too. That was another of Barksdale's methods of obtaining flawless performance . . . which would surely lead to another scene with Naomi . . . and another sleepless night . . .
and more of those nagging stomach pains . . .
and yet another imperfect performance for Barksdale . . .

Loudspeaker: IGNITION MINUS TWENTY MINUTES . . .
The monitor lights at console twenty-three blinked routinely.
"Keller," said the voice in the earphone. "Report, please."
"Control, this is Wallace at monitor twenty-four. I don't believe Keller is feeling well. Better send someone to cover fast!

Loudspeaker: THE COUNT IS STOPPED AT NINETEEN MINUTES THIRTY-THREE SECONDS.
"This is Control, Wallace. Assistance has been dispatched and the count is on temporary hold. What seems to be wrong with Keller?"
"Control, this is Wallace. I don't know. His eyes are open and fixed on the monitor but he won't respond to my questions. It could be a seizure or . . . a stroke."

Discussion Questions

1. What are the relevant behavioral issues here?
2. In this case Keller became ill. What other behavioral patterns might be expected from employees experiencing excessive job or home pressure?
3. Is there any way of avoiding the more serious manifestations (as with Paul Keller) of pressure on the job? Explain.
4. Are there any early warning signs given by employees under pressure? If so, what are they?
5. What is the proper role of the supervisor here? Should he attempt counseling?

Special Project

Prepare and submit a documented research paper on the subject, *Negative Pressure and Productivity*: *Some Causes and Some Answers*.

Selected References

Books

Levinson, H. *et al. Man, Management, and Mental Health*. Cambridge, Massachusetts: Harvard University Press, 1963.
Levinson, H. *Executive Stress*. New York: Harper & Row, 1970.
McLean, A. A., and Taylor, G. C. *Mental Health in Industry*. New York: McGraw-Hill, 1958.
Maier, N. R. F. *Psychology in Industry*, New York: Houghton Mifflin Company, 1965, Chapter 16.
Miner, J. B. *The Management of Ineffective Performance*. New York: McGraw-Hill, 1963.

Anthologies

Fleishman, E. A. *Studies in Personnel and Industrial Psychology*. Homewood, Illinois: The Dorsey Press, 1967. Fraser, D. C. "Recent Experimental Work in the Study of Fatigue," p. 540.
Hampton, D. R., Summer, C. E., and Webber, R. A. (Eds.). *Organizational Behavior and the Practice of Management*. Glenview, Illinois: Scott, Foresman and Company, 1968 "Leavitt, H. "Frustration: The Roadblock," p. 374.

Articles

Argyris, C. "Organizational Effectiveness Under Stress," *Harvard Business Review*, May–June 1960, p. 137.
Burke, R. J. "Effects of Aging on Engineers Satisfactions and Mental Health: Skill Obsolescence," *Academy of Management Journal*, December 1969.
Buyniski, E. F. "Stress—Sickness—Supervision," *Personnel Administration*, July–August 1962.

NO MORE CODDLING ... NO MORE PLEAS

"I regret gentlemen," said Walter Demby, "that my General Sales Manager, John Foote, was not able to meet with you today. He could have provided you with more precise detail regarding the use of our products in your particular application. I hope my discussion of other similar applications will suffice until John can get back to you with additional information."

Walter Demby chatted several more minutes with representatives of this potentially large customer. They were all pleasant and positive in their tone, but Demby knew they had clearly planned to meet with Foote today to discuss specific details and not generalities. Although they agreed to meet next week with Foote, Demby had the feeling they were now leaning toward a competitor's product. Demby knew he could have sold them today had he the time to prepare for the meeting, but Foote had all the data and Foote was designated to make the presentation.

As Demby drove back to the office his anger toward Foote continued to grow. This was the last straw! This time there would be no more coddling . . . no more pleas for self-discipline. This time Foote would get the message simply and clearly.

Demby stopped for gasoline and took a moment to phone his secretary.

"Candice, this is Walt Demby. Has Mr. Foote come in yet?"

"Yes he did, Mr. Demby. About twenty minutes ago."

"Did you tell him I was with the people at Markham?"

"Yes I did."

"And?" asked Demby.

"Mr. Foote appeared to be very upset with himself."

"He ought to be," muttered Demby. "Where is Foote now?"

"I asked Mr. Foote to wait in your office until you returned . . . just as you had asked."

"And no visitors?" asked Demby.

"No visitors," replied Candice.

"Good. I should be there in twenty minutes."

Walter Demby had worked out exactly what he would say to Foote and also developed answers to Foote's likely replies. This time he would get right to the basic issue. This time he would do what should have been done with Foote over a year ago.

By the time Demby arrived back at his office his emotions had somewhat subsided. Candice Brown was typing sales reports when he entered. Demby pointed a finger at the door marked, W. Demby, DIRECTOR OF MARKETING. His secretary nodded affirmatively.

"Bring in more coffee, Candice. I'm going to need some too."

Inside, Walter Demby placed his attache case next to his desk and hung up his suitcoat. John Foote was seated on the sofa facing Demby's desk, his face in his hands. Demby sat at his desk and waited.

"Walt, I . . . I don't know what to say." Foote spoke slowly and his words were soft and choked with emotion. "I was out late last night and had a few drinks . . . I just don't know how it happened but I . . . I apparently didn't hear the alarm clock go off . . ."

"You didn't hear the alarm clock because you were bombed out of your mind! A few drinks? You probably made every bar in town after you left work yesterday. You didn't hear the alarm clock because you were lousy, stinking drunk!"

"I'm sorry Walt . . . Lord knows I'm sorry. I just didn't realize I drank so much . . . I didn't feel it at the time . . . didn't feel sick or anything."

"Well, you felt it this morning. You slept off your giant drunk while I had to substitute for you over at Markham. They were expecting *details*

173

this morning, Foote... details that you had developed. I did the best I could without hard data but..."

"I'll call Ollie over at Markham this afternoon," replied Foote. "I'll set up another meeting for next week and give them the detailed presentation then. A few days won't matter much."

"I've already set up a meeting for next week between you and the Markham people," replied Demby.

"Oh, good ... good," Foote said, a slight smile appearing on his face.

"Good?" Demby roared. "Is that all you can say you dumb sonofabitch?"

"Walt ... I mean that ..." Foote stammered.

"The Markham account is as good as dead. Did you hear me Foote? The Markham account is D...E...A...D...! We lost that account because my esteemed and talented Sales Manager, John Foote, is a drunk!"

A knock at the door provided Foote with a short reprieve from the verbal whipping.

"Yes?" Demby called out.

"The coffee you asked for, Mr. Demby."

"Come in, Candy."

Candice Brown brought in a tray with two cups and a small pot of coffee. Sensing her interruption at a very delicate moment, Candice placed the tray on Demby's desk and started to leave.

"Thank you, Candy," said Demby, adding, "no calls for the next thirty minutes, please."

Demby poured coffee for Foote and himself.

"Did you look at yourself this morning, John? Your eyes are red, you haven't shaved, and you look pale. If the meeting were now instead of eight o'clock I *still* couldn't let you handle it.

Foote felt his chin. "Walt, I was so shook when I woke up and looked at the time that I forgot all about shaving. You know this is not the appearance I normally make."

"I'll grant you that," replied Demby, "but the issue is not how you look today. The issue, John Foote, is that you have a problem with alcohol which has been getting progressively worse."

"Walt, you know I've had problems. When my son, Bill, was killed in that freak skiing accident I thought I would go out of my mind. Then Loretta and I started to have some difficulties ..."

"Stop it, John!" Demby appealed. "You know I understand the tragedy of Bill's loss to you ... but that was over four years ago. You've got to stop using it as an excuse to drink."

"I was improving, Walt, but when Loretta left me ..."

174

"Loretta left you because she was sick and tired of covering for an alcoholic husband. And, I'm tired of covering for you, John. I can't do your job and mine."

Demby took a sip of coffee before dropping the bombshell.

"I'm letting you go, John . . . as of today."

The words stunned Foote and he spilled part of his coffee on the dark carpeting. Instinctively, Foote began to blot the spill with his handkerchief.

"Forget it, John. The stain won't show."

John Foote put his handkerchief away and looked across the desk at his boss.

"Walt, today was an isolated case. I was feeling sorry for myself last night. It won't happen again . . . I swear it won't."

"I'm sorry, John, but I'm so damned sick of hearing that same old broken record. Maybe letting you go is the only way to wake you up to what you're doing to yourself. You drank heavily before Bill died . . . no one really believes your drinking started with that. Loretta left you and you still kept on drinking . . ."

Foote now became more vocal in his own defense.

"Now wait one second, Walter Demby. I admit I've had problems at home but a man should be judged by his total output at work and not his home life." Foote paused, adding, "And my record for eight years with this company is a good one."

"It used to be, John. You were one fine salesman and a great sales manager. But, for the past year, we've been carrying you. Your good record is part of ancient history."

Foote started to reply but Demby cut him off.

"You're a sick man, John. You're overweight and you've had high blood pressure for years. Two months ago you told me your doctor also found high cholesterol and tri-glyceride levels. Stay on the 'sauce' much longer, John, and you'll kill yourself."

Demby shook his head.

"I'm sorry, John. I've tried . . . I really have . . . but my decision is final. You will simply have to work out your problem on someone else's time. We can't run a clinic here."

Discussion Questions

1. How do you feel about Demby's decision? Discuss.
2. Could this termination have been prevented? How?
3. What other alternatives might have been considered on the day of the case?

4. How far should a supervisor go in working through problems such as this with an employee?

5. An employee once remarked wryly, "Sure, we have a company policy on alcoholism but it's not enforced. If we cracked down, several members of top management would be among the first to go." Explain the organizational implications of this statement.

Special Project

Most larger organizations have adopted guidelines and developed policy statements for supervisors regarding the problems of excessive use of alcohol among employees. Some organizations also conduct special training programs to help their managers effectively deal with job-related problems caused by alcohol.

Conduct a survey of local organizations regarding their policies on this subject. Are some policies more effective than others? Why?

Of Special Interest to Industry Groups

What is the official and unofficial policy of your company toward alcoholism? Does it need to be updated?

Selected References

Anthologies
Leadership on the Job. New York: American Management Association, 1966. Trice, H. "Identifying the Problem Drinker on the Job," p. 234.

Articles
Buchanan, H. "How Companies Are Dealing With Alcoholism," *Personnel*, November–December 1966, p. 19.
Dutton, R. E. "Industry's $2-Billion Headache—The Problem Drinker," *Personnel Journal*, June 1965, p. 303.
Kelley, J. W. "Case of the Alcoholic Absentee," *Harvard Business Review*, May–June 1969, p. 14.
MacMillan, M. H. "The Threshold of Tolerance," *Personnel Journal*, February 1970, p. 98.
Maier, N. R. F. "How to Get Rid of an Unwanted Employee," *Personnel Administration*, November–December 1965.
Springborn, B. "The Axman Cometh," *Industry Week*, January 12, 1970, p. 37.
Steinmetz, L. "The Unsatisfactory Performer: Salvage or Discharge," *Personnel*, May–June 1968, p. 46.

Literature
Alcohol and Alcoholism. (Public Health Service Publication No. 1640), National Institute of Mental Health, Chevy Chase, Maryland 20015 (free, single copies). Superintendent of Documents, U.S. Government Printing Office, Washington, D.C. 20402 (In quantity, 50¢ each).
Alcoholism in Industry—Modern Procedures, Christopher D. Smithers Foundation, 41 East 57th Street, New York, NY 10022 (Price $1.00).
Detour—Alcoholism Ahead, Public Relations Department, Kemper Insurance Group, 4750 North Sheridan Road, Chicago, Illinois 60640 (50 copies free. Additional, 5¢ each).

Management Guide On Alcoholism and Other Behavioral Problems, Public Relations Department, Kemper Insurance Group, 4750 North Sheridan Road, Chicago, Illinois 60640 (50 copies free. Additional, 5¢ each).

Manual on Alcoholism (The), Order Handling Unit, American Medical Association, 535, North Dearborn Street, Chicago, Illinois 60610 (50¢ per copy).

What To Do About the Employee With a Drinking Problem, Public Relations Department, Kemper Insurance Group, 4750 North Sheridan Road, Chicago, Illinois 60640 (50 copies free. Additional, 5¢ each).

DEPARTMENT CHAPLAIN

Kay Kellogg was nearing completion of the monthly departmental report when she was interrupted by her secretary, Lynn Wainscott.

"Excuse me, Dr. Kellogg, but Dr. Scheffner would like to see you."

"Did you explain I'm tied up with budgets and reports," Kay replied somewhat irritated.

"I did, but Dr. Scheffner insisted. He says it's personal and very urgent..."

"Oh, no!" Kay Kellogg moaned softly, removed her reading glasses, and rubbed her eyes."

"Excuse me?" asked Miss Wainscott.

"Nothing... nothing at all, Lynn. Ask Dr. Scheffner to come in, and hold all phone calls for about fifteen minutes."

Lynn Wainscott started to leave the office of the Chairman of the English Department when Kay Kellogg added, "Lynn, do a favor for me please. If Dr. Scheffner is still in the office with me after twenty minutes, I want you to interrupt and tell me the Dean of Arts and Letters wishes to see me immediately."

Lynn Wainscott appeared puzzled.

"Dr. Scheffner tends to be... well, somewhat lengthy at times," said Dr. Kellogg, defensive of her planned tactic. "And I must complete this report today."

A few moments later, Theodore Scheffner closed the door behind him and sat in the chair next to Kay Kellogg's desk.

"Kay, I know how busy you are this week, but I just had to see you," began Dr. Scheffner. "I need your advice more than I've ever needed it before."

"What can I do for you, Ted?" asked Kay calmly, feeling she was about to hear a repeat of a now familiar theme.

"It's Eva. She's going to leave me... she wants a divorce." Scheffner spoke rapidly and nervously, quite in character of a stereotype of a smallish, middle-aged English professor.

177

"I'm sorry to hear that Ted," replied Dr. Kellogg. "Perhaps it will be like the last time. Maybe she's only upset and will settle down in a few days."

"No, no," Scheffner countered. "This time she really means it. She plans to leave for good and take the children."

"She must be very angry about something."

"Not angry . . . Eva isn't angry," replied Scheffner, "My wife is sick . . . she's sick!"

Scheffner's eyes darted rapidly from Kay Kellogg, up, down, across the room, and back again to Kay. His breathing was short and he picked nervously at the cuticles of his fingers as he talked.

"Surely you're overreacting?" asked Kay.

"I'm not at all. Eva's out of touch with reality. She wants a big house in the suburbs . . . a house she knows we can't afford. She says it's my fault we don't have it . . . claims we don't have anything."

"Eva should understand the salary limitations of your position here at City College."

"She should," shouted Scheffner. "But she doesn't. She doesn't care what I do . . . she doesn't understand what I do . . . she has no respect for me or my work."

"Oh, I'm sure Eva respects you as a . . ."

"Not true!" replied Scheffner crisply. "To Eva, I am a failure. She has no respect." Scheffner paused. "Kay, yesterday I worked at home because I had no scheduled classes. In the afternoon Eva had several neighborhood women over for tea and, although she was whispering in the other room, I overheard her remarks about me. She told the other women not to talk too loud or Mr. Maladroit would be disturbed."

"Mr. Maladroit?" asked Dr. Kellogg.

"Yes," replied Scheffner. "That is her warped impression of me."

"And then you had an argument?"

"After her guests left I told her what I had heard and we argued for several hours. Then she announced she was leaving me."

Kay Kellogg placed her hand over Scheffner's.

"Ted, I'm terribly sorry for you and Eva, but I really don't see what I can do."

"Talk to her, Kay," pleaded Scheffner. "Explain the critical educational role we play with these young people. Somehow make her understand how valuable my contribution is."

"Ted, I really don't feel it's my place to . . ."

Scheffner broke in before she finished.

"Let me tell you how bad it is. Eva even has the gall to criticize my work at the college. Imagine! She told me that the children of several of her friends purposely registered for another section of Nineteenth Century American Literature because my classes had the reputation of being dull . . . me dull?"

"Not dull . . . not exactly," replied Dr. Kellogg. "But a number of students do request other sections in preference to yours."

"Lazy . . . they're getting lazier all the time."

"I don't think so, Ted. We've spoken of this before . . . of the need to keep American literature classes vital and alive so students will feel enriched by the classroom experience and want to read more on their own.

"Well?" asked Scheffner.

"Well," replied Kay Kellogg, "You promised last semester to modify classroom content and upgrade emphasis on themes to which young people can relate so that the content of the literature will have meaning as well as the literary style and quality."

Kay Kellogg continued.

"Ted, you know all authors rise and fall in popularity with the times. I don't think we should fight it even though we have our own preferences or we'll turn off our captive audiences. I've already suggested the reintroduction of the works of Stephen Crane and Richard Henry Dana to stress the importance of literature in shaping thoughts on the nature of conflict and man's intolerance to man. So far you haven't even reworked your classroom plan much less actually introduced the material."

"Yes, I know," admitted Scheffner. "So much is involved in rebuilding a course which is so well balanced. And it's so difficult to concentrate on your work when you're married to such a hateful woman as I am."

Kay Kellogg sat back in her chair.

"Ted, perhaps it's best that you stopped in today. Frankly, your work has been suffering the past two semesters or so. Your lectures lack the enthusiasm and spirit they once had and your selection of readings leaves most students quite cold."

Kay Kellogg took a deep breath and continued.

"You will simply have to make major content and format changes in your courses or I will be unable to recommend a full professorship for you in the next academic year. Additionally, I insist you complete your manuscript on the life of William Cullen Bryant and submit it for publication by the start of the next semester. The department typists are complaining about the senseless re-work of already completed chapters and the vague future publication date has already become somewhat of a departmental joke."

The office was quiet for a moment.

"Those are very severe words, Dr. Kellogg," replied Dr. Scheffner at last. "Publish or perish . . . shape up or ship out."

"I'm sorry," replied Dr. Kellogg.

"No, don't be sorry. You're right, of course." Scheffner paused, then added. "The book *would* be completed . . . my classes *would* be restructured . . . and my mind *would* be on my work as an instructor if I didn't have these problems with Eva. Dr. Kellogg, will you please help me with Eva?"

"Ted, it's not my place. Have you talked to your physician?"

"No, Eva has him all mixed up with a variety of fictitious illnesses. He'd only give her another prescription to get her out of his office."

"Perhaps your clergyman might be able to help?"

"Reverend Dinsman is a very old man," Scheffner countered. "I doubt if he can hear much less listen and solve marital problems."

Kay Kellogg was greatly distressed and bit her lip to keep from shouting out her feelings both as a boss and a woman.

"Ted, perhaps you and Eva should see a marriage counselor," she said at last. "A counselor might be able to get you two to communicate again."

"We tried that route too . . . and it didn't work either. We agreed to go about three months ago but after two meetings we both felt it was a waste of time . . . that we could solve our own problems better."

"But you haven't as yet . . ."

"No, of course we haven't because Eva's sick. She won't listen to any man. But she'd listen to you, Kay . . . I know she would. She has lots of respect for you. You could help me by getting Eva to see how ridiculous her attitudes are toward me and my work."

"Ted, I really don't . . ."

"Dr. Kellogg. I'm afraid I must interrupt." It was Lynn Wainscott. "Dr. Johnstone has asked you to come over to his office immediately."

"I won't detain you," said Scheffner. "The Dean is a very impatient man. Can we talk again soon?"

"Yes," replied Kay Kellogg quietly, "We'll talk again . . . soon."

Discussion Questions

1. Define Dr. Scheffner's problem as seen by:
   (a) Ted Scheffner.
   (b) Eva Scheffner.
   (c) Kay Kellogg.
2. Regarding the conversation in this situation:

(a) What did Kay Kellogg handle well? Discuss.

(b) What did Kay Kellogg handle poorly? Discuss.

3. Was Kay Kellogg's role more difficult to play because she is a woman counseling a male employee? Discuss.

4. How would you have handled this situation?

5. To what extent should a supervisor become involved in the personal problems of an employee?

(a) Should he initiate discussion to probe for possible personal problems if an employee's work performance is poor?

(b) Should he offer assistance only if an employee asks for help or advice?

(c) Should he avoid this problem entirely?

6. One supervisor recently said, "I don't fool around with anyone's personal problems. I send the guy to Personnel for counseling on most problems or to the company doctor if he has a medical problem or needs a 'shrink.'[1]" Comment on this statement.

Special Projects

1. What do the experts say about counseling employees on personal problems? Prepare a well-documented research paper titled, *The Role of the Supervisor in Personal Problems of Employees*.

2. There is some indication that Scheffner was trying to say it was all but impossible for him to resolve the problem and begin to improve his work performance. Read *Games People Play* by Dr. Eric Berne or a similar work on Transactional Analysis and relate the conversation in this situation to one or more "games."

   Note. A well-intentioned supervisor can be inadvertently trapped into playing a "game" on personal problems.

3. Effective counselors often use a technique called *mirroring* or *reflecting* to keep the other person talking and to have him better see the significance of his own statements. Find out how mirroring or reflecting works and then re-write this case study to illustrate how the conversation would be likely to progress.

   For example:

   > SCHEFFNER: It's Eva. She's going to leave me. She wants a divorce.
   > KELLOGG: She wants a divorce?
   > SCHEFFNER: Yes, she's upset with me and my work. Claims I'm a maladroit who isn't getting anywhere in life.
   > KELLOGG: Not getting anywhere?

   And so forth. Make your dialogue as realistic as possible.

   Offer presentations in class and discuss the value of this technique in employee counseling.

Selected References

Books
Levinson, H. *Emotional Health: In The World of Work*. New York: Harper & Row, 1964.

[1]Psychiatrist.

Anthologies

Hampton, D. R., Summer, C. E., and Webber, R. A. (Eds.). *Organizational Behavior and the Practice of Management*. Glenview, Illinois: Scott, Foresman and Company, 1968. Berne, E. "Games," p. 380.

Huseman, R., Logue, C., and Freshley, D. *Readings in Interpersonal and Organizational Communication*. Boston, Massachusetts: Holbrook Press, Inc., 1969. Meyer, H., Kay, E., and French, J. "Split Roles in Performance Appraisal," p. 296.

Koontz, H., and O'Donnell, C. *Management: A Book of Readings*. New York: McGraw-Hill, 1971. Huber, G. "Motivation and Competence," p. 435.

Articles

Business Management. (Editors of) "Should Employers Meddle in Family Problems?" April 1964.

Delahanty, D. "Three Aspects of Nonverbal Communication In The Interview," *Personnel Journal*, September 1970, p. 757.

Gould, M. I. "Counseling for Self-Development," *Personnel Journal*, March 1970, p. 226.

Holzman, R. S. "The Price of Advice," *Management Review*, January 1966.

Levinson, H. "What You Can Do When A Problem Is Personal," *Management Review*, April 1967.

Shama, J. M. "Role of the Department Head in a University," *Training and Development Journal*, June 1971, p. 35.

Zima, J. P. "Counseling Concepts For Supervisors," *Personnel Journal*, June 1971, p. 482.

CASE STUDY CROSS REFERENCE

Although located elsewhere in this book, the following problem situations are also valuable in the study of Section 7:

Individual Identity, Values, and Ethics

"*The* point is that I have to decide to stay or leave with the Hanna team. If I stay, I lose the one big chance still open to me. If I leave, I risk a lawsuit, loss of reputation, and certainly some loss of dignity. If it really gets bad, Livingston might drop me, too, and then I can really consider myself blacklisted."

EARL TANNER
It's Not an Ordinary Job Offer

INTRODUCTION

What frustrations exist for man in a complex work environment if he cannot identify with his work or others repeatedly fail to recognize his individuality and separate contributions? How can personal value systems and individual feelings about moral or ethical standards affect the feelings and productivity of others? Who is to judge right from wrong?

Cases in This Section

Some People Just Don't Care Anymore

A discussion group brainstorms the problem of low motivation in a particular job classification. The nature of the problem is elusive although the symptoms are clear ... lack of motivation or lack of identity ... or both?

This Letter Could Get Me Fired

A small group successfully completes a difficult project ... recognition is in order ... but for whom? Singling out one employee frustrates another ... possible group dissension ... a question of values for the supervisor.

Dr. Berkowitz and the Ethics Committee

A research proposal is submitted to a hospital ethics committee for consideration . . . medical knowledge will be advanced but the test population poses questions of ethics and consent.

A Little Moonlight Could Be Too Much

After-hours activities by a company designer creates a dilemma for the president . . . there is no proof of trade secrets leakage . . . but some circumstantial evidence . . . should the employee be confronted? . . . what are the legal aspects?

It's Not an Ordinary Job Offer

When the state-of-the-art in an organization is largely developed by one individual, what are his obligations and loyalties . . . can the man be separated from the knowledge? Group loyalties and fuzzy legal precedence are also involved. What is ethical behavior?

SOME PEOPLE JUST DON'T CARE ANYMORE

Author's note. This case can be studied independently or in conjunction with two cases presented in earlier sections. These related cases are:

- *Now, About the Question of Leadership* (Leadership Section).
- *Let's Take a Vote* (Decision Making Section).

If used independently, participants should at least read the two referenced cases in sequence to provide proper background and perspective.

Setting. The Superintendent's Office of a large modern postal facility. There is a large conference table around which a number of people are seated.

Participants. Eight men and two women — primarily postal supervisors, carrier route examiners, and finance personnel from various city locations. One person is a trainer-consultant. They are officially assembled as a problem solving team.

Cast

Name		Title	Basic Attitude
Wrigley	(M)	Superintendent	Strong opinions
Hernandez	(M)	Route Examiner	Enthusiastic
Evans	(M)	Assistant Superintendent	Positive but cautious
Blackman	(M)	Assistant Superintendent	Reserved but positive
McCleary	(M)	Finance Examiner	Humorous but positive
Lowell	(F)	Customer Service Representative	Concerned
Smith	(M)	Superintendent	Somewhat negative
Cline	(F)	Finance Examiner	Swings with the majority
Fisher	(M)	Route Examiner	Tired and somewhat bored
Saxbe	(M)	P.S.M.I. Trainer[1]	Officially neutral

Two hours have passed since the group first convened (see *Now, About the Question of Leadership*). The group has elected Wrigley as its permanent leader and Blackman has been designated as data recorder. After considerable discussion (see *Let's Take a Vote*), the group has selected a problem area they wish to analyze and improve. They now begin their analysis:

> BLACKMAN: (*Printing on large flip chart*) The Postal Service problem this group has decided to analyze and improve is *MIS-SENT MAIL TO DIRECT FIRM HOLDOUTS*. Okay group, what do you want me to write next?
>
> WRIGLEY: Perhaps we should start brainstorming some possible alternative solutions since we've now stated the problem.
>
> LOWELL: I'm afraid I won't be any help at all on this problem unless it's explained to me in detail. Being a Customer Service Representative, I really have little knowledge of specific operations in the main mail distribution center.
>
> CLINE: I'm in the same position as Mrs. Lowell. I need some clarification too.
>
> HERNANDEZ: Perhaps I can help. First, there is no need to understand the entire incoming or outgoing city mail system in order to have a feeling for the magnitude of the problem. Basically all mail is hand-sorted in most of the steps of its movement from one place to another. Letter clerks essentially sort mail piece-by-piece for

[1]P.S.M.I. — Postal Service Management Institute.

hours on end, placing each letter in its proper bin or slot. The work is fatiguing and endlessly repetitive. If most clerks were not dedicated and well-trained, mail sorting would be chaotic, with mail being constantly routed from one wrong bin to another. As it is, we do have enough mis-sent mail to consider it a problem worthy of improving.

LOWELL: How about the automatic Letter Sorting Machines I've heard so much about?

WRIGLEY: In many sorting operations we have already introduced time saving equipment which also reduces the number of errors. The L.S.M.s[2] do make a significant difference, although there is still the possibility of error. A human being still reads the address and then key punches a code which triggers movement of that particular piece of mail to its proper bin destination to await a secondary sorting. We use the L.S.M.s largely in breaking down incoming mail on the Primary Sort.

McCLEARY: It's like this, Mrs. Lowell. Most mail reaching a major city like Dallas is bagged simply, Dallas. This mail typically is processed through the Letter Sorting Machines in what we call the Primary Sort. After this operation, with some exceptions, the incoming letters have been organized into Sectional Centers or city areas. Another sort is then necessary to further break down the mail to specific postal stations. This is the so called Secondary Sort and the place where much of our problem lies.

EVANS: A mail clerk on Secondary Sort reads addresses of mail which has been sent to his Sectional Center and "sticks" each piece into the proper postal station slot or bin. From this point mail moves to the specific postal station where it will be sorted again for street address and then delivered by carrier.

BLACKMAN: I've drawn a schematic representation of the process on the flip chart which should clarify the steps:
(*See diagram, p. 187*)

CLINE: Thank you Mr. Blackman. Your diagram is appreciated although I believe that Mrs. Lowell and I basically understand the process . . . it's just some specific steps which are confusing.

LOWELL: Yes. But we've mentioned *Firm Holdouts*. I don't know what that means and I see it on Mr. Blackman's diagram.

McCLEARY: It's like this. Assume Big Business X or Large Company Y receives a lot of mail each day. It makes sense to have this mail culled out during the Secondary Sort so that it won't have to be re-sorted at the individual postal station.

[2]Letter Sorting Machine.

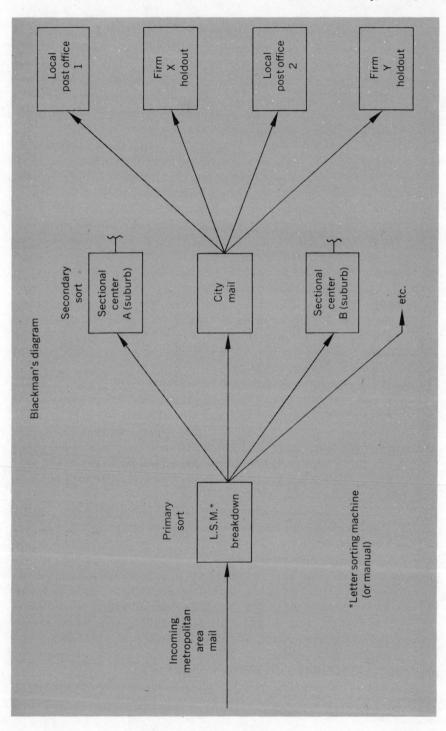

Blackman's diagram

Secondary sort

Primary sort

Incoming metropolitan area mail

L.S.M.* breakdown

Sectional center A (suburb)

City mail

Sectional center B (suburb)

etc.

Local post office 1

Firm X holdout

Local post office 2

Firm Y holdout

*Letter sorting machine (or manual)

LOWELL: I see it now. A Secondary Sort clerk may have several bins *exclusively* for large firms or organizations in addition to the regular postal station bins. If he throws a firm letter into the post office bin in which that firm is located it only has to be sorted out again later at the station.

BLACKMAN: Exactly. The system is logical but it means more work for the mail clerk. Extra bin locations to memorize, you know . . .

WRIGLEY: Right. It takes a great deal of concentration and care to rapidly break down and "stick" the mail. Remember each clerk "sticks" over twenty individual pieces of mail each minute . . . each into one of over 200 bins or cubicles in front of him!

BLACKMAN: You can see that the chance for error is enormous.

EVANS: For one thing, fatigue sets in. We're talking about identification and correct sorting of maybe a thousand pieces of mail per man per work tour (8 hour shift)!

SMITH: The job can be damned boring too. That's more the reason we have errors than the fatigue thing.

FISHER: It's more than that, Smith. Some people just don't give a fig about the quality of their work . . . they just don't care. Some guys will sort mail with no concern for whether it's correct or not.

McCLEARY: Hey! I wondered when Smith and Fisher would turn on. Welcome to the group fellas!

SMITH: Knock it off, McCleary. I'll contribute to the group whenever there's anything interesting being discussed. The problem is how to motivate these guys and gals who throw mail to be accurate as well as fast.

FISHER: It's more than that. How do you motivate a man to *care* about his job? I tell you, this younger generation just doesn't care anymore. Why, when I started with the Post Office Department back in . . .

McCLEARY: (*interrupting*) Are you going to tell us that story again, about how you and Ben Franklin used to throw mail together . . . (*general laughter*)

SAXBE: The group is wandering.

WRIGLEY: We sure are. Let me summarize and maybe then we can proceed. Mail can be mis-sorted accidentally at almost any step in the handling process. Naturally, all rehandling is inefficient and costly . . . and should be minimized. But, with the direct firm holdout bins we have a special problem if mail is mis-sent . . . the customer complains.

SAXBE: I'm afraid I need a bit of clarification here.

WRIGLEY: When mail for specific companies is culled out at the Secondary sort it is not re-checked later. Most of this mail goes directly to the company via the local station. No letter carrier sorting is involved as with the usual house to house deliveries.

SAXBE: I still don't see . . .

WRIGLEY: If clerks at Secondary Sort are careless, Company A gets some Company B mail. Company A reposts the mail for Company B. Company B is upset that their mail is delayed and Company A informs us that they should not have to be in the mail sorting and delivery business.

SAXBE: The problem is crystal clear.

SMITH: I wish the answer was. I don't see that there is any way we can possibly motivate these guys to do their job correctly. It's like Fisher said . . . they just don't care anymore.

FISHER: *You said it,* Mr. Smith.

SAXBE: Is this a problem with all mail clerks, all young mail clerks, some of both, or neither?

(*momentary silence*)

EVANS: Your point is well taken and we should really develop better data on this. Although the younger clerks are more vocal in their complaints about the job, I would venture a guess that we have some problem clerks in all age ranges.

BLACKMAN: I suspect you're right. It is a minority of clerks which give us most of our problems. The majority are quite conscientious about their work.

WRIGLEY: Poor clerks are weeded out eventually. Our problem is to make good clerks out of fair clerks and acceptable clerks out of marginal clerks.

HERNANDEZ: I have an idea. Why don't we poll the group and have each one of us come up with at least one possible alternative to improve accuracy of mail sorting for direct firm holdouts. You know, brainstorm for ideas.

CLINE: That sounds like an excellent idea. Maybe Mr. Blackman can jot them down so we don't lose the thoughts.

WRIGLEY: All right, in order then. What do you propose to improve mail sorting accuracy?

McCLEARY: Bonuses for high accuracy-low error sorting.

EVANS: A unit award for the group that had the best accuracy record over a period of time.

BLACKMAN: A big E for excellence posted in the work area.

LOWELL: Could a clerk put a slip of paper in with each batch of this company mail that said, sorted by Ed Johnson?

SMITH: You can't do that, Mrs. Lowell! The Union would never buy it!

189

HERNANDEZ: Don't be so negative, Smith. Remember, we're brain-storming. Let Mrs. Lowell's idea stand.

WRIGLEY: Okay, let's go on. Mrs. Cline?

CLINE: Oh, I don't know. Could the company mail be spot-checked by a supervisor?

FISHER: Why are we wasting all this time when the answer is obvious! Spike the case![3] It's the only way to ensure accuracy.

SMITH: Too expensive, Fisher. But I see no reason why we can't use random spiking. Those guys should do a better job if they never know when someone will be checking up on them.

HERNANDEZ: How about altering the coffee break structure. I think some of those people get pretty tired near the end of their shift and errors usually increase when people are tired.

WRIGLEY: We might suggest that companies use distinctive colored envelopes for their regular return mail such as invoices and bills.

BLACKMAN: (*still writing down suggestions from group*) Not bad . . . not bad at all! Any more wild ideas?

(*momentary silence*)

EVANS: As I look at our suggestions, they seem to boil down into these basic groupings:

1. Individual recognition with money rewards.
2. Group recognition with money or symbols.
3. Improved checking by supervision.
4. Altering work patterns.

(*general agreement from group*)

LOWELL: Do we really feel that more supervision or closer super-vision will work? Isn't that sort of a negative approach to management?

SMITH: Not with these people it isn't. They're just after that ol' paycheck every two weeks. They couldn't care less about their work.

FISHER: (*distressed*) We keep going around and around. Smith has the answer. Let's devise an improved checking and inspection system and quit wasting so much time.

HERNANDEZ: I don't think that's the answer at all. Some of us have worked out on the floor sorting mail. It's tiring work. You really have to concentrate. You want to do a good job but there are millions of letters to sort . . .

WRIGLEY: And it never ends. When you sort a million letters, there are a million more to sort!

[3]*Spike the case:* a 100 percent accuracy verification of any given batch of sorted mail by another person, usually a supervisor.

HERNANDEZ: Man, out there on the floor it's easy for a guy to finally say, "Why should I care? No one cares about me. I'm just another body sorting through a never-ending stack of mail."

LOWELL: You see the problem then as the mail clerk having little or no personal identity with his work?

HERNANDEZ: That's right, Mrs. Lowell. Take my sister, for instance. She works on an assembly line at the toy factory. When she's out shopping she can point to a toy or a doll and say, "I put the shoes on." She can see her work in the final product.

LOWELL: And you can't do that with mail sorting?

HERNANDEZ: That's it.

EVANS: It's not all that bleak. Chances are better than ever now for clerks to obtain better Postal Service assignments.

BLACKMAN: Our problem is with the man *while* he is a clerk. How do we improve his motivation? Will it go up if he has greater production job identity?

McCLEARY: Almost anything would help.

HERNANDEZ: AMEN!

SAXBE: The group is beginning to focus on job or product identity as one factor in a person's interest in his work. Perhaps it is the answer here . . . perhaps not . . . but we should try to be more specific.

WRIGLEY: Okay, what specific things could be done to increase product or job identity among mail clerks? Mrs. Lowell had an idea before. She said that each clerk could possibly put a name slip into each batch of mail, particularly when the next stop for the mail was directly to the customer as in the case with our direct firm holdout mail.

McCLEARY: I think that's a good idea. Only a fool would put his name slip in a batch of bad mail. (*pause*) I can see it now . . . a bright red packing slip which says, "This mixed up mail was processed by P. Fisher."
(*general laughter*)

FISHER: Not funny, McCleary. It's the end of my duty tour and I'm tired. I don't need you picking on me.

WRIGLEY: Let's stay on the right track here . . .

CLINE: I think Mrs. Lowell has a good idea. I think something could be done along the lines of improving personal identity.

EVANS: It's done in private industry and I can only assume it works.

BLACKMAN: Let's not get hung up on just one approach to this identity problem. Surely there are others . . .

SMITH: I tell you you're fighting windmills. Identity isn't the problem. Those mail handlers don't know the meaning of the word! I say pay them good wages, set standards, check their work, and get rid of those who can't cut the mustard!

FISHER: I'm with you, Smitty.

LOWELL: Has anyone bothered to ask a mail clerk recently?

(*momentary silence*)

WRIGLEY: I suggest we take a short break. Perhaps after that we can sharpen our attack on the problem. What do you think, Mr. Saxbe?

SAXBE: I think that your problem is one of great significance not only to the Postal Service, but to many industrial, business and governmental jobs. I'd like to see this group do something positive to improve the situation. However, as a group, you're beginning to have process problems again. Let's talk about it after break.

Discussion Questions

1. As one management approach to the problem of repetitive work, Smith commented, "I say pay them good wages, set standards, check their work, and get rid of those who can't cut the mustard." Discuss the ramifications of this philosophy.
2. Mrs. Lowell felt that motivation would be improved if the clerks could identify better with their work. Is this the answer? Discuss.
3. A personalized packing slip was suggested to go with each batch of firm holdout mail. What other specific approaches could be used to improve job identification in this situation?
4. What other techniques or methods might be used to improve accuracy in mail sorting which the discussion group only briefly mentioned or forgot entirely?
5. Is this problem typical of other businesses or industries as well? Discuss.

Special Project

Find out how local businesses cope with problems in repetitive operations and lack of product or job identification. Select several target industries, companies, or businesses in your local area which, you feel, share the problem discussed in this case. Some *possibilities* are:

1. Typing pool in an insurance company.
2. Automobile assembly.
3. Draftsmen in a large department.
4. Electronic assembly.

Contact the Personnel Manager of the company by letter, telling him of your interest, and request a meeting at his facility for a small group (4 maximum) from your class. He may be able to provide many answers or help you to interview a person more familiar with the problem.

Have several such teams check other organizations and have all present oral reports in two or three weeks.

Of Special Interest to Business and Industrial Groups

What, if anything, is your organization doing about the problem of personal identification with product or job? Or, is it necessary? Discuss.

Selected References

Books

Foulkes, F. K. *Creating More Meaningful Work*. New York: American Management Association, 1969, Chapter 4.

Friedmann, G. *The Anatomy of Work*. New York: Free Press of Glencoe, 1961, Chapters 3, 4.

Gellerman, S. W. *Management by Motivation*. New York: American Management Association, 1968, Chapters 6, 8.

Likert, R. *New Patterns of Management*. New York: McGraw-Hill, 1961.

Maier, N. R. F. *Problem Solving Discussions and Conferences*: *Leadership Methods and Skills*. New York: McGraw-Hill, 1963.

Schein, E. H. *Process Consultation: Its Role In Organization Development*. Reading, Massachusetts: Addison-Wesley, 1969.

Tiffin, J., and McCormick, E. J. *Industrial Psychology*. Englewood Cliffs, New Jersey. Prentice-Hall, 1965, pp. 467–468.

Anthologies

Fleishman, E. A. *Studies in Personnel and Industrial Psychology*. Homewood, Illinois: The Dorsey Press 1967.
 Smith, P. C. "The Prediction of Individual Differences in Susceptibility to Industrial Monotony," p. 546.
 Smith, P. C. "The Curve of Output as a Criterion of Boredom," p. 556.

Hampton, D. R., Summer, C. E., and Webber, R. A. (Eds.). *Organizational Behavior and the Practice of Management*. Glenview, Illinois: Scott, Foresman and Company, 1968. Kolb, H. D. "The Headquarters Staff Man in the Role of a Consultant," p. 518.

Leavitt, H. J., and Pondy, L. R. (Eds.). *Readings in Managerial Psychology*. Chicago, Illinois: University of Chicago Press, 1964.
 Crutchfield, R. S. "Conformity and Character," p. 315.
 Maslow, A. H. "A Theory of Human Motivation," p. 6.
 Thompson, J. D., and Tuden, A. "Strategies Structures and Processes of Organizational Decision," p. 496.

Articles

Argyris, C. "Resistance To Rational Management Systems," *Innovation*, Number Ten, 1970, p. 28.

Davis, S. "Building More-Effective Teams," *Innovation*, Number Fifteen, 1970, p. 32.

Schwartz, S. J. "A Cure for the 'I Don't Care' Syndrome," *Personnel Journal*, July 1971, p. 528.

Slocum, J. W. Jr., Miller, J. D., and Misshauk, M. J. "Needs, Environmental Work Satisfaction and Job Performance," *Training and Development Journal*, February 1970, p. 12.

Wohlking, W. "Structured and Spontaneous Role Playing: Contrast and Comparison," *Training and Development Journal*, January 1971, p. 8.

Booklets

What's Wrong With Work? Organization Development Program Group, Industrial Relations Committee, National Association of Manufacturers, 277 Park Avenue, New York, NY 10017 ($2.50 per copy).

THIS LETTER COULD GET ME FIRED

There are a number of problem situations which are guaranteed to give most managers sweaty palms or an ache in the gut, problems which they wish would go away, but won't . . . problems which never seem to get any easier regardless of how many times the role has been played before.

Victor Lord would admit to this. Seasoned by years of production management experience, Lord still finds certain management decisions to be emotionally difficult. He still finds it difficult to terminate an employee particularly when the choice must be made between two good people. Another difficult task for Lord is to have to discipline an employee who feels his work is satisfactory. Still another is having to choose one good man for promotion over another. "What do you say to him," asks Lord, "when the unsuccessful candidate still feels he is the better choice?"

Lord once said to an associate, "The worst part about management is having to make those decisions which help one person or group and hurt another in the process. It's not only difficult at the time but difficult afterward as you review your decision in retrospect. You keep asking yourself, did I make the proper choice? Did I really? Management is a lousy business whenever anyone gets hurt."

It is now 2:55 p.m. In exactly five minutes, Victor Lord, Production Manager, will meet with one of the five supervisors who report to him. The man is Kyle Branch, the capable and aggressive supervisor of Production Scheduling. The subject of the meeting (requested by Branch) is to discuss Lord's feelings about a Special Recognition Award for a young man in Branch's section.

This will not be an easy meeting, thought Lord. Unless it is handled well, some one will get hurt . . . perhaps the wrong person.

The issue is individual recognition, and on the surface it would appear to be no problem. Branch had summed up the situation in his interoffice memorandum submitted to Lord several days before:

> *To:*   Victor Lord
>   Production Manager
> *From:* Kyle Branch
> *Subject:* Special Recognition Award
>
> As you are already aware, several persons in our Production Scheduling Section have been working with company computer specialists on a new computerized Production Scheduling System. This effort has been far more difficult than we originally anticipated but, in recent weeks, we have made major breakthroughs and the system should be operable by the end of the year.
>
> Not only should the new system save thousands of dollars in direct costs each

year, but it is expected to substantially improve production line balancing and reduce current product scheduling problems.

While several of my people have been involved in this work I feel that Henry Jackson should be considered for the *Special Recognition Award* for his outstanding analytical contributions. Henry is a highly motivated young man who, in time, could be this company's first Negro executive.

I realize that the award can only be made by the President but a recommendation from you would significantly improve Jackson's chances.

Could we get together next week to discuss this in greater detail?

Lord had heard of Henry Jackson before. The man was generally known to be both talented and anxious to assume greater responsibility. Under other circumstances Lord would have been more than pleased to favorably act upon the recommendation of his supervisor.

But, yesterday Lord received another note, handwritten, and sent through the company mails in a confidential envelope. It was from Eileen Rogers, one of Kyle Branch's people, and the content made it evident that this case of special recognition would require a long hard look before a decision was made.

Eileen Rogers' note read:

DEAR MR. LORD:

Although I hardly know you, I feel that you are the only person to whom I could turn about a problem which exists in Production Scheduling.

The problem is this. I have been working with Henry Jackson and Bert Finney on the new computerized Production Scheduling System. I can't speak for Mr. Finney but I personally feel that because my supervisor, Mr. Branch, and Henry Jackson are good friends, I have not received near the credit I deserve for my efforts.

I don't see why one person should be constantly singled out in a team effort and be given credit for the work of others.

I realize that this letter could get me fired, but I felt it had to be written for the record.

EILEEN ROGERS

It was now 3:00 p.m. Kyle Branch would be in Lord's office in a few moments. Lord ponders his alternatives:

1. Show the note to Branch and ask for an explanation.
2. Let Branch develop his argument for giving the award to Jackson. Without telling Branch about Eileen Rogers' note, ask penetrating questions about others on the team and their respective contributions.
3. Ask Branch about his friendship with Jackson and try to determine if this has biased his recommendation. Don't mention the note from Eileen Rogers.
4. Defer a decision about the award after hearing Branch's arguments.

Then call in Eileen Rogers for a private discussion to further probe her version of the situation.

5. Call in the whole team and discuss the situation.

This meeting with Branch would have to be handled very carefully, Lord thought, and even then, someone was likely to get hurt.

Discussion Questions

1. What potential problems exist if Lord shows Eileen Rogers' note to Kyle Branch?
2. What potential problems exist if Lord sees Eileen Rogers without informing her supervisor (Branch) of the note?
3. Henry Jackson is black. Does this affect the problem situation?
4. What would you do if you were Victor Lord? Explain.
5. In some organizations there is an unwritten but generally followed rule which says: The manager should never bypass a subordinate supervisor and discuss a problem directly with an employee. This cuts the supervisor out of the communications loop and makes him look like a "flunky." Discuss this philosophy.
6. In a few organizations there is a rule (usually stated as policy) that any employee who feels his supervisor has not reasonably handled a situation may directly take the problem to a higher level of management for reevaluation. Discuss this philosophy.
7. Discuss this case relative to the concepts of open or authentic communication.

Special Project

The so-called open door policy often stated by executives and managers is difficult to achieve in most organizations. Research and prepare a written report which outlines some of the practical barriers or obstacles to a true open door policy. Some obstacles are:

1. Internal political problems.
2. Status differences.
3. Secrecy.
4. Intensive competition.
5. etc.

Selected References

Books

Argyris, C. *Integrating The Individual and The Organization*. New York: Wiley, 1964.

Kellogg, M. S. *What To Do About Performance Appraisals*. New York: American Management Association, 1966.

Ready, R. K. *The Administrator's Job: Issues and Dilemmas*. New York: McGraw-Hill, 1967.

Anthologies

Hampton, D. R., Summer, C. E., and Webber, R. A. (Eds.). *Organizational Behavior and the Practice of Management*. Glenview, Illinois: Scott, Foresman and Company, 1968.

Dearborn, D., and Simon, H. "Selective Perception," p. 162.

Leavitt, H. "Frustration: The Roadblock," p. 374.

Leavitt, H. "Perception: From The Inside Looking Out," p. 155.

Huseman, R., Logue, C., and Freshley, D. *Readings in Interpersonal and Organizational Communication.* Boston, Massachusetts: Holbrook Press, Inc., 1969.

Boynton, R. P., and Wright, D. S. "Communication Gap: Is Anybody Up There Listening?" p. 448.

Meyer, H., Kay, E., and French, J. "Split Roles in Performance Appraisal," p. 296.

Schultz, R. S. "How to Handle Grievances," p. 310.

Timbers, E. "Strengthening Motivation Through Communication," p. 203.

Wiksell, M. J. "Talking It Over *Is* Important," p. 236.

Leadership on the Job. New York: American Management Association, 1966. Sayles, L. "On-The-Job Communication: Why Isn't It Easier?" p. 37.

Articles

Burke, R., Faber, F., and Bresver, B. "Managing Interpersonal Differences," *Personnel Journal,* May 1970, p. 408.

Fielder, F. E. "Style or Circumstance: The Leadership Enigma," *Psychology Today,* March 1969, p. 38.

Kuhn, D. G., Slocum, J. W. Jr., and Chase, R. B. "Does Job Performance Affect Employee Satisfaction?" *Personnel Journal,* June 1971, p. 455.

Sikula, A. F. "Value and Value Systems: Relationship to Personal Goals," *Personnel Journal,* April 1971, p. 310.

Zaleznik, A. "Management of Disappointment," *Harvard Business Review,* November–December 1967, p. 59.

DR. BERKOWITZ AND THE ETHICS COMMITTEE[1]

"Somehow the drug acted to destroy all organisms built on a unicellular structure or less. It had no effect on organ systems — groups of cells organized into larger units. The drug was perfectly selective in that respect.

In fact, Kalocin was the universal antibiotic. It killed everything, even the minor germs which caused the common cold. Naturally, there were side effects — the normal bacteria in the intestines were destroyed, so that all users of the drug experienced massive diarrhea — but that seemed a small price to pay for a cancer cure."

MICHAEL CHRICHTON
The Andromeda Strain
p. 265

Many hospitals have long had ethics committees, composed of doctors not directly involved with patient care, to rule on unusual techniques for treatment or on the use of controversial drugs. Their number has increased sharply in recent years, due largely to a decision in 1966 by the National Institute of Health not to award research grants to hospitals or other

[1]This case was suggested by an article probing the dilemmas of medical research which appeared in the *Wall Street Journal* on April 14, 1971.

197

institutions which did not have one. At the time there were 371 committees and their number has rapidly increased to nearly two thousand.

Hospital ethics committees, composed of from three to fifteen doctors, meet regularly to rule on proposals by researchers and physicians. In many cases a project wins approval without encountering any difficulty with the committee.

In cases where a particular project is questioned, ethics committees and researchers often work out compromises. Compromises typically take the form of altering specific study parameters, modifying one or more aspects of treatment, or by varying drug dosage.

The work of an ethics committee is extremely sensitive. On one hand, the committee must be certain the patient's rights are being protected, that he indeed is receiving the best possible medical treatment. On the other hand, the advancement of medicine must always be considered. Often the task is exceedingly complex and the committee members must act on insufficient knowledge of the risks and benefits involved.

In some cases serious conflicts can arise between medical specialists and the ethics committees, particularly when a specific procedure has never been used before or where a controversial drug is suggested. The recent dispute between Dr. Irene Berkowitz and the ethics committee of the Lincoln (Nebraska) Cancer Center illustrates one view of the nature of these conflicts.

"We are all aware, doctors," began Dr. Berkowitz, "that certain types of cancer trigger a high level of calcium in the blood which can kill a patient far faster than the cancer itself. Prevention of this calcium buildup in certain patients has been advocated for several years as one weapon to prolong life."

Dr. Berkowitz continued her presentation to the ethics committee. "I have been particularly impressed with calcitonin,[2] the recently discovered hormone produced by the thyroid gland. Studies to date indicate the amount of calcium in a person's blood may be at least partly regulated by calcitonin. Lippmann and Schrock offered a recent paper on the possibility of using injections of calcitonin to control calcium levels and prolong life. Lippmann also suggests that calcitonin may have other therapeutic value relative to the cancer itself but his studies are inconclusive."

Dr. Berkowitz passed out copies of her calcitonin research proposal to the nine member board of ethics.

---

[2]Calcitonin is an actual experimental drug. Dr. Berkowitz, the Lincoln Cancer Center, other persons, and institutions mentioned in this case are all fictional.

"Before we can intelligently consider calcitonin in the war against cancer, we must determine whether or not the hormone does indeed control calcium and how it does so. To prove this we need a group of normal children whose thyroids produce calcitonin and a group of children without thyroids producing this hormone so that the two groups can be compared.

"I would prefer it to be otherwise but the study will require the use of children rather than adults. Normal calcium deposits increase with age and, at this stage, I feel research results with adults would yield inconclusive results."

"Dr. Berkowitz, exactly what will the test or tests require of the children?" The question was from Dr. Carl Aymond, chairman of the ethics committee.

"Thank you, Dr. Aymond. I should have discussed that earlier." Berkowitz thumbed through a copy of the proposal she had just distributed. "You'll find the complete test outline on page six," said Berkowitz. "While tedious, the test itself poses little risk to the children. The test requires three hour calcium injections into the bloodstream and blood samples taken every half hour to determine calcitonin levels from which we can assess the relationships between the two chemicals."

"I for one don't like it," said Dr. Anton Melke. "Is there no alternative?"

"I'm afraid not," replied Berkowitz. "Several other techniques have been suggested, but there appears to be no other way to determine the calcium and calcitonin relationship except by their direct interaction in two distinct control groups."

"It bothers me as well," added Dr. Ruth Cregar. "For how long a period will the children be involved?"

"A total of four days of injections and blood sampling. Some in the group will be tested once each week for four weeks. Others will be on a one day per month cycle for four months. The calcium deposition will be nominal and the risks quite small . . ."

"Nevertheless," interrupted Melke, "there is a risk involved for the children."

"Yes," replied Berkowitz, "a small risk."

A momentary lull followed as several members of the ethics committee reviewed sections of the proposal and exchanged comments among themselves. Finally, Dr. Eugene Livermore spoke.

"Dr. Berkowitz," said Livermore, "I am most upset about your proposed use of mentally retarded children in the project. Your proposal calls for most of the children in the group whose bodies produce no calcitonin to be drawn from the Nebraska Exceptional Children Centers at Lincoln and Omaha.''

"That is correct, Dr. Livermore," replied Dr. Berkowitz.

"Why use mentally retarded children?" asked Dr. Cregar.

"Why use institutionalized children?" asked another panel member.

"Yes," added Dr. Aymond. "This is a most serious situation. On all new medical techniques and drugs it is imperative that the consent of the participant be obtained directly if he is a responsible adult and the consent of a parent or guardian be obtained if the participant is a minor. The question of what constitutes consent from institutionalized children is a very difficult one."

"Can't other subjects be found who are intelligent enough to give consent to the study?" asked Melke.

"I, too, have been concerned about the medical and legal implications of using institutionalized children," replied Dr. Berkowitz. "But again, there appears to be no alternative. Only one in every 30,000 babies is born without a thyroid gland and more than half of these have an I.Q. far less than 90. The result is that many members of this very tiny group are in institutions for the mentally retarded. There is virtually no place else to find them."

Discussion Questions

1. Should the ethics committee agree to or deny this project? Discuss the implications of their decision.
2. How can the rights of the children be represented?
3. What parallels can be drawn to this situation outside the field of medicine? What is the process or procedure by which these are resolved?
4. Relate the case to *The Programmed Decision* presented earlier in this book. In what ways are they similar?

Special Projects

1. Do the larger hospitals in your area have ethics committees? Select a class research group to contact a hospital regarding the operation of the committee. Remember, allow ample time for formal inquiry and clearly state your proposed line of questioning.
2. Someone always stands at the fringe of man's knowledge, be it medicine, art, or space technology. Read the fictionalized account of medicine and surgery during the period of the Spanish inquisition as told in *Divine Mistress*, by Frank G. Slaughter. Compare and contrast the events in that book with the situation described in this case.

Selected References

Books
Crichton, M. *The Andromeda Strain*. New York: Dell Publishing Company, 1970.
Slaughter, F. G. *Divine Mistress*. New York: Pocket Books, A Division of Simon and Schuster, 1969.

Anthologies
Huseman, R., Logue, C., and Freshley, D. *Readings in Interpersonal and Organizational Communication*. Boston, Massachusetts: Holbrook Press, Inc., 1969.
    Nirenberg, J. S. "Communicating for Greater Insight and Persuasiveness," p. 239.
    Potter, C. J. "Persuasiveness—Powerful Tool," p. 252.
Koontz, H., and O'Donnell, C. *Management: A Book of Readings*. New York: McGraw-Hill, 1968.
    Barnard, C. I. "The Environment of a Decision," p. 92.
    Clark, J. W. "A Tentative Statement of Ethical Guides," p. 639.
Leadership on the Job. New York: American Management Association, 1966. Marquis, V. "It's A Question of Ethics."
Leavitt, H. J., and Pondy, L. R. (Eds.). *Readings in Managerial Psychology*. Chicago, Illinois: University of Chicago Press, 1964.
    Asch, S. E. "Opinions and Social Pressure," p. 304.
    Hovland, C. I. "Studies in Persuasion," p. 179.

Articles
Fitzpatrick, G. D. "Good Business and Business Ethics," *Advanced Management Journal*, October 1965.
Hagen, W. W. "Ethics in Business," *Advanced Management Journal*, April 1965.

A LITTLE MOONLIGHT MAY BE TOO MUCH

Carl Welch and Bob Mitchell were already seated and about to order lunch when Howard Robinson arrived at the restaurant. Welch rose and motioned to Robinson who was looking for their table.

"Over here, counselor," called Welch.

"Sorry I'm late," Robinson said as the two men shook hands, "but I was delayed in court this morning and then traffic was unusually heavy in the downtown area."

"No problem, Howard. We've been here only a few minutes ourselves ... Howard, I'd like you to meet Bob Mitchell, my Director of New Product Design."

Mitchell and Robinson exchanged greetings and all three ordered lunch. After the waiter left, Carl Welch got directly to the purpose of the meeting.

"Howard, a situation has developed within my company which is of great concern to Bob and myself. We talked about it at length the other day and decided we really needed the expertise of an attorney."

"Be happy to help if I can," replied Robinson. "What seems to be the problem?"

"It concerns one of the designers on Bob's staff so I'd like him to tell you the details," said Welch.

"It started out innocently enough," Mitchell began. "A few weeks ago I was having a casual conversation with Frank Ennis about how we spend our free evenings and weekends. Ennis told me he had recently become involved most evenings with a neighbor of his on a project of mutual interest. Ennis is one of our better electronics designers and we have a good working relationship so I pursued the subject a little more."

Mitchell continued.

"I inquired as to the nature of the project and Ennis said it was an electro-mechanical device which could switch incoming phone calls to another phone number if the person being called was away."

Robinson interrupted. "You mean Ennis was designing and building this switching device with his neighbor?"

"Apparently so," replied Mitchell. "Ennis told me his neighbor was a reasonably successful inventor who had several major patents to his credit. Now elderly, the inventor neighbor spent most of his time in his garage workshop and had been working for some time on the device. Ennis was assisting him evenings and weekends in the development and prototype[1] work.

"I thought very little of it at the time," said Mitchell. "In fact I almost envied Frank in the sense that it sounded like something I might enjoy tinkering with myself . . . if I had an inventor for a neighbor.

"Two weeks later I asked Frank how his project was coming along and he said the work had progressed to the point where he and his inventor friend had formed a company to market the product . . ."

Carl Welch interrupted. "This was supposedly a company in name only since the product had yet to be perfected let alone ready for manufacturing and marketing."

"That's right," said Mitchell. "My first concern was that one of my best designers was going to leave and form his own company. More power to him, of course, but I hated to lose the man."

Howard Robinson broke into the conversation for points of information.

"Are you concerned about an employee conflict of interest in terms of

[1] First working model.

him moonlighting or has he been using company time to work on his outside project."

"I must emphasize," added Mitchell, "that I saw no evidence so far which suggests Ennis is using company time for a personal effort but . . ."

"Then, you'll have to assume he isn't," Robinson replied. "I'm afraid I don't quite see the issue as yet . . ."

"We think the issue is privileged company data," said Welch, "but we can't prove it yet and we're unsure of our legal position . . ."

"Please explain," said Robinson.

"In long discussions with Ennis about the proposed device," said Mitchell, "he told me more than I feel he originally intended. While Ennis never said so, I believe part of the electronics package which he is designing into his device is a nearly perfect copy of a proprietary design of ours. In a sense I believe he's stealing company secrets for his own personal use."

"I see," said Robinson. "Have you confronted Ennis with this?"

"We thought that would be unwise without talking to you first, Howard," said Welch. "We certainly wouldn't want to unjustly accuse a man of stealing company secrets if he isn't. At the same time each day we wait to find proof we may be injuring ourselves as an organization. That's why we came to you, Howard. What should we do at this point?"

Discussion Questions

1. What action should be taken with Frank Ennis and his moonlighting project?
2. Can this situation be resolved without legal action? How?
3. Unless the material is copyrighted or patented, can the company prohibit Ennis from using it? Explain.
4. Suppose the material is only company confidential (not patented or copyrighted) and Ennis is familiar with it (as he obviously is): Can a distinction be drawn between using this material in a new personal business venture and seeking employment with a competitor and then disclosing the information? Explain.

Special Projects

1. Two issues are involved here:

   (a) Moonlighting (usually a job with another organization).
   (b) Company confidential data (maintaining confidentiality).

   How do business firms in your area resolve these difficult problems? Conduct a sample survey of representative organizations and report in class.
2. Prepare a well-documented research paper on, *The Nature and Extent of Industrial Espionage and Loss of Trade Secrets.* Include data on what is being done to prevent

such losses. Stress the human behavioral aspects of the problem from both the organization and employee point of view.

Selected References

Books

Evans, C. G. *Supervising R & D Personnel.* New York: American Management Association, 1969.

Greene, R. M. *Business Intelligence and Espionage.* Homewood, Illinois: Richard D. Irwin, Inc., 1969.

Stessin, L. *Employee Discipline.* Washington, D.C.: BNA Incorporated, 1960, Chapter 8.

Articles

Abel, W. "The Company and The Inventor," *Innovation,* Number Four, 1969, p. 28.

Allen, T. "Who Guards The Gate?" *Innovation,* Number Eight, 1969, p. 33.

Badawy, M. K. "Understanding The Role Orientations of Scientists and Engineers," *Personnel Journal,* June 1971, p. 449.

Freed, R. N. "Protecting Valuable Information," *Innovation,* Number Eleven, 1970, p. 59.

Lawler, E. E. "The Paycheck as an (Expensive) Communication Device," *Innovation,* Number Three, 1969, p. 48.

Lewis, J. "Protecting A New Technology Takes More Than Patents," *Innovation,* Number Fifteen, 1970, p. 24.

Meyer, H. "Is Your Pay Plan Full of Cobwebs?" *Innovation,* Number Fourteen, 1970, p. 56.

Walton, R. "The Inventor and The Company," *Innovation,* Number Four, 1969, p. 36.

Young, R. "No Room for the Searcher," *Innovation,* Number Eleven, 1970, p. 51.

IT'S NOT AN ORDINARY JOB OFFER

After the usual Friday evening hello kiss in the doorway of his home, Earl Tanner took his wife's hand and they walked into the living room. By the time they reached the plush gold sofa, Mildred was well into the problem she had earlier in the day with the television repair service.

"Millie," Tanner interrupted, "can we please skip the TV repair details?"

Mildred Tanner normally expected her husband to be exhausted from work by Friday evening, but tonight she sensed something different about this mood. Earl was unusually preoccupied about something.

"Well . . . sure, Earl. I just thought you were interested since it was you who suggested calling the repair service."

"Sorry, Millie," for a moment his expression softened to a slight smile and he affectionately reached out and clasped both hands against his wife's small shoulders. "I didn't mean to cut you off that way but we have to talk. I mean I have something so fantastic to tell you that . . ." His voice swelled with excitement.

"Tell me! Tell me!" teased Mildred now beginning to assume Earl's solemn entrance was put on.

"I'm not joking, Millie." The smile disappeared.

"All right, Earl. Sit down and I'll mix us a drink while you're talking."

"In a minute," he countered and gently pulled his wife down beside him on the sofa. "It's about a job offer I got today."

"Is that all, Earl Tanner?" Mildred pulled away and started to rise. "You had me half scared to death for a moment. I thought maybe you saw Dr. Lewis today and he . . ." Mildred paused, then continued. "What's wrong, Earl? You've had several offers over the past four years."

"It's not an ordinary job offer."

"What's not ordinary?"

"One-hundred-thousand-dollars." Earl said each word slowly and deliberately as if he were counting them.

"One-hundred-thousand-dollars?" Mildred slumped back to the sofa. "I don't believe it! Who? Where?"

"Livingston Industries here in Los Angeles." Earl's tone and appearance were almost matter-of-fact, but he could sense the shock of sheer joy building within his wife. He grinned as she groped for words.

"But, Earl, even at an organization as large as Livingston Industries wouldn't you practically have to be the president to make a hundred thousand dollars a year?"

"I would be the president . . . at least president of the Military Electronics Division . . . reporting directly to Marshall Livingston himself."

"Oh, darling. I'm so happy for you I could . . ." Mildred threw herself against her husband and gave him a long, rewarding kiss.

"Enough! Enough!" Earl pleaded, pulling himself away at last. He rose, removed his suitcoat and threw it across a chair. "I didn't say I was taking the job. I said it was offered for my consideration."

"But how can you possibly turn down a hundred thousand dollars?"

"I might."

"Earl, if you're letting loyalty to Quintronics get in the way of an opportunity like this . . ." She hesitated. "Why you made Quintronics what it is today and they still treat you like a college physics professor!"

"Thirty-five thousand dollars and director of a two-hundred man engineering team is hardly poor treatment for . . . a former college physics professor," replied Tanner crisply.

"Why defend the company now! Any other Friday evening you'd be drowning your frustrations with Quintronics in a double Manhattan." Typical of her annoyance, Mildred fussed with the hem of her dress, avoiding her husband's eyes.

As if on cue, Earl walked to the bar and started to mix the drinks.

Still looking away, Mildred continued. "How many times have Bert and Cash Quinlan made it plain to you, to Bob Emerson, and to the other professionals that *they own the company* and intend to keep it that way? Why, at the last Christmas party, Cash's stupid wife gloated about his ability to buy any talent he needed. Earl, as long as you stay there you're just a brain for hire . . . to be picked at their prices!"

Tanner walked back to the sofa, a Manhattan in each hand, and placed them on the coffee table. Then he sat down and looked directly at his wife. "Today Marshall Livingston offered me a hundred thousand dollars to leave Quintronics and take over his Military Electronics Division. Isn't that brain picking at a higher price?"

"I hardly see the comparison," replied Mildred. "First, the money is almost triple what you earn plus a presidency. I'll bet there's more you haven't told me, too."

Earl sipped before answering. "Yes, a sizable package of stock options, auto and personal expense accounts, and a promise of hands-off as long as I keep the Division profitable and growing."

"Well, then, when do you start?"

"It's not that simple, Millie."

"Why not? Isn't it a firm offer?"

"Oh it's firm all right! Marshall Livingston personally made the offer at lunch today. That headhunter[1] Jerry Gollob set up the meeting very discreetly. Until the moment I met Livingston I thought Gollob was just handing me a line about the opportunity of a lifetime. No Millie, it's quite firm. Livingston laid it out very clearly."

"Earl, after eight years with Quintronics you need a change. And this is more than a change. It's a wonderful opportunity for you to work for someone who appreciates your creative mind. What can you possibly lose? Financially we could gain so much too."

"Millie, I've spent all afternoon weighing gains against losses until I can hardly think straight . . ."

"I certainly can't see any problem," replied Mildred.

"Don't be so damned naive! At one hundred thousand dollars Livingston could have his pick of a thousand top level executives. Of these, a computer could sort out a dozen or more with Ph.D.s. And, most of these would have more executive experience than I have. Logically, I'm a second-rate contender for the job!"

[1]Professional job placement counselor.

"Earl Tanner, you've earned that job and I'm sure you're the best man Marshall Livingston could possibly . . ."

"Stop it, Millie!" Earl began to pace back and forth between a chair and the sofa. "Livingston isn't buying my brain for tomorrow's ideas alone. That wouldn't bother me so much. He has more practical things in mind. The hundred thousand is to buy both me and my cooperation to bring Bob Emerson, Larry Gordon, Hammel, Templeton, and five or six more key engineers from Project Hanna. In a week Livingston could have Project Hanna after Quintronics spent five years and eight million dollars in development!"

Tanner walked to the bar for a refill. Obviously stunned, Mildred followed her husband to the bar and sat on a stool as he mixed a second round.

"How does Livingston figure he'll get the entire team?"

"Simple. He said that reliable sources inside Quintronics indicate that most of the men would leave if I asked them."

"Is it true?"

"I think so—and Livingston seemed positive. One of my engineers may already be on his payroll."

"And if they don't join you?"

"I produce one Project Hanna team or *no* presidency and *no* one hundred thousand dollars!"

They were both silent for a moment. Earl stepped out from behind the bar and sat on the stool next to his wife.

Mildred considered the implications of Earl's statements.

"There's no law that binds a man to his job. What he knows is his wherever he goes. Project Hanna belongs to you as much as it does to Quintronics."

"Millie, if the key men on Project Hanna quit for Livingston, Bert and Cash Quinlan will slap a multi-million dollar trade secrets lawsuit against Livingston Industries, against me, and against every John Doe who leaves. They'll use the old story—*unfaithful employees steal secret formula from unsuspecting and faultless employer*. It will be front-page news in the *Journal* as well as all the local papers."

"Could they win?"

"I don't know. Trade secrets suits have never followed a predictable pattern as far as I know. I asked Livingston and he felt it would never get to court, assuming they even attempted to sue. Fear of reprisal statements about gross mismanagement might deter them."

207

"That's a good point," Mildred said.

"But it's not *the* point," replied her husband. "*The* point is that I have to decide to stay or leave with the Hanna team. If I stay, I lose the one big chance still open to me. If I leave, I risk a lawsuit, loss of reputation, and certainly some loss of dignity. If it really gets bad, Livingston might drop me, too, and then I can really consider myself blacklisted."

"Then it would be back to the university?"

"Most likely."

"How much time do you have?"

"Livingston wants to know by 5 p.m. next Monday after I talk to the key engineers."

"You mean *if* you talk to them."

"Millie, I'm so confused. I don't even know whether I have the right to make the decision alone. It's their futures too."

Mildred put her arm behind her husband and began to rub the back of his neck.

"This is going to be one hell of a long weekend," said Tanner.

Mildred nodded.

Discussion Questions

1. What should Earl Tanner do?
2. Should Tanner involve the other members of the Project Hanna team?
3. All professionals at Quintronics sign a patent agreement as a condition of employment. Does this procedure protect Quintronics in the situation as described?
4. What conditions should be created within a company to prevent the occurrence of this type of situation?

Special Project

Assume you are General Manager of a high-technology organization such as Quintronics. Working for you in the research and engineering departments are some of the most capable and respected people in your industry. Your company is less than a year old and, to date, has developed few formal personnel policies.

Develop:

1. An overall philosophy (credo) regarding employees.
2. A set of working rules or personnel relationships which will facilitate better communications, trust, and loyalty between organization and employees.

Prepare this statement of policy and submit as a formal class project.

Selected References

Books

Hinrichs, J. R. *High-Talent Personnel: Managing a Critical Resource.* New York: American Management Association, 1966.

Likert, R. *The Human Organization: Its Management and Value.* New York: McGraw-Hill, 1967.

Maslow, A. H. *Eupsychian Management.* Homewood, Illinois: Richard D. Irwin, Inc., 1965.

Miller, B. *Managing Innovation For Growth and Profit.* Homewood, Illinois: Dow Jones–Irwin, Inc., 1970.

Anthologies

Hampton, D. R., Summer, C. E., and Webber, R. A. (Eds.). *Organizational Behavior and the Practice of Management.* Glenview, Illinois: Scott, Foresman and Company, 1968. Strauss, G. "The Personality vs. Organization Theory," p. 261.

Leavitt, H. J., and Pondy, L. R. (Eds.). *Readings in Managerial Psychology.* Chicago, Illinois: University of Chicago Press, 1964. Martin, N. H., and Sims, J. H. "Power Tactics," p. 217.

McKinsey and Company (Eds.). *The Arts of Top Management.* New York: McGraw-Hill, 1971. Copisarow, A. C. "The Future Impact of Technology on Management," p. 280.
Hertz, D. B. "The Successful Innovators," p. 308.
Patton, A. "Motivating Tomorrow's Executives," p. 192.

Articles

Allen, T. "Who Guards The Gate?" *Innovation*, Number Eight, 1969, p. 33.

Baram, M. S. "Trade Secrets: What Price Loyalty?" *Harvard Business Review*, November–December 1968, p. 66.

Breton, E. J. "Caution: Fragile Inventive Talent; Handle with Care," *Innovation*, Number Nineteen, 1971, p. 44.

Chartier, R. "Managing The Knowledge Employee," *Personnel Journal*, August 1968, p. 558.

Coleman, R. J., and Riley, M. J. "The Chief Executive: His Personality Characteristics and the Firm's Growth Rate," *Personnel Journal*, December 1970, p. 994.

Dewhirst, H. D. "Impact of Organizational Climate On The Desire To Manage Among Engineers and Scientists," *Personnel Journal*, March 1971, p. 196.

Fielder, F. E. "Engineer the Job to Fit the Manager," *Harvard Business Review*, September–October 1965, p. 115.

Fitzpatrick, G. D. "Good Business & Business Ethics," *Advanced Management Journal*, October 1965.

Freed, R. N. "Protecting Valuable Information," *Innovation*, Number Eleven, 1970, p. 59.

Hagen, W. W. "Ethics in Business," *Advanced Management Journal*, April 1965.

McClelland, D. C. "Business Drive and National Achievement," *Harvard Business Review*, July–August 1962, p. 99.

Mahler, W. R. "Should Some Chief Executives Get Out of the Kitchen?" *Training and Development Journal*, January 1970, p. 4.

Mendell, J. S. "The Case of The Straying Scientist," *Harvard Business Review*, July–August 1969, p. 4.

Miller, T. F. "How to Slow the Turnover Flow," *Personnel Journal*, May 1968, p. 321.

North, D. "Life Among the People Brokers," *Innovation*, Number Three, 1969, p. 42.

Park, F. "With Your Money and My Brains," *Innovation*, May 1969, p. 56.

Paster, I. "The Indispensable Man," *Personnel Journal*, March 1970, p. 246.

Patton, A. "The Coming Scramble for Executive Talent," *Harvard Business Review*, May–June 1967, p. 155.

Roberts, E. "What it Takes to be an Entrepreneur . . . and to Hang on to One," *Innovation*, Number Seven, 1969, p. 46.
Yaney, J. P. "The Management of Innovation," *Personnel Journal*, March 1970, p. 224.

CASE STUDY CROSS REFERENCE

Although located elsewhere in this book, the following problem situations are also valuable in the study of Section 8:

Group Conflict and
Team Development

"I don't want him in that meeting tomorrow!" Campana stormed, breathing heavily from pent-up anger and frustration.

"Who?" asked Guy Frederick, Government Marketing Director.

"You know damned well who I mean . . . I don't want Horace Pardee and those other used car salesmen from corporate headquarters messing up in thirty minutes what we've taken most of a year to achieve!"

EDDIE CAMPANA
Used Car Salesman from
Corporate Headquarters

INTRODUCTION

Conflict between individuals and groups usually leads to negative attitudes and counterproductive behavior. How can such conflicts be resolved before serious damage is done to weaken the team or the organization? What is meant by team and organizational development? How can it be achieved? What is the proper role of the manager in resolving conflict and developing teamwork?

Cases in This Section

The Momentum of Success

Sweet success of last year . . . some changing attitudes across the country affect a respected magazine, its publisher, and editor . . . strong feelings on both sides clash on future editorial policy. Must loss of a key man be the only way to resolve the conflict?

I Love You, Shirley, But . . .

Love is beautiful but team dissension is not . . . uneven work loads . . . covering up for the boss . . . slipped schedules . . . jealousies and conflicting statements.

Used Car Salesman from Corporate Headquarters

A year of careful planning may end in disaster if a controversial person attends a high level meeting . . . the boss should know better . . . the obvious corporate influence . . . a threat of resignation.

Where Do We Go from Here?

Several executives discuss the recent past in which the termination of a young employee had serious repercussions . . . are the standard rules still viable? . . . should we adopt a new posture in the light of changing values? . . . giving away the ball game?

Teach Them to Be Managers

Can managers manage under the leadership of a benevolent autocrat? A training program is suggested but the professor refuses . . . status . . . power . . . paternalism. What is the basis for manager development?

THE MOMENTUM OF SUCCESS

There was something about Eldon Caulfield's facial expression which told Dan Brace that the next few minutes would not be particularly pleasant. At first, Brace pretended not to notice the publisher as he quietly entered the editorial office. Brace continued to edit copy for a future issue of *The New Englander* as his boss slipped off his rubbers and hung up his overcoat and hat. Yes, thought Brace, this might well be the encounter he had been anticipating for several weeks.

"Foul weather out there," said Caulfield, quite aware that his entrance had been ignored.

Dan Brace looked up, put his pencil aside and pushed his swivel chair back from the desk.

"If it continues like this for one more week I think I'll take that job with the *St. Petersburg Herald*," said Brace.

Dan Brace generally enjoyed needling his boss about leaving *The New*

Englander for greener pastures, a threat all editors periodically use. This time though as he said the words he could see Caulfield was not in a laughing mood.

"Although it's possible New York might manage to muddle on without you, Brace, I doubt if St. Petersburg could survive the shock," said Caulfield dryly as he rubbed his hands and started opening cabinet doors at random in the cluttered office.

"The brandy is in the credenza," said Brace and he waited while Caulfield poured himself a small glass.

"I won't waste any words with you, Dan," said Caulfield at last. "I always have a transparent feeling when I don't get right to the point."

"Okay," said Brace placing his hands behind his head and placing his feet on the desk. "Let's get to the point. Let me guess. You're upset with our current series on the plight of cities?"

"Yes, partly . . . but there are a few other things as well . . ."

"Let me guess again," said Brace. "You've just come back from another meeting with the money men and they're getting nervous. Is that it?"

"Yes, Dan, and they have some good reasons too," said Caulfield firmly. "We're receiving a large volume of mail from public officials denouncing the city series. These people can make a lot of noise, and bad publicity is definitely not what the Board of Directors want."

Brace shook his head in disgust.

"Eldon Caulfield, did you make *any* attempt to remind the Board that less than two years ago their quaint period piece, fondly known as *The New Englander*, was teetering on the brink of bankruptcy?"

Caulfield took another sip of brandy and stared out the window into the darkness broken only by heavily blowing snow.

Brace continued, "As I recall, the Board was very nervous then. After twenty years of garden party writing, theater news, social chit-chat, and Long Island trivia, *The New Englander* was going broke! The momentum of success from another era had finally run out. Advertisers were leaving in droves . . ."

"Yes," Caulfield countered, "I was one of the voices for change at the time. I fought to revise and update our format and style. Wasn't it I who brought you to New York and billed you as 'the bright young literary talent from San Francisco'?"

"And, all modesty aside," interrupted Brace, "it seems to me I've done just that. I added a new masthead, new typestyle, and a whole fresh series of 'right-now' articles by the best talents in America." Brace got up from behind the desk and walked over to Caulfield. "Moreover, last month's circulation and avertising revenue were the highest in the last six years."

"We're not fools, Dan...none of us. You, I, and the Board are all keenly aware that Dan Brace is largely responsible for turning around *The New Englander* from a losing American institution into a national sounding board for contemporary problems."

"Then," replied Brace, "may I kindly ask if I have done all these wonderful things for *The New Englander*...what in the devil is the problem?"

"The Board feels that two years ago the country wanted controversial materials prepared by responsible persons in and out of public office but the wave has passed and it's now time to soften our editorial stance."

"Back to tasteful but bland?" asked Brace.

"Certainly not," replied Caulfield. "But a softer stand on specific issues and the re-introduction of general family interest and life style articles appear to be in order."

Brace simulated a lengthy regurgitation to clearly make his feelings known regarding the proposed new editorial policy.

"I'm sorry, Dan," said Caulfield, his voice rising and becoming quite harsh, "but I'm beginning to swing around to the Board's position. National sentiment is switching to moderation and, instead of following the obvious trend, you insist on using even more radical and explosive materials."

Dan Brace said nothing but crossed the room, bent over a table of editorial clippings, and began to sort through them.

Caulfield walked over to Brace. "Well," he said.

"Well, what?"

"Well," said Caulfield, "haven't you got anything to say?"

"Sure," replied Brace firmly. "Tell the Board to sack me. Give me two weeks termination pay and I'll take the Florida job."

Caulfield placed his hand on Brace's shoulder as a conciliatory gesture. "Don't be so bullheaded, Dan. First, you and I both know there is no Florida job waiting. Secondly, the Board has no intention of losing you."

"Funny way they have of showing it," replied Brace cynically. "What are their terms for me to retain my prestigious position with *The New Englander*?"

"For one thing the series, *The Ten Worst Cities in America* is to be canceled immediately. Several large advertisers headquartered in target cities have threatened to pull out their ad copy. However, the last straw for the Board was the resolution at the National Conference of Mayors last week condemning the series as muckraking journalism."

"No," said Brace calmly as he returned to his desk and lit a cigarette.

"Second," said Caulfield, "your proposal to run a condensation from the book, *Radical in Prison*, before it's released in hardback is denied. The Board feels that *The New Englander* is not the proper place for advertising the extreme views of Juan Escobar."

"Those two items specifically," said Caulfield, "plus more of a light touch in future issues . . . a more moderate stand.

Dan Brace sat down, put out the cigarette and placed his chin in his hands. "Mr. Caulfield, I suppose it was too much to wish that since I do not advise the Board in monetary matters, they would not advise me on editorial matters." Brace paused. "It appears that everyone is either a literary critic or editorial expert these days."

"I'm sorry, Dan," said Caulfield, "but I agree with the Board. These steps must be taken."

"You're forcing me to resign, you know."

"I hope it won't come to that Dan . . . I really hope it won't."

Discussion Questions

1. What can be done *now* to defuse the conflict between Dan Brace and the Board of Directors?
2. How might the conflict have been corrected earlier?
3. Assuming Brace stays, what general guidelines could be developed so that similar problems can be avoided in the future?

Special Project

Assume you are placed in a leadership role in which you must work with two parties (or two groups) both necessary to the operation, but antagonistic to each other. Some *possible* examples are:

(a) Literary people — Editorial board.
(b) School newspaper — School administration.
(c) Product research — Product sales.
(d) Medical research — Medical ethics boards.
(e) etc.

How can you maximize the efforts of each without increasing "natural" antagonisms and suspicions? How can you develop teamwork or a "you win — I win" relationship between the parties?

Make whatever reasonable assumptions are necessary to support discussion of the subject. Be as specific as you can relative to policies, actions, and so on. Avoid generalities and platitudes.

This can best be done using several discussion groups of 3–4 persons each. Allow 30 minutes for small group discussion and an equal amount of time for oral group reports.

Selected References

Books
Beckhard, R. *Organization Development: Strategies and Models*. Reading, Massachusetts: Addison-Wesley, 1969.
Greenewalt, C. H. *The Uncommon Man: The Individual In The Organization*. New York: McGraw-Hill, 1959.

Anthologies
Hampton, D. R., Summer, C. E., and Webber, R. A. (Eds.). *Organizational Behavior and the Practice of Management*. Glenview, Illinois: Scott, Foresman and Company, 1968. Cartwright, D., and Lippitt, R. "Group Dynamics and the Individual," p. 307.
Huseman, R., Logue, C., and Freshley, D. *Readings in Interpersonal and Organizational Communication*. Boston, Massachusetts: Holbrook Press, Inc., 1969. Galbraith, J. R. "Influencing the Decision to Produce," p. 219.
Leavitt, H. J., and Pondy, L. R. (Eds.). *Readings in Managerial Psychology*. Chicago, Illinois: University of Chicago Press, 1964. Ginzberg, E., and Reilley, E. "The Process of Change," p. 208.

Articles
Burke, R., Faber, F., and Bresver, B. "Managing Interpersonal Differences," *Personnel Journal*, May 1970, p. 408.
Genfan, H. "Managing Change," *Personnel Journal*, November 1969, p. 910.
Harley, K. "Team Development," *Personnel Journal*, June 1971, p. 437.
"Organizations: Tops, Bottoms, and Turmoil," *Industry Week*, May 4, 1970, p. 26.
Zacks, G. "How We Rebuilt Our Company," *Innovation*, Number Sixteen, 1970, p. 50.

I LOVE YOU, SHIRLEY, BUT...

Author's note. The National Weather Service (formerly U.S. Weather Bureau) has been quietly making major advances in the science of meteorology in recent years, primarily through the use of the computer methods in weather forecasting. By matching current meteorological conditions in a given geographic area against past comparable weather data stored in memory banks, the accuracy of prediction is sharply improved. In this hypothetical situation a group of computer service bureau programming specialists are assisting the National Weather Service in a new programming effort. An unusual ingredient is added to the team mix and morale begins to decline.

In retrospect, Jim Sparling could see the growing signs of discontent in his group, the minor schedule points which were missed, the lack of enthusiasm, and the general coolness of the Service Bureau team toward Fred and Carolyn. If he had been more perceptive several months ago, Sparling felt he might have had several additional options in dealing with the problem. But now, his back was to the wall.

216

Francene Lang was the one who finally confronted Sparling with the problem last Friday afternoon after it had been festering within the small computer programming staff for two or three months. Sparling had been clearing up the last few pieces of paperwork from his desk when Francene stopped by and asked to see him. She appeared troubled so Sparling closed the door of his office for privacy.

SCENE 1: FRIDAY AFTERNOON

"Francene, I don't know what your plans are for the weekend, but I intend to take it easy for a change . . . probably a little golf on Saturday and I know I'll watch a football game on television Sunday afternoon."

It was obviously small talk but Sparling felt that Francene would get to her problem in her own way.

"Mr. Sparling, I have terribly mixed feelings about what I'm going to tell you. First, I'm afraid I'm going to spoil your weekend. And I know that Fred Ashford and Carolyn Witter are going to be very angry with me . . . but someone has to tell you because the whole team is falling apart."

"Say, you really sound serious . . ." replied Sparling, still with a slight smile, although he sensed concern in her words.

"I wish someone else would have done this . . . but no one had the nerve to tell you . . ."

"Tell me what, Francene?"

"That Fred and Carolyn are in love and planning to get married." Francene blurted out the words and waited for Sparling's reaction.

Jim Sparling roared with laughter and shook his head in disbelief.

"Francene you're too much . . . too much I tell you! For a moment I thought you were serious . . ."

"I am serious, Mr. Sparling. Fred and Carolyn are planning to get married."

"But Fred Ashford is *already* married!" said Sparling. "And Carolyn is a child. I don't believe it."

"It's true," replied Francene. "You probably didn't notice it because you don't work as closely with them as we programmers do. They've been having an affair for some time. It started almost immediately . . . a few days after Carolyn was hired as a Data Collection Assistant and assigned to work with Fred on the National Weather Service program.

"Well," said Sparling, "I knew Fred was delighted with his new assistant. He raved to me at the time about how capable and helpful she was and what an asset she would be on the National Weather Service contract. But, I never thought there was anything else . . ."

Sparling stopped and mentally reviewed the implications of this information.

"Francene, if what you say is true, then I'm personally disappointed at the behavior of a middle-aged married employee falling for a girl who could pass for his daughter. And I regret the personal consequences for Fred and his wife, Shirley. But, quite frankly, I don't see how it affects us at the Service Bureau or the contract with the National Weather Service in particular."

Francene Lang hesitated before answering, perhaps deciding whether or not she should continue.

"Mr. Sparling, the National Weather Service project team is very demoralized, and we may miss our contract delivery date because of Fred and Carolyn."

"How's that?"

"The job was going quite well. Fred Ashford is a good leader and a fine programmer. He had excellent rapport with his staff and with our customer, the National Weather Service. But, a few days after Carolyn was hired, he lost interest in all the details of the job." Francene took a deep breath and continued. "He lost interest in everything . . . except Carolyn."

Sparling stroked his chin as he thought back to past conversations with Fred Ashford. It was true there had been a few schedule slippages and more logic rework than usual, but not enough to cause any concern to Sparling. Ashford had dismissed the problems as being inconsequential. Besides, thought Sparling, the contract administrator for the National Weather Service had never complained to him. For all intents and purposes everything was just fine.

"Exactly what is the problem, Francene?" Sparling asked.

"The problem is that the rest of us are doing their work. The staff is covering for the boss and his mistress, and we don't like it one bit!"

Francene Lang had been with the Service Bureau for over three years. Young, attractive, and successfully combining a career and marriage, Francene was one of the finest female computer specialists Sparling had known. It was doubtful she had any reason not to be telling the truth.

"How is the staff covering?" asked Sparling.

"Rich Small started preparing the weekly progress reports because Fred had dropped the ball. Ernie Quevada now debugs portions of the National Weather Forecasting computer program which Fred used to personally handle. Walter King and I are both doing data collection on daily temperature variations for the Eastern Seaboard for the years 1955 to 1965. This was one of the jobs Carolyn was supposed to handle. But, most of all, we cover by taking phone calls and making excuses when Fred and Carolyn aren't at the National Weather Service offices with the rest of the team."[1]

Sparling was perplexed.

"What do you mean, Francene? The only time Fred and Carolyn aren't in Rockville[2] would be when they're here at the office in Falls Church, Virginia or in the car between here and there."

"That's one of the things which really upsets the rest of us on the National Weather Forecasting project so much . . . that they can get away with it."

"Get away with what?" pleaded Sparling.

"You assume Fred and Carolyn are at the National Weather Service, and NWS personnel assume they are at our offices in Falls Church. Only the staff knows they're off somewhere together while we do the extra work to keep the program from coming apart."

"How bad is it?" asked Sparling.

"Morale is bad . . . really shot. I expect several resignations in the next week or so because no one wants to be associated with an unsuccessful program."

Francene leaned toward the Director of the Washington Service Bureau and pleaded, "Do something, Mr. Sparling. Do something before it's too late!"

SCENE 2: MONDAY MORNING

"It's true," said Fred Ashford, "I am in love with Carolyn and she's in love with me and I've never felt better in my whole life!"

When Sparling confronted Fred Ashford with his knowledge of the affair he had expected a denial or anger. Instead, Ashford glowed as he spoke openly and frankly about Carolyn and himself.

"Carolyn is the most wonderful, warm, and understanding person I've ever met," continued Ashford. "We didn't plan it . . . we were just working together and it happened . . . we were right for each other. Imagine, a beautiful young girl like that falling for a plain, middle-aged guy like me! Imagine!"

---

[1]Although not necessarily typical of all Service Bureaus and other consultant computer programming services, it is quite common to have service personnel work at the client or customer offices rather than their own. This eases interface problems with client personnel and computer equipment.

[2]Rockville, Maryland. A suburb of the District of Columbia where the National Weather Service and several other government agencies are located.

"Does Shirley know?" asked Sparling.

"Yes. I finally told her Saturday. First she insisted I was joking. Then she told me I was becoming senile. Then she cried for over three hours. On Sunday she was calm and in control of herself. She admitted we had drifted apart years ago. Then I said, 'I do love you Shirley, but I'm out of my mind over another woman.'"

"I hate to bring you back to reality, Fred," said Sparling, "but you may be out of a job as well."

Ashford stared at his boss in disbelief.

"What do you mean, out of a job? How does my personal life affect my position with the Service Bureau?"

"For starters," replied Sparling quite crisply, "the Weather Forecasting contract is in schedule trouble. Your staff is near the point of mutiny, you've neglected your leadership responsibilities and others have had to do your work and Carolyn's in addition to their own."

Ashford started to speak but Sparling went on.

"Add to all that the distinct possibility that you and Carolyn have been charging time on a government contract while you have been on . . . personal business?"

"That's not true," replied Ashford. "Carolyn was hired primarily as my administrative assistant and, regardless of our feelings for each other, we have not cheated on the contract or acted improperly on the job. Often between the office and Rockville we would stop for lunch or coffee . . . but only for a few minutes. Jim, you've known me too long to think I'd cheat you and the company."

"How about the covering up and extra staff work load?" asked Sparling.

"No one has an extra work load." Ashford was quite emphatic. "All jobs have been discussed and delegated to the most capable person or persons. And, as for the covering up, most of that is the product of small minds which assumed we were at some cheap motel if we weren't with the rest of the group."

Both men were silent. Sparling tapped a ball point pen, making numerous small dots on his desk blotter, as he carefully thought out his strategy.

"What you do with your life is your business Fred, except when it affects our business, which is developing computerized information systems. Therefore, I am terminating Carolyn Witter immediately. I want you to stay out on site, pull your team together, and get this contract completed. And, I want a daily report by phone on your progress. I'm doing this because the project is too far along to bring in a new project leader. But let me make myself perfectly clear . . . any more foul ups and you and Miss Witter can get married in the unemployment office!"

Discussion Questions

1. Why was Carolyn Witter terminated and not Fred Ashford? Was this fair? Discuss.
2. Do you concur in keeping Ashford as the project leader? Why?
3. Can Ashford be effective in redirecting his team toward successful completion of the project? Explain.
4. What approach should Ashford use with his team to regain their acceptance of him?
5. If you disagree with Sparling's decision, how would you have solved this situation?

Special Project

Organizations often have specific rules and policy statements on husbands and wives working in the same company or department, or the hiring of relatives and close friends of either sex.

Obtain copies of several of these policy statements and discuss in class. Discuss the advantages and disadvantages of each from both the viewpoint of the organization and the employees.

Selected References

Books
Blake, R., Shepard, H., and Mouton, J. *Managing Intergroup Conflict in Industry.* Houston, Texas: Gulf Publishing, 1964.
Lawrence, P. R., and Lorsch, J. W. *Developing Organizations: Diagnosis And Action.* Reading, Massachusetts: Addison-Wesley, 1969.

Anthologies
Hampton, D. R., Summer, C. E., and Webber, R. A. (Eds.). *Organizational Behavior and the Practice of Management.* Glenview, Illinois: Scott, Foresman and Company, 1968.
  Bennis, W., and Shepard, H. "A Theory of Group Development," p. 164.
  Katz, D., and Kahn, R. "Organizational Change," p. 555.
Huseman, R., Logue, C., and Freshley, D. *Readings in Interpersonal and Organizational Communication.* Boston, Massachusetts: Holbrook Press, Inc., 1969.
  Buchanan, P. C. "How Can 'We' Gain 'Their' Commitment?" p. 211.
  Rogers, C. R. "The Characteristics of a Helping Relationship," p. 269.
Leavitt, H. J., and Pondy, L. R. (Eds.). *Readings in Managerial Psychology.* Chicago, Illinois: University of Chicago Press, 1964.
  Cartwright, D., and Lippitt, R. "Group Dynamics and the Individual," p. 286.
  Cohen, A. M. "Changing Small-Group Communication Networks," p. 391.
  Sherif, M. "Experiments on Group Conflict and Co-operation," p. 408.

USED CAR SALESMAN FROM CORPORATE HEADQUARTERS

Two secretaries had to scurry out of the way as Eddie Campana stormed down the hall, quite unaware of their presence. Reaching the door of the

Director of Government Marketing, Campana stepped inside and slammed it shut behind him.

"I don't want him in that meeting tomorrow," Campana stormed, breathing heavily from pent-up anger and frustration.

"Who?" asked Guy Frederick, Government Marketing Director.

"You know damned well who I mean . . . I don't want Horace Pardee and those other used car salesmen from corporate headquarters messing up in thirty minutes what we've taken most of a year to achieve!"

"Settle down Ed," said Frederick softly. "I'm on your team, remember?"

"Settle down? I and my entire proposal preparation team have spent months working with Engineering to develop a presentation plan for the Air Force Survey team . . . not to mention another year of research and development before that. Then this company has the incredible stupidity to invite two clowns from corporate headquarters to take part. I tell you, Guy, it won't be a presentation, it'll be a fiasco . . . a farce!"

"Let's get our facts straight, Ed," replied Frederick. "I received a phone call from Ralph Conners just a few minutes ago, probably just before he called you. I had no intention of having corporate headquarters represented at this meeting but then I'm not in charge of the Communications Systems Division."

"But Conners should know better," pleaded Campana.

"Look, Ed," said Frederick, "we've got to begin facing the fact that the high flying Communications Systems Corporation we both joined two years ago is now merely one of fourteen separate and not so autonomous divisions of Empire Industries. Remember, Ed? Do you recall the liquidity crunch which almost wiped us out just when our equipment development plans were moving into high gear?"

"Yes, I remember all of that, but . . ."

"Empire Industries came along with an offer to buy us out lock, stock and barrel when the bankers refused to extend our notes or offer additional credit . . . all that at a time when market conditions wouldn't tolerate another speculative public stock offering. Jay Fishman jumped at the chance to save his company even though he knew it would mean his resignation and a replacement from Empire Corporate offices."

"Guy, I know Ralph Conners was the Empire choice to run our Division, but Ralph is a real savvy executive. You'd think he could separate the specialized marketing approach required by this Division from his loyalties to Empire."

"I suppose so," replied Frederick, "but someone back at Corporate probably insisted they be represented at our meeting with the Air Force and Conners had to go along. It's a price we have to pay for being bankrolled by a major financial conglomerate ... they can pull the strings whenever they want."

"But it's patently stupid! Tomorrow at ten o'clock, after months of preparation, an Air Force Survey Team will tour our facility. Our carefully planned tour will show them our capabilities for micro-electronic assembly, process control, inspection and reliability testing, clean room operations and security procedures. After luncheon we plan to present our detailed approach for developing a Darkness Terrain Analyzer under a sole source contract ..."

"None of that is changed," interrupted Frederick. "The plans for tomorrow are the same as before except that Horace Pardee and Norbert Brodsky of corporate marketing will be part of the Division team which will host the Air Force Survey."

"Everything is changed!" bellowed Campana. "Have you ever been in a meeting with Pardee or Brodsky?"

"No," replied Frederick, "I guess I haven't. I recall meeting Brodsky once when he visited our facility last May, but I don't believe I've met Horace Pardee."

"You'd know if you did," growled Campana. "He's a pompous corporate type, lacking both finesse and tact."

"Come on now, Ed, Pardee can't be that bad?"

"But he is, Guy ... he's bad news. I attended a meeting at Empire several months ago and had the bad fortune of meeting him then. He's shallow, acceptable for the luncheon circuit or for broad marketing statements but he has no technical depth even in products with which he should be familiar. On something as complex as the Darkness Terrain Analyzer he'll be way out of his environment."

"I'm sure Pardee will realize that and leave the more technical aspects to you and your presentation team."

"That's the biggest problem," replied Campana. "From what I recall, Mr. Horace Pardee dominated the meeting I attended and made a fool of himself in the process. Maybe they can generally keep him in line at Corporate but he'll blow our entire planned presentation the first time he opens his mouth!"

"Are you sure?" asked Frederick.

"Positive."

"What do you want me to do?"

"Guy, you're closer to Ralph Conners than any of the rest of us. Get Conners to stop Pardee from attending at all. If he can't, then, somehow, muzzle Pardee tomorrow. And, pass this on to Mr. Conners as well . . . if Pardee gives the Air Froce representatives a bad impression of our operation I promise to submit my resignation tomorrow evening. That's not a threat, Guy, it's a promise. This whole thing means too much to me."

Discussion Questions

1. List and discuss the alternatives open to Guy Frederick.
2. Of these alternatives, which are more likely to improve rather than impair the:
   (a) Corporate—Division relationship?
   (b) Frederick—Conners relationship?
   (c) Frederick—Campana relationship?
3. How might this apparent crisis have been averted?
4. What long term team building approaches might be used to strengthen the ties of the acquired Communications Systems Corporation with Empire Industries?

Special Project

Prepare a well-documented research paper title, *Corporate Adoptions: The Parent-Child Relationship* or any similar title which explores the working relationships between large conglomerates or financial holding companies and their operating divisions or subsidiaries.

Alternate. Have each class member research and report on several corporate-division relationships and present their findings in class. What organizational patterns are evident? For what apparent reasons are some successful and others not? Products and markets are obviously important but are any human relationships patterns evident? Discuss.

Note. Excellent sources for recent data are such magazines as *Fortune, Forbes, Business Week,* and others which stress the organizational and philosophical attitudes of companies.

Selected References

Books

Bennis, W. G. *Organization Development: Its Nature, Origins, and Prospects.* Reading, Massachusetts: Addison-Wesley, 1969.

Blake, R., Shepard, H., and Mouton, J. *Managing Intergroup Conflict in Industry.* Houston, Texas: Gulf Publishing, 1964.

Ginzberg, E., and Reilley, E. *Effecting Change in Large Organizations.* New York: Columbia University Press, 1957.

Jackson, T., and Spurlock, J. *Research and Development Management.* Homewood, Illinois: Dow Jones–Irwin, Inc., 1966, Chapter 6.

Anthologies

Effective Communication on the Job. New York: American Management Association, 1963. Famularo, J. "Cooperation or Conflict in Working With Other Managers," p. 291.

Hampton, D. R., Summer, C. E., and Webber, R. A. (Eds.). *Organizational Behavior and the Practice of Management.* Glenview, Illinois: Scott, Foresman and Company, 1968. Sayles, L. R. "The Change Process in Organizations: An Applied Anthropology Approach," p. 691.

Huseman, R., Logue, C., and Freshley, D. *Readings in Interpersonal and Organizational Communication.* Boston, Massachusetts: Holbrook Press, Inc., 1969.
   Fergason, G. "Keeping Management Informed," p. 163.
   Scott, W. "Communication and Centralization of Organization," p. 79.

Koontz, H., and O'Donnell, C. *Management: A Book of Readings.* New York: McGraw-Hill, 1968.
   Likert, R. "Measuring Organizational Performance," p. 608.
   Odiorne, G. S. "Coaching a Winning Management Team," p. 483.

Leavitt, H. J., and Pondy, L. R. (Eds.). *Readings in Managerial Psychology.* Chicago, Illinois: University of Chicago Press, 1964. Thelen, H., and Dickerman, W. "The Growth of Groups," p. 382.

Articles

Beckhard, R. "The Confrontation Meeting," *Harvard Business Review,* March–April 1967, p. 149.

Grote, R. C. "Effect of Leadership Changes On A Work Group," *Training and Development Journal,* July 1971, p. 18.

Kelly, J. "Make Conflict Work For You," *Harvard Business Review,* July–August 1970, p. 103.

Lippitt, G. L., and Schmidt, W. H. "Crises in a Developing Organization," *Harvard Business Review,* November–December 1967, p. 102.

Luneburg, W. V. "The Role of Management in an Atmosphere of Crisis," *MSU Business Topics,* Autumn 1970, p. 7.

Margulies, N. "Implementing Organizational Change Through an Internal Consulting Team," *Training and Development Journal,* July 1971, p. 26.

WHERE DO WE GO FROM HERE?

Last Tuesday Gordon Blue was terminated by his supervisor on the grounds that he was an insubordinate troublemaker. The supervisor was backed up by his manager, Bill Kelly, the Director of Manufacturing, and Blue left that very day.

Reaction was swift and intense, particularly among the younger people in the company. Blue was no troublemaker, went their argument. He was a talented young Production Scheduler who was arbitrarily terminated for his choice of dress and political opinions.

Attitudes of people in the company were so divided on the issue that little effective work was done for the remainder of the week. With the exception of machine paced jobs, most job time was consumed in an endless discussion of the pros and cons of the Blue case.

By Friday morale had sagged badly in the organization. Paula White, a young clerk in the Documents and Records section submitted her resignation, citing the Blue case as her reason. That day Bill Kelly was also asked

by an unofficial committee (which claimed to speak for the entire manufacturing group) to reverse his decision and re-hire Blue. Kelly was
polite but refused to reconsider his decision. Several members of the
group threatened to quit but no additional written or oral resignations
were received as of 5:00 p.m. Friday afternoon.

It is now Saturday morning. Top Line Hardware Manufacturing Company is quiet except for a meeting in the office of the president, Tom
Overhill. Overhill, greatly disturbed by the events of the prior week, has
hurriedly called this meeting with his key personnel to review the Blue
case and to take a long hard look at existing company policies and attitudes
toward employee dress, appearance, and work habits. In attendance are
Bill Kelly, Ned Baxter, the Director of Marketing; and Louis Farmer,
Office Manager.

OVERHILL: Bill, could you give us one last summary of the Blue case?

KELLY: Gordon Blue has been with Production Scheduling for about
two years. His attendance and absenteeism records were good and
he was an adequate, but not outstanding, performer. He had
received two small raises during his employment.

FARMER: And on the negative side?

KELLY: I'd say very emotional, particularly relative to subjects not
related to the job, and prone to get into loud debates with almost
anyone on anything.

BAXTER: Such as?

KELLY: Oh, politics mostly . . . particularly world involvements, national priorities, equality among men and nations, redistribution of
wealth . . . you know, things like that.

OVERHILL: Radical left involvement?

KELLY: Don't know for sure . . . perhaps, but more likely just an overzealous young man.

BAXTER: Well, I was in Philadelphia most of last week so I really
don't know what happened.

KELLY: Blue worked for Bob Darby and Darby long ago expressed
his concern to me about Blue's political views . . .

FARMER: A lot of us are political. I can get pretty heated about some
issues too.

KELLY: Darby was concerned only about Blue's activities here at work
. . . passing out leaflets for one cause or another, having hopeless
petitions signed, or collecting money for various peace and
brotherhood causes.

OVERHILL: That alone may have been reason to terminate the man.
Everyone knows my feelings about things like that on company
time.

BAXTER: Was it on company time?

KELLY: Blue said no and Darby said yes. I suspect it was both. But Darby didn't terminate Blue for his political activities at work.

FARMER: I hope not or it will set a precedent for wedding collections, retirement collections, baseball World Series lotteries and so on . . .

OVERHILL: There's a lot more of *that* business than I like, but, in the interests of time, I feel we should stay with the Blue case and its implications.

KELLY: Blue's work was suffering. He was talented as his supporters say, but he was going in too many directions at the same time. He was probably also ineffective in several of his outside causes because he was spreading himself so thin. As a Production Scheduler he had repeatedly fallen behind in his paperwork and forced others to carry part of his load.

OVERHILL: And had Darby taken the proper disciplinary actions?

KELLY: Certainly. He spoke with Blue the first time. The second time a formal discipline action notice was placed in Blue's personnel folder.

BAXTER: But aren't three formal discipline notices necessary for termination?

KELLY: Ordinarily, yes. However, this time Darby challenged Blue on a petition being circulated during work time. Blue was defiant and Darby threatened to write him up again.

OVERHILL: And?

KELLY: Blue told Darby where he could . . . (*clears his throat*) shove his "mundane establishment job." Their discussion became more heated and Darby let Blue go on grounds of insubordination.

BAXTER: Isn't Darby at fault too?

KELLY: Partially, but Bob Darby is one of our best men . . . usually very cool and clear-headed. I believed him when he said Blue purposely goaded him into it. Regardless of what others said, I had to back one of our best managers . . . or our top staff would have fallen apart.

FARMER: I suppose you're right . . .

OVERHILL: He certainly is. The Blue–Darby encounter should have been avoided, but it happened. Their emotions got the best of them and Darby acted in good faith. Bill Kelly backed up his subordinate manager as he should have done. It would be ridiculous for me to reverse that now. (*Pause*) No, we have to consider the Blue case to be closed.

FARMER: For the record, Bill, did Gordon Blue's appearance or mannerisms have anything to do with the dismissal?

KELLY: None whatsoever.

BAXTER: Well, where do we go from here?

OVERHILL: That's exactly the reason for this meeting . . . to determine where we go from here. It's time we took a fresh look at ourselves from a personnel policies and procedures point of view.

BAXTER: You don't mean giving in to the kids, do you?

OVERHILL: Oh, hell no! But I can spot a morale problem a mile away. I want to develop a new way of working together in which future conflicts get resolved in such a way that *all parties win* as opposed to Darby winning and Blue losing.

KELLY: Then you really do support Blue?

OVERHILL: No, Bill, not in the sense of what he was doing at work. But I see Blue as a man who has talent, a man we hired and trained. Then we terminated him and lost his skills forever. Why? Why couldn't this have been caught earlier and the conflict resolved? Don't we know how to work together . . . to communicate?

FARMER: What are you suggesting?

OVERHILL: I'm not sure and that's why we're here. I think we should brainstorm new approaches to resolving internal conflicts of any type before they boil over. Something is wrong with the system. I say let's make the system more workable so we don't lose talent like Gordon Blue.

KELLY: But at the same time not alienate those among us who may disagree with Blue?

OVERHILL: I think so.

KELLY: But not compromise quality or quantity of production?

OVERHILL: That goes without saying. I'm socially minded, too, but I'm also in this business to make an acceptable profit for the stockholders.

BAXTER: It will probably mean upsetting the traditional chain of command with respect to internal communication.

OVERHILL: Possibly. And, frankly, I'm not sure I'll like what we develop. Gordon Blue is a symbol of changing times. We're going to have to adapt our traditional means of communicating and resolving conflicts to meet entirely different sets of future situations.

FARMER: How do you suggest we begin?

Discussion Questions

1. Separate, define, and discuss the issues involved in this case.
2. How should this management team approach these difficult problems?
3. What are the positive and negative implications for the organization if the proposed policy changes are significant?
4. Read the case study, *A Highly Motivated "Kook,"* Section 6 and correlate the issues defined there with those presented in this case.

Special Project

Define basic policy issues developed in this case and assign these as project topics to several participants or participant teams. Have each develop a *new written policy* and offer for verbal critique in class at a later session.

Then, compile these sets of personnel policies developed by the class and submit to a local respected personnel manager or administrative manager for his analysis. On what grounds did he have objections? Were your policies incomplete, lacking in scope or depth, or naive? Or, did you give *him* food for thought?

Note.   If industry analysis is contemplated, first obtain a copy (probably free on request to your professor) of the Personnel Policies and Practices Handbook of any local medium sized or large company. Use this as a guide to subjects and scope but avoid a reworded replica of the original. Be fresh and inventive, considering people as the human resources they are . . . but be practical.

Selected References

Books

Beckhard, R. *Organization Development: Strategies and Models.* Reading, Massachusetts: Addison-Wesley, 1969.

Ginzberg, E., and Reilly, E. W. *Effecting Change in Large Organizations.* New York: Columbus University Press, 1957.

Ready, R. K. *The Administrator's Job: Issues and Dilemmas.* New York: McGraw-Hill, 1967.

Walton, R. E. *Interpersonal Peacemaking: Confrontations and Third Party Consultation.* Reading, Massachusetts: Addison-Wesley, 1969.

Anthologies

Effective Communication on the Job. New York: American Management Association, 1963. Halford, J. "Rumor Must Be Reckoned With," p. 116.

Hampton, D. R., Summer C. E., and Webber, R. A. (Eds.). *Organizational Behavior and the Practice of Management.* Glenview, Illinois: Scott, Foresman and Company, 1968. Tannenbaum, R., Weschler, I., and Massarik, F. "Sensitivity Training for the Management Team," p. 539.

Huseman, R., Logue, C., and Freshley, D. *Readings in Interpersonal and Organizational Communication.* Boston, Massachusetts: Holbrook Press, Inc., 1969. Davis, K. "The Organization That's Not on the Chart," p. 156.

Koontz, H., and O'Donnell, C. *Management: A Book of Readings.* New York: McGraw-Hill, 1968. Odiorne, G. S. "Coaching a Winning Management Team," p. 483.

Leadership on the Job. New York: American Management Association, 1966. Halford, J. "The Care and Feeding of the Grapevine," p. 63.

Leavitt, H. J., and Pondy, L. R. (Eds.). *Readings in Managerial Psychology.* Chicago, Illinois: University of Chicago Press, 1964. Jackson, J. M. "The Organization and Its Communication," p. 486.

Articles

Athos, A. G. "Is the Corporation Next to Fall?" *Harvard Business Review,* January–February 1970, p. 49.

Bradley, G. E. "What Businessmen Need to Know About the Student Left," *Harvard Business Review,* September–October 1968, p. 49.

Davey, N. G. "The Consultant's Role In Organizational Change," *MSU Business Topics*, Spring 1971, p. 76.

Delbecq, A. L. "Sensitivity Training," *Training and Development Journal*, January 1970, p. 32.

Greiner, L. E. "Patterns of Organizational Change," *Harvard Business Review*, May–June 1967, p. 119.

Lippitt, G., and Schmidt, W. H. "Crises in a Developing Organization," *Harvard Business Review*, November–December 1967, p. 102.

Mann, E. K. "Sensitivity Training: Should We Use It?" *Training and Development Journal*, March 1970, p. 44.

Pine, F. S. "The Executive Rap Session," *Personnel Journal*, September 1970, p. 732.

Scanlan, B. K. "Sensitivity Training—Clarifications, Issues, Insights," *Personnel Journal*, July 1971, p. 546.

Booklets

Team Building in Church Groups. Geyer, N., and Noll, S. Valley Forge, Pennsylvania: Judson Press, 1970 ($1.00 each).

TEACH THEM TO BE MANAGERS

"Is there anything I can get for you, Professor Marquardt? Some coffee perhaps?" Frank Engberg was obviously enjoying being host in his sumptuous office and, at the same time, somewhat apprehensive about having an industrial psychology professor as a guest.

"No thank you, Mr. Engberg," I replied. "I'm just fine."

"Then you must have one of these cigars." Engberg opened a dark antique wood carved box. "I've been hooked on these since Ben Strauss offered me my first one."

"I'm sorry, I don't smoke. But, please, have one yourself," I replied.

"Think I will," replied Engberg. "A fine cigar is just what a man needs after lunch."

In the few moments that it took Engberg to light up I scanned his office. It was beautifully decorated in a soft woody masculine theme. Everything, from the deep plush carpet on the floor to the attractive prints hung on richly paneled walls, was an elegant statement of achievement and status.

"You like the office?" asked Engberg noting my apparent interest.

"Yes, I certainly do. It's most attractive."

"It came with the job. Years ago when I first started as a salesman here at Zelsco, I used to sit across the desk where you are now and take my orders from Ben Strauss. Never thought then that Old Ben Strauss would retire and I'd become president of Zelsco."

"How long has Strauss been retired?" I asked.

"A little less than a year now. When his children had grown and married

Ben decided to sell the firm he created and personally ran for seventeen years. He took an offer from a small conglomerate and is now touring Europe with his wife."

"And that is when you became president?" I asked.

"Yes," replied Engberg. "At the time I was Sales Manager of a four man sales staff and the logical choice for the job."

"Logical choice for the job?" I mirrored back to keep Engberg talking.

"Well," said Engberg, "I suppose that sounds immodest but you could count Ben Strauss' possible replacements on one finger and I was the one."

"Why was that?" I asked.

"You didn't know Strauss or you wouldn't have to ask, Dr. Marquardt. He was an absolute dictator in all major decisions and in the day-to-day operation of the company. Lots of people simply couldn't work for him."

"An unpleasant person?"

"Oh, no!" replied Engberg. "Strauss was one of the nicest men you'd ever want to meet. He knew all of his employees by name and a lot about their families, too. But things had to be run his way."

A little confused, I probed deeper into the legacy of Ben Strauss.

"As a leader, was Strauss close to his employees?"

"I'm not exactly sure I know what you mean," Engberg said. "He was warm and personable. Everyone looked up to Strauss as a father figure who was in complete charge of his family."

"That's part of the answer I was looking for. Was he easy to talk to when problems developed?"

"Hardly," replied Engberg. "There was never any question about who was in charge here. There was Strauss the big boss and the rest of us workers. When there were problems he would sit in this fine office . . . no one else in the company had a private office . . . and dictate decisions or arbitrate disputes."

"This office was a status symbol?" I asked.

"It sure was. In this office and behind this desk Ben Strauss was bigger than life and we were small and unimportant by comparison."

"But you stayed with the company."

"True," replied Engberg. "Somehow Strauss never intimidated me as much as he did most of the others. Besides, I was in sales and spent more time in Columbus, Knoxville, and Memphis than I did here at the office."

"Well, Mr. Engberg," I said, "what exactly do you feel I can do for you or Zelsco?"

"Dr. Marquardt, we have a supervisory leadership problem here at Zelsco which stems from what I've already told you. Ben Strauss was a great guy, but he failed to develop any real leaders out in the plant. There isn't a man out there who can stand on his own two feet and make a simple decision. I want to develop individual leaders out there who won't keep coming in to me to make every decision. I also want to develop a team concept . . . a management team. That's why I called you in, Dr. Marquardt."

"And what do you feel I can do for you?" I asked.

"Run a management training program here for my supervisors. Teach them how to make decisions, to delegate, to communicate. Bring them up to speed on all that recent behavioral stuff. In other words, Dr. Marquardt, teach them to be managers . . . something they didn't have to be under Ben Strauss."

"I'm sorry, Mr. Engberg," I said after a few moments of thought. "I could develop and conduct a management training program for your supervisors but, at this point, it would be a waste of money."

Discussion Questions

1. Why does Dr. Marquardt feel that a training program now will be a waste of money?
2. What should be done now to start developing a management team?
3. What environmental conditions are prerequisites to team development?
4. What is the proper role of Frank Engberg in any proposed team development program?
5. What is the proper role of an outside consultant such as Dr. Marquardt in any proposed team development program?

Special Project

Prepare a research paper on the subject, *Organization Development: Recent Experiences in Business and Industry.*

Selected References

Books
Bennis, W. G. *Changing Organizations: Essays on the development and evolution of human organizations.* New York: McGraw-Hill, 1966.
Myers, M. S. *Every Employee a Manager.* New York: McGraw-Hill, 1970.

Anthologies
Hampton, D. R., Summer, C. E., and Webber, R. A. (Eds.). *Organizational Behavior and the Practice of Management.* Glenview, Illinois: Scott, Foresman and Company, 1968. Guest, R. H. "Organizational Change: The Effect of Successful Leadership," p. 716.

Articles
Coleman, R. J., and Riley, M. J. "The Chief Executive: His Personality Characteristics and the Firm's Growth Rate," *Personnel Journal,* December 1970, p. 994.

Cone, W. F. "Management Development: The Need For An Eclectic Approach," *Training and Development Journal*, September 1970, p. 26.

DuBrin, A. J. "Management Development: Education, Training or Behavioral Change," *Personnel Journal*, December 1970, p. 1002.

Eitington, J. E. "Assessing Laboratory Training Using Psychology of Learning Concepts," *Training and Development Journal*, February 1971, p. 2.

Ford, G. A. "Four Steps Are No Longer Enough," *Training and Development Journal*, July 1970, p. 29.

Gannon, M. J. "The Case Observational Method: A New Training Technique," *Training and Development Journal*, September 1970, p. 39.

Herman, S. M. "What Is This Thing Called Organization Development?" *Personnel Journal*, August 1971, p. 595.

Hinrichs, J. R. "Two Approaches to Filling the Management Gap," *Personnel Journal*, December 1970, p. 1008.

James, J. "Training for Leadership," *Training and Development Journal*, May 1970, p. 34.

Johnson, G. R. "Building A Staff-Hire or Train?" *Personnel Journal*, March 1970, p. 222.

Levinson, H. "A Psychologist Looks At Executive Development," *Harvard Business Review*, September–October 1962, p. 69.

Morreale, R. A. "Some Common Fallacies of Management Development," *Personnel Journal*, November 1969, p. 899.

Morrisey, G. L., and Wellstead, W. R. "Supervisory Training Can Be Measured 'Objectively' On The Job!" *Training and Development Journal*, June 1971, p. 12.

Parry, S. B. "The Name Of The Game . . . Is Simulation," *Training and Development Journal*, February 1971, p. 28.

Paster, I. "The Indispensable Man," *Personnel Journal*, March 1970, p. 246.

Prieve, E. A., and Wentorf, D. A. "Training Objectives—Philosophy or Practice?" *Personnel Journal*, March 1970, p. 235.

Scheer, W. D. "Do We Throw The Book Away and Start Over?" *Personnel Journal*, March 1971, p. 189.

Stolz, R. K. "Executive Development: New Perspective," *Harvard Business Review*, May–June 1966, p. 133.

Varney, G. H. "Why Hasn't Management Development Worked?" *Training and Development Journal*, July 1970, p. 55.

Yeager, J. C. "Management Development: An Act of Faith," *Training and Development Journal*, June 1971, p. 6.

CASE STUDY CROSS REFERENCE

Although located elsewhere in this book, the following problem situations are also valuable in the study of Section 9:

Section 9

Technology and the Future

"I used to feel the same way," said Falk. "Now I'm not so sure. Progress in all fields is accelerating at an incredible rate. In only one human lifetime man first flew at Kittyhawk and stepped on the surface of the moon. People are beginning to come apart emotionally because of the impermanence of things, the incredible changes taking place around them, their feeling of utter frustration in a vastly complex society of machines and systems which engulf them daily. I really don't believe we're ready for a youth pill."

EMORY FALK
Reversing the Physiological Clock

INTRODUCTION

Is the past a reliable guide to the present? Is the present a reliable guide to the future? What are the future impacts of today's emerging technologies? How will people feel and behave in increasingly complex work environments? What is the proper role of the organization in anticipating and planning for future change? What is the role of the organization now and in the future relative to new social and economic demands placed upon it by the community of man?

Cases in This Section

The Tissue Issue

Most everything seems to pollute our environment...or does it? A scholarly attack has a major effect on a large corporation...a planned counterattack...two old friends on different sides of the issue...no one dares reverse his official position.

Trouble in Toyland

Corporate minutes tell it all . . . a nice, big company besieged on all sides by social, political, and economic problems . . . bad public relations or inept management?

Wonderful Friday

The four day work week isn't here yet . . . but it may not be far off . . . two sides of the issue are developed . . . some possible new behavioral issues which will have to be faced.

Letter from a Retired Employee

Some provocative questions are raised by a retired employee and posed for future managers to ponder . . . what is the proper role for the company in preparing employees for change? Should the work environment be too comfortable?

Reversing the Physiological Clock

Has the future arrived? Will man's most fatal disease be controlled? A shocking announcement by a major drug company . . . the research appears to be sound . . . some possible implications on social and religious issues . . . are we really ready for the impact?

THE TISSUE ISSUE

Environmentalists have spread the word across the land: Shun colored toilet paper. It pollutes worse than white paper. But does it really?

Item from *The Wall Street Journal*
October 21, 1970

"This has got to stop!" stormed Trevor Bates at the special Monday morning strategy meeting. The president of Caminol Paper Company slammed his copy of Sunday's newspaper on the conference table for emphasis.

"We've been taking brick-bats for some time now on the pollution problem and, so far, have successfully answered most of our critics. This one has me worried though . . . Carl Pollard is a nationally recognized environmentalist as well as chemist. Even if he's dead wrong on this one we're still going to have a public relations problem for a year or more. And, if he's right . . . our entire marketing program will have to be restructured!"

Several executives nodded agreement and hurriedly exchanged comments. It was evident though that not everyone at the hastily called meeting had seen the article to which the president was referring. Realizing that no time had been available to distribute an agenda prior to the meeting, Bates handed the newspaper to Roy Stanley, Vice-President, and head of the Household Products Division.

"Roy, why don't you read the lead paragraphs since your people will be most directly involved in this."

Stanley picked up the paper, adjusted his glasses, and began to read.

DYES IN COLORED TOILET TISSUE POLLUTE!

"Noted scientist, Dr. Carl Pollard, head of Environmental Sciences at the State University, today urged the public not to buy colored or tinted toilet tissue, facial tissue, and related household paper products. The problem, said Dr. Pollard, is that the dyes used to tint these paper products do not break down with the paper itself in ordinary sewage or septic systems. The result is an additional pollutant load on our already inadequate waste disposal systems, rivers, and lakes.

"Asked if he wasn't making a mountain out of a molehill, Dr. Pollard commented, 'Any additional water pollution from an unnecessary source for the sake of fad or vanity is intolerable!'

"Dr. Pollard refused to name specific offenders but he did nod affirmatively when Caminol Paper was mentioned by one reporter. Caminol, a local manufacturer of household paper products, has been a leader in the production and marketing of colored paper products. So far the company has not made any comment."

Stanley put the paper down and removed his glasses.

"My home phone started ringing the moment the story broke," he said. "If it wasn't a reporter it was some crackpot threatening me in the name of humanity. I told the press that an official statement would be released Monday or Tuesday and then called Dave Lerner in Research for his opinion. Dr. Lerner believes that Pollard has blown this whole thing out of proportion and I asked Dave to attend this special meeting so he could give you his technical analysis."

Dr. David Lerner rose and spoke with the help of notes he had made on several small cards.

"After I received the phone call yesterday from Mr. Stanley I contacted several of my assistants and we met at the laboratory for a technical conference. We were joined at my request by Dr. Erwin Manners, Chief Chemist at Midland Chemical, our major dye supplier.

"Our review of all dyes and dye concentrations used in Caminol paper products led us to no new conclusions about their effects in disposal systems. As originally planned, when we first introduced color six years ago, all dyes are fully biodegradable . . . that is, they decompose naturally and do not inhibit the decomposition of the tissue products in any way.''

Lerner continued.

"We are prepared to assist in the preparation of any public statements to that effect. My assistant, Amy Nelson, will be available to the Public Relations Department as necessary to develop our technical position in lay language.''

Trevor Bates was obviously pleased by the quick reaction to the crisis by Stanley and Lerner. He complimented them and was visibly relieved to know that no pollution problem existed. Bates then routinely asked for questions and it became apparent that the problem was not totally resolved.

"We can issue rebuttal statements to the public,'' offered Jim Clark of Public Relations. "But how do we keep Carl Pollard from repeating his grandstand performance of last weekend? What we really need is a statement from him that he wasn't talking about our company.''

Roy Stanley turned to David Lerner.

"Dave,'' asked Stanley, "you know Carl Pollard quite well, don't you?''

"I did my doctoral work under his direction twelve years ago, but I have only seen him two or three times since.''

Stanley pressed his point.

"How do you evaluate him? Would Pollard back down if he were asked to do so when presented with a solid technical analysis by someone . . . like yourself, whom he greatly respects?''

David Lerner thought for a moment.

"Pollard is no fool,'' replied Lerner. "He's as brilliant as he is versatile. And, while he was always a master of overstatement to make a point, I feel he is serious about this issue and may not back down gracefully . . . even if proved wrong.''

"But you will *try*, David, won't you?'' Stanley's question was clearly a directive.

Lerner nodded in agreement and the meeting was adjourned.

Several days later Lerner made an appointment to see his former instructor. Pollard was cordial but the reminiscences were brief.

"David, I assume you are here on behalf of your company to have me modify my recent pollution comments.''

Lerner was not surprised at Pollard's directness and was equally direct in his reply.

"Frankly, yes. I'm as personally concerned about pollution as you are but feel you've selected the wrong target. Caminol has been making excellent progress in its program to remove water pollutants from its paper processing operations.''

"That is another subject we could debate all day," replied Pollard, adding, "you're here to talk about dye pollution!"

After momentary hesitation, Lerner stated the official Caminol position.

"Caminol can fully document the safety and pollution-free nature of all dye materials. We prefer to release the data with you on our side. However, if necessary, it could be presented in a manner which questions your research integrity."

"So, David, it would come to that?"

"With my deepest regrets, Carl. But you must see our point. The public demands color coordinated paper products and we are a competitive, profit-making paper manufacturer."

"And we are back to the power of the dollar?" asked Pollard.

"Carl, I am a scientist with a sense of ethics no less than yours. If I were not convinced that all of our dyes are fully biodegradable I would not continue at Caminol."

"Tell me," replied Pollard, "how do you know you are not adding to the pollution load?"

"The dyes in the pastel products are used in such minute quantities that . . ."

"But," interrupted Pollard, "you continue to move toward darker colors and more complex dye structures. How can you be sure?"

"Industry standards indicate that we are well below the limits . . ."

Pollard interrupted again. "Industry standards mean nothing! They do not limit practices which are against the best public interest. One of my reasons for public comment was to force outside impartial study of the entire subject."

Lerner felt he was not making progress and tried another approach.

"Carl, if it were up to me I would drop the entire color program irrespective of possible pollution. Color is more costly than white and the competition is horrendous. But the public loves color even though we might prefer to produce only white."

"Come now, David. That statement hardly absolves your company of blame. I am well aware that even your white products are created with extensive use of whitening ingredients which themselves are pollution suspects."

"Carl, now you're being totally unrealistic. The public would never buy grey toilet tissue."

"Perhaps not, David. Have you asked them?"

Lerner now realized that Pollard had no intention of modifying his public position.

"I assume then that you will not help us?"

"No, David, I cannot. I feel I have an obligation to make the public aware of industrial pollution regardless of intent or magnitude. I will not make an exception even for a friend and colleague."

Discussion Questions

1. What action should next be taken by Caminol Paper Company?
2. Is it possible to reconcile the views of these two scientists? How?
3. What is the proper role for a company such as Caminol in:
    (a) Neutralizing its waste products in the manufacturing process?
    (b) Offering products which are totally biodegradable?
    (c) Telling its side of the story to the public.
    (d) Working with appropriate city, county, state, and federal anti-pollution agencies?

Of Special Interest to Industrial Groups

Discuss the progress being made by your company to limit environmental pollution.

Special Project

Obtain the services of a qualified person from a local industry to speak to your group about the progress being made by his organization with regard to air or water pollution. Have him emphasize such items as:
    (a) The scope (magnitude) of the problem.
    (b) Alternatives for solution.
    (c) Cost tradeoffs.
    (d) Product or process changes (if any).
    (e) Difficulties involved.
    (f) Relations with governmental agencies.

Selected References

Books
Miller, B. *Managing Innovation For Growth and Profit*. Homewood, Illinois: Dow Jones–Irwin, Inc., 1970.

Anthologies
Drucker, P. F. (Ed.). *Preparing Tomorrow's Business Leaders Today*. Englewood Cliffs, New Jersey: Prentice-Hall, 1969. Drucker, P. "Business and the Quality of Life," p. 74.
McKinsey and Company (Eds.). *The Arts of Top Management*. New York: McGraw-Hill, 1971. Ansoff, I., and Stewart, J. "Strategies for a Technology-Based Business," p. 290.
Clee, G. H. "The New Manager: A Man for All Organizations," p. 146.

Articles
Bennis, W. "How to Survive in a Revolution," *Innovation*, Number Eleven, 1970, p. 2.

Fubini, E. "What Are The Consequences Of What We Are Doing?" *Innovation*, Number Thirteen, 1970, p. 21.

McKee, E. "The Blunders Companies Are Making Over Pollution Control," *Innovation*, Number Sixteen, 1970, p. 24.

Perlmutter, H. "Corporate Markets and the Human Condition," *Innovation*, Number Nine, 1970, p. 56.

Ruina, J. P. "Can We Control The Goose That Is Laying The Golden Eggs?" *Innovation*, Number Sixteen, 1970, p. 36.

Shapero, A. "The Blobocracy Blight," *Innovation*, Number Twenty-one, 1971, p. 2.

TROUBLE IN TOYLAND

*Minutes of the Annual Meeting of the Stockholders
of Record — Children's World Manufacturing Corporation*

President Waldo M. Tembler called the annual meeting of the stockholders, Children's World Manufacturing Corporation, to order at 3:07 p.m. at the Senator Hotel in New York. Although the meeting was scheduled to start at 2:00 p.m., persons representing themselves as the Committee to Spare Our Children From Needless Violence blocked the entrance to the main ballroom, barring stockholders and delaying the proceedings. When hotel security guards arrived, Mr. Tembler asked the protesters to step aside, stating that if they did, he would allow them to voice their feelings at the meeting.

Mr. Tembler welcomed the stockholders to the meeting and expressed confidence that Children's World would retain its title as the largest toy manufacturer in the world. A jibe of "bigness does not mean niceness" from the audience was shouted down by other stockholders. Mr. Tembler then completed his short opening remarks.

At 3:15, Roger V. Capp, Treasurer, reported gross corporate sales for the fiscal year (including all wholly owned subsidiaries in the United States, Mexico, Europe, and Asia) as 823 million dollars and consolidated net profits at 103.5 million dollars.

At 3:30, Arnold Ruttenberg, Corporate Director of Marketing, presented new toy items which would be ready for the wholesale trade well in advance of the Christmas season. Among these were Hector the Household Robot, the Astronaut Space Chase Game, and Black Lisa, the doll with the enchanting smile and a face everyone will adore. Ruttenberg was interrupted by a stockholder who identified herself as "Mrs. Ellen Trueblood, one of the black women in the New Jersey doll assembly plant."

Mrs. Trueblood claimed to have long ago suggested changes in the design profile of Black Lisa which were totally ignored. Mrs. Trueblood went on to say that, as currently designed, Black Lisa was a young parody of the "old pancake lady" and would be an affront to the entire black community. Mr. Ruttenberg thanked her for her comments but said hers was only one opinion. He said Black Lisa was a design composite created after extensive market research with children of all colors, races, and nationalities.

Mr. Ruttenberg also answered questions from stockholders regarding suits filed by the Consumer Protection League of New York State alleging deceptive packaging of small toys. Mr. Ruttenberg noted that large protective boxes and related containers are often necessary to ensure damage-free product shipment, storage, and display.

Regarding the no contest plea entered by Corporate attorneys in response to the federal suit filed under the Truth in Advertising Act, Mr. Ruttenberg stated that advertising agencies were often overzealous in their use of animation effects on television. Some toys do appear to be larger, faster, or better on television than they do in real life said Mr. Ruttenberg, but it was a constant problem to place each toy in its best light considering the competitiveness of the industry. Mr. Ruttenberg added that a plea of no contest was not a guilty plea but merely a statement not to use such practices or methods in future advertisements.

At 4:10 p.m., Martin B. Prescott, Director of Corporate Design, spoke of future industry and company developments. He also re-emphasized the extensive design research which preceded the manufacture of Black Lisa. On the subject of product reliability, Mr. Prescott reminded the audience not to place too much importance on the long-running syndicated newspaper feature which condemned most toy manufacturers (and specifically Children's World) for purposeful and willful built-in toy obsolescence. Mr. Prescott added that product reliability in all toy and game lines had undergone major study in the last six months and only a few product adjustments were found to be required. These changes have already been incorporated into future production runs.

Responding to questions from a spokesman of the Committee to Spare Our Children from Needless Violence, Mr. Prescott stated:

(a) Fewer war oriented toys were now being produced and fewer still were in the design stages due to changing public attitudes.

(b) The company was currently reviewing its long sponsorship of the television program, Western Conflict, but no final decision had, as yet, been made.

All planned presentations completed, president Tembler opened the podium to questions on any subject related to corporate activities.

Mr. Juan Alonzo argued that the E.E.O.[1] agreements to which the company and the Union had agreed, worked specifically in favor of women and blacks. He said unless something was done soon to improve job opportunities for Mexican-Americans, particularly in the office and professional areas, formal protests might well be invoked at the East Los Angeles and Phoenix facilities. Mr. Tembler replied that the E.E.O. provisions were fair to all but that he would personally instruct Darrin McCall, Personnel Manager, to review all promotions made in the last twelve months.

Sarah Fish of Queens called for a reduction of salaries and bonuses to officers but was ruled out of order, shareholders having previously authorized by majority vote the officers' salaries and bonuses to which she alluded.

John Ruskin Bench, a stockholder who described himself as "a proud American," accused the company of buying doll clothes and small mechanical parts from mainland China. The accusation was vigorously denied. Bench then asked if the company planned future procurements from Communist China. Mr. Tembler stated that world conditions were changing and the possibility did exist for the future. At this point Mr. Bench became very vocal and abusive and was escorted from the meeting by a security officer.

There being no further business to be discussed, the meeting was adjourned at 5:25 p.m.

> Respectfully submitted,
> VERNON T. CULHANE
> Corporate Secretary

Discussion Questions

1. List, define, and discuss the issues developed in this problem situation.
2. Which are (are not) appropriate at this type of meeting?
3. Were responses adequate? What might have been done differently to improve credibility with stockholders on specific issues?
4. Why is corporate credibility essential?
5. What is the proper role of the modern large corporation in social, environmental, and political areas?

Special Project

Prepare a well-documented research paper on how major corporations see their role in the community and as a partner in social and economic improvement. This will require extensive data collection from business, newspapers, magazines, and television newscasts. Beware of generalizations, obtain correct quotes, and make sure your data are sound.

[1]Equal Employment Opportunity.

Selected References

Anthologies
Luthans, F., and Wortman, M. S. *Emerging Concepts in Management.* Toronto, Canada: The MacMillan Company, 1969. Petit, T. A. "The Doctrine of Socially Responsible Management," p. 44.

Articles
Brodey, W. "If You Can't Support The Revolution Let The Revolution Support You," *Innovation*, October 15, 1970, p. 12.
Carr, A. Z. "Can An Executive Afford a Conscience?" *Harvard Business Review*, July–August 1970, p. 58.
Carr, A. Z. "Is Business Bluffing Ethical?" *Harvard Business Review*, January–February 1968, p. 143.
Crissy, W. J. E. "Image: What Is It?" *MSU Business Topics*, Winter 1971, p. 78.
Frey, D. N. "The Colossus That is Detroit," *Innovation*, Number Six, 1969, p. 2.
Hopper, K. "Has America Turned Its Back on the Factory?" *Innovation*, Number Nineteen, 1971, p. 24.
Horman, C. "The War Against War Research," *Innovation*, Number One, 1969, p. 30.
Horman, C., and Lindgren, N. "How The Auto Industry Has Managed (Or Not Managed) Its Crisis," *Innovation*, Number Thirteen, 1970, p. 2.
Mertes, J. E. "The Genesis of the Corporate Image," *MSU Business Topics*, Winter 1971, p. 35.
Perline, M. M. "Organized Labor and Social Responsibility," *Personnel Journal*, June 1971, p. 487.
Rodos, D. L. "Product Liability: Tougher Ground Rules," *Harvard Business Review*, July–August 1969, p. 144.
Saxon, G. Jr. "Annual Headache: The Stockholders Meeting," *Harvard Business Review*, January–February 1966.

WONDERFUL FRIDAY

The four day work week is now being adopted by an ever-increasing number of offices, shops, and manufacturing facilities across the country. For some it is working to the advantage of management and employees alike. Others have had difficulty adapting to the change or have reverted back to five days.

As increasing numbers of firms, unions, and individual managers consider the possibility of switching to a four day week, they naturally look to those who have adopted this work pattern and those who have experimented with it in the hope of learning from their experiences. One executive recently obtained the following reactions to his informal survey on the subject:

For the Four Day Work Week
> WORKER: "It's great! It splits the week in two and I get in a lot of bowling and camping."

WIFE: "I get to see my husband more and we do more things together. I wish it had happened years ago when the children were young. Most children suffer, you know, from having their father away from home so much."

ECONOMIST: "Every firm is in a constant struggle for survival. The one which is first with new and innovative approaches to achieving its tasks may have a competitive advantage . . . all other things being equal, of course."

WORKER: "A lucky break for me. With the kids in college I need the extra money. Having Friday off, I took a job bartending afternoons and evenings each weekend at a local club."

PERSONNEL MANAGER: Primarily, we noted an improvement in attitudes among the workers. On the positive side they see it as something which management really did more for the employee and less for management. On the negative side they know how many job applicants we've had lately. Ready competition for their jobs is obvious."

SUPERVISOR: "We work thirty-six hours now instead of forty. I didn't believe it at first, but we actually produce more in thirty-six hours than we did before in forty. Morale is high and absenteeism is way down."

MANAGER: "The statement you just heard (by the supervisor) is correct. I don't find it surprising when you look at the arithmetic. Assume a worker earned $4.00 per hour before or $160.00 for a full forty hour week. Now he works four days of nine hours each and earns the same $160.00. That's equivalent to $4.44 per hour. To top it off, management pays a bonus of four hours at the old forty hour base rate ($4.00/per hour) if the worker is here all four days . . . that is, no absences in a given week. You can see what that does for morale and attendance. For example:

Old Rate—40 hours at $4.00 = $160.00
Old Rate (one absence) 32 hours at $4.00 = $128.00
New Rate—36 hours at $4.44 = $160.00 + (bonus) = $176.00
New Rate (one absence) 27 hours at $4.44 = $120.00 and *no bonus.*
Not all companies use our system though."

COMPANY PRESIDENT: "Fortunately our work output is easily measured. We tracked production on a day-by-day basis since the change and overall productivity is up . . . per worker and for the company as a whole. That's what was supposed to happen, but I wasn't sure about the idea until I saw it for myself."

MANAGEMENT CONSULTANT: "The key to success is effective planning. You have to ensure that customers, employees, and suppliers all favorably adjust to the idea well in advance."

FOREMAN: "One way we save is pretty obvious. We used to lose fifteen to twenty minutes each morning for equipment start up and an equal amount each evening for clean up. The time is the same now but we work an extra hour."

VICE-PRESIDENT: "To make it work we had to take a hard stand on all overtime work . . . that is, over nine hours per day. Overtime pay differentials could easily wipe out the gains. So far, we've been fortunate."

UNION OFFICIAL: "The time is right for the four day week. It will put more people to work and reduce the chronic unemployment problems in this country. We have been able to successfully re-write four day work week agreements for nine hour days. But, we won't negotiate for four days of ten hours at straight time."

Against the Four Day Work Week

SOCIOLOGIST: "For many an extra day of personal time will be difficult. New behavioral patterns toward leisure will have to be developed. People may tend to spend too much money at first. Mass advertising for leisure activities may create new needs."

PSYCHOLOGIST: "Work is one significant form of structuring time and some people simply cannot exist without pre-structured days. They literally don't know what to do with their new found time and it can cause various forms of anxiety and neurosis. I liken it to the problems of retirement for many male workers."

WORKING WIFE: "My husband has Friday off, but I don't. So, he's at home messing up the house . . . cooking for himself . . . you know. Mostly he watches television. I'm sorry it ever happened."

SOON-TO-BE WORKING WIFE: "It was an economic necessity. We need the money since John's company went to the four day week and he lost all the regular overtime he used to get. He suggested taking a weekend job but I argued that we'd never be together then. At least we'll still have Saturday and Sunday together."

OFFICE MANAGER: "One practical difficulty is that we must have the office open five days each week even though the shop works four. Most of our customers and suppliers all work a five day week and they expect someone to be here on Friday. We use a skeleton work force to man the office on Fridays but this requires a personnel rotation plan and someone is always upset."

INDUSTRIAL ENGINEER: "Our operation requires the use of high fixed cost capital equipment. To be efficiently used it should be run as intensively as possible. If it were cost effective (no premium for overtime or weekends) we would run seven days a week. As it is, we lose four hours production time from each machine each week under the thirty-six hour concept. Our prices will probably have to go up."

BUSINESS CONSULTANT: "I see the four day week as a realistic idea for certain manufacturing areas but it lacks credibility in service related industries."

WORKER: "We had to give up regular coffee breaks as part of the new agreement. I know I get an extra day off but it's more like a sweat-shop now."

WORKER: "Management is more vocal than ever about tardiness, work habits, dress on the job, and the whole bit . . . they let you know constantly that they have a steady stream of applicants and you had better not screw up! What we really need more than ever before is a Union."

SUPPLIER: "That company refuses to accept shipments on Fridays and I've had to completely rework my delivery schedule for the remaining four days. They save money at my expense! I end up paying overtime premium two or three nights a week."

PERSONNEL MANAGER: "I'm concerned about the amount of moon-lighting. Two jobs are more possible with the four day week but people still need a certain amount of rest . . . and I don't want them resting here!"

Discussion Questions

1. List the various pro and con arguments and discuss.
2. What appear to be the major behavioral advantages of the four day work week:
   (a) From the viewpoint of the worker?
   (b) From the viewpoint of the organization?
3. What appear to be the major behavioral drawbacks to the four day work week:
   (a) From the viewpoint of the worker?
   (b) From the viewpoint of the organization?
4. Discuss ways in which the disadvantages to both employees and management can be minimized.
5. The management consultant in this case said, "The key to success is effective planning." Explain his statement. What forms of planning would be most critical?

Of Special Interest to Industrial and Business Groups

Suppose your company were now contemplating a switch to the four day work week. What would be the immediate advantages? What special problems would have to be resolved?

Special Projects

1. If an organization in your area has recently adopted a shorter, four day work week, find out how the change has affected productivity, morale, absenteeism,

turnover, and attitudes. What problems are still involved? How are they solving them?

2. Prepare and submit a well-researched paper on the advantages and disadvantages of the four day work week.

Selected References

Books
Drucker, P. F. *The Age of Discontinuity: Guidelines To Our Changing Society*. New York: Harper & Row, 1969.

Anthologies
McKinsey and Company (Eds.). *The Arts of Top Management*. New York: McGraw-Hill, 1971.
    Copisarow, A. C. "The Future Impact of Technology on Management," p. 280.

Articles
Kleinschrod, W. A. "The New Hours," *Administrative Management*, March 1971, p. 18.
"The Endless Weekend," *Life Magazine*, September 3, 1971.
"The Spreading Four-Day Week," *Newsweek Magazine*, August 27, 1971.
Wheeler, K. E. "Small Business Eyes the Four Day Work Week," *Harvard Business Review*, May–June 1970, p. 142.

LETTER FROM A RETIRED EMPLOYEE

1139 Grace Street
Denver, Colorado
September 21, 19—

Mr. Edmund Forrester
President
Rocky Mountain Express Company
540 Capital Drive
Denver, Colorado

DEAR MR. FORRESTER:

I retired two weeks ago after forty-one years with Rocky Mountain Express Company. You know that, of course. I want to thank you again for the fine retirement party and the wonderful speech you made about me and my long years of service with Rocky Mountain.

This may sound odd, but I am already enjoying being retired. I spend more time with my garden, do more reading than ever, and find I enjoy sharing the home activities with my wife.

I've also had more time for thinking and reflecting. Frankly, I've thought a lot about my years at Rocky Mountain. I was turning thirty the day your proud father brought you in to the office in a blanket to show you off to us. He always made us part of his family and we always thought of him as part of ours.

Jobs were scarce when I started. In those days a man felt he was lucky to have any job which would feed and clothe his family. Employers didn't talk then about vacations, fringe benefits, and things like that. The standard work week was 48 to 50 hours.

I was a truck dispatcher's assistant then in our old office on Front Street. It seems so ancient now. The clerks prepared and copied most documents in longhand because the office had only one manual typewriter. Remember when we actually wore green eyeshades and used those old roll top-desks? No, I guess you wouldn't recall any more although your father often brought you to the office.

How all of that changed! How different the young men were when they returned from Europe and the Pacific after the war. Eager, aggressive men they were. Some were just crazy truck jockeys but many were dreamers who saw new ways of doing things. They got your father to update his fleet of trucks as soon as commercial vehicle production resumed and they modernized the office too.

Last year, I watched another new breed of young men install the computer system. They said it would optimize truck loadings and schedules, prepare lowest cost shipping points from warehouses across the country, and handle all billing and general accounting. Our whole staff of clerks in 1949 couldn't keep up with just the western states and today, one machine does it for the entire country!

I didn't plan to wander through days gone by in this letter but it's hard for an old man not to. What I really wanted to do is pose two questions for your consideration now that your uncle has died and you, alone, run the company.

1. I've lived through a period of great change in our operations. It hasn't been easy. I've had to re-learn a lot and, in recent years, I guess I didn't contribute much anymore. I hear future changes will be even more rapid and dramatic. So, this is my question: Shouldn't you be preparing your employees for changes yet to come? Remove the fear of the unknown and make change work to your good rather than against it. I recall how we all feared that first punched card tabulating machine the company bought. We all thought we would lose our jobs. I guess you know what I mean.

2. Even more seriously, I've finally begun to question the paternalism your father nurtured and which, I always thought, was one of the finest things about the company. Two way loyalty, he called it. Be good to us and you'll always have a job.

Well, I kept my job for forty-one years. I dispatched trucks for forty-one long years. I wonder now if I had quit in 1943 after a run-in with your father what I might be doing now. Maybe I would have started my own business or become an artist or musician.

I wonder now if in some way it was cruel punishment being a truck dispatcher all those years. I never did learn a trade, never worked for anyone else. It was too nice at Rocky Mountain. I was too comfortable to leave . . . or was I afraid to leave?

Who was at fault if, indeed, there was fault? Was I to blame? Your father? The system of organizing work? Perhaps no crime was committed but, I now wonder, could I have made a greater contribution in my short life if I wasn't so *comfortable* at work?

What, Mr. Forrester, should your responsibilities be toward employees in the future? An old retired truck dispatcher raises these questions for you and future managers to ponder.

Most affectionately,
JOHN B. APPLETON

Discussion Questions

1. Define and restate the questions posed by Appleton.
2. What are the implications of change as suggested by Appleton?
3. Discuss Appleton's concern as an old man that he had only one job all of his working life. From a behavioral point of view is this:
   (a) good?
   (b) bad?
   (c) neither?
   (d) unknown?
   (e) of no concern to us?
4. Would modern career counseling techniques as we now understand and use them have prevented this problem? Why? How?
5. Are there other aspects of the job environment (perhaps not envisioned by Appleton and probably created by as yet undiagnosed environmental conditions) which might go undetected by career counseling and job coaching and yet have serious effects on employees? Explain your ideas.

Special Projects

1. Have the class define and debate the issues suggested in Discussion Question 3.
2. What is innovation? What is meant by an innovative organization? How does an

organization become innovative? Prepare a report on the subject of *The Innovative Organization*.

Selected References

Books
Rohrer, Hibler, and Replogle (staff). *Managers For Tomorrow*, New York: The New American Library, 1965.

Anthologies
Drucker, P. F. (Ed.). *Preparing Tomorrow's Business Leaders Today*. Englewood Cliffs, New Jersey: Prentice-Hall, 1971.
  Boettinger, H. M. "The Impact of Technology," p. 50.
  Diebold, J. "The Information Revolution," p. 61.
Leavitt, H. J., and Pondy, L. R. (Eds.). *Readings in Managerial Psychology*, Chicago, Illinois: University of Chicago Press, 1964.
  Leavitt, H. and Whisler, T. "Management in the 1980's," p. 578.
  Simon, H. A. "The Corporation: Will It Be Managed By Machines?" p. 592.
McKinsey and Company (Ed.). *The Arts of Top Management*. New York: McGraw-Hill, 1971.
  Neuschel, R. P. "Leadership Styles and Organizational Achievement," p. 40.

Articles
Anshen, M. A. "The Management of Ideas," *Harvard Business Review*, July–August 1969, p. 199.
Drucker, P. F. "Management's New Role," *Harvard Business Review*, November–December 1969, p. 49.
Gibson, J. L., and Klein, S. M. "Employee Attitudes as a Function of Age and Length of Service: A Reconceptualization," *Academy of Management Journal*, December 1970, p. 411.
Peckham, M. "The Corporation's Role in Today's Crisis of Cultural Incoherence," *Innovation*, May 1971, p. 30.

REVERSING THE PHYSIOLOGICAL CLOCK

"Future shock is the dizzying disorientation brought on by the premature arrival of the future. It may well be the most important disease of tomorrow."

"This is the prospect that man now faces. Change is avalanching upon our heads and most people are grotesquely unprepared to cope with it."

ALVIN TOFFLER
Future Shock
pp. 13, 14

Part 1 — Disclosure

The marketing executives began to arrive, first alone and in pairs and later in larger groups as nine o'clock approached. Most had flown in the night before from major marketing centers in New Orleans, Houston, Los Angeles, and Portland, with two coming from as far west as Honolulu. Upon arrival at J. F. K. International and Newark Airports all were met by company cars and driven to convenient motels for the night in suburban Grayslake, New Jersey.

Chad Martin, South Central Regional Marketing Manager for Goodhill Pharmaceutical Laboratories, was as unprepared for what was about to take place as any of the other marketing personnel who arrived at Goodhill corporate headquarters that Monday morning. Officially it was a quarterly marketing meeting. The time was right but, contrary to usual practice, no pre-meeting agenda had been mailed out.

As Chad entered the architecturally bold Goodhill corporate building, he sensed there would be something different about today's meeting. At 8:50 a.m. the main audio-visual conference center was nearly filled. Martin used the few minutes to renew acquaintances with personnel from other cities, many of whom were normally not on the invitation list for quarterly meetings. All were as confused as Martin about the purpose or scope of the meeting.

At nine, A. Kenneth Post, Director of North American Marketing Operations, took the podium microphone and made several general comments before introducing Hardy M. Van Zelst, the Chief Executive Officer of the multinational pharmaceutical firm.

A man with a brilliant mind, Van Zelst was internationally respected for his successful efforts in steering an old-line drug manufacturing firm into its present position as a leader in pharmaceutical research and development. Although a Swiss, Van Zelst spoke flawless English and this morning his words would stun an audience long conditioned to hearing regular progress reports on man's dramatic progress in medicine.

"Gentlemen," began Van Zelst, "I believe I can say without reservation that we stand at the threshold of a future free of most human pain and suffering. In the last hundred years man has conquered the most dreaded of his ancestor's diseases. Tuberculosis, malaria, syphyllis, and poliomyelitis for instance, have been contained. Treatment or prevention of major diseases has been made possible for millions of persons the world over. In recent years we have also made significant progress in treating many cancer forms and in effecting release from pain for persons suffering from disabling arthritis. Proudly, Goodhill Laboratories has been in the forefront of this eternal battle against disease."

Van Zelst continued.

"But all of our past achievements may well pale by comparison to what you will hear today. Perhaps the best kept secret in our organization's history will be publicly unveiled through the various news media today concurrent with this meeting. After five years of relentless research, we at

Goodhill may finally have shaped the delicate key to the eternal question of senescence.[1] As incredible as it seems, we may have discovered what Ponce de Leon could not, *the fountain of youth!*"

It was five minutes before Kenneth Post's gavel led the group back to order and Van Zelst was able to continue.

"I regret having to release the news to you in such dramatic form and without the usual advance notice," said Van Zelst. "But it has been necessary to maintain the highest degree of secrecy around our research activities to prevent any premature rumors until our efforts yielded promising results. Two separate research programs over a six year period have provided extensive data which now leads us to believe that the human physiological clock can be slowed . . . stopped . . . or even reversed!

"I will now introduce Dr. Kurt von Offer of our Belgian subsidiary and an internationally acclaimed chemist. Following him will be Mrs. Sylvia Lanier, noted biologist and bio-chemist who will speak for the efforts of our American team. Each research team has probed the problem differently and there are some specific areas of disagreement which you will probably hear. However, I must emphasize, both studies show such promising results that our final product or products may well be a composite of the two techniques. First, Dr. Kurt von Offer . . ."

Dr. von Offer acknowledged the applause and requested the lights be dimmed. He then used a series of projected transparencies to vividly illustrate his presentation.

"For years," started Dr. von Offer, "I and many of my colleagues have felt that the process of aging might not be as inevitable as we have always assumed. We have asked ourselves endless questions. Why do some organs fail prematurely and why do others remain quite functional up to the point of death? Why do some organ systems have the miraculous ability to regenerate their cellular structure while others cannot? Our research has concluded that aging in specific organs and for the body as a whole . . . is in fact nothing more than a form of disease!"

Dr. von Offer paused and scanned the silent audience.

Chad Martin felt compelled to ask the question obviously on everyone's mind.

"Dr. von Offer," asked Martin rising from his seat, "perhaps I am out of order but, if I understand you correctly . . . and aging is a disease . . . then are we to assume that it is a disease which can be medically treated?"

"The question is appropriate," replied von Offer. "In a general sense

---

[1] Aging.

you are quite correct. Our research has shown the cause of aging to be molecular cross-linkage of vital cells. By a process somewhat similar to that by which a normal cell becomes dysfunctional and cancerous, it appears that in aging, separate vital cells become cross-linked or knotted with each other. This cross-linking reduces the ability of each individual cell and entire cell systems to perform their required functions. With time these vital cells begin to die, metabolism slows down, tissues lose their elasticity and dry out. The blood vessels eventually become stiff and clog . . . bone and cartilage become brittle."

Dr. von Offer continued.

"The physical effects of aging are obvious: reduced mobility and organ effectiveness. In addition the body loses its natural defenses against many other diseases so common to the aged."

Von Offer showed numerous transparencies of the aging process to the group.

"We are now working on a search for micro-organisms or possibly nucleic acid enzymes which will digest or untie the knots binding these vital molecules. By this approach we may not only be able to slow the aging process but possibly reverse it."

Dr. von Offer was again interrupted by a question from the floor.

"Sir. As a former pre-med student who decided to pursue pharmaceutical marketing, I'm concerned about your enzyme approach. How would this process work on necessary molecular cross-linking such as in muscle tissue?"

Von Offer adjusted his glasses.

"That, sir, is one of our greatest problems at present," he replied quietly. "The micro-organism must be perfectly selective. Selectivity and effectivity are the keys to our eventual success. Within one to two years we believe we will have the answer."

After several more questions and answers, Dr. von Offer completed his presentation. Hardy Van Zelst then introduced Mrs. Sylvia Lanier whose introductory comments mirrored those of von Offer.

"The American research team has also studied the effects of molecular cross-linking. Our stress, however, has been placed less on removing existing cross-linkage and more on the prevention of cell cross-linking.

"Unfortunately our approach favors those who are now young, those whose vital cells are currently free of extensive cross-linking. Emotionally we would prefer to offer longer life to those who are now older but we differ with Dr. von Offer on the practicality of this approach.

"In this area we face many obstacles. It is not evident why vital cells cross-link. The most promising approach is the free radical theory . . . essentially the oxidation of cells."

Mrs. Lanier concluded her presentation and called for questions.

"How long would you estimate until the pill is perfected?" asked one marketing representative.

"One to two years until sufficient experimental data can be presented to the F.D.A.[2] for their analysis . . . another one to three years until it is available to the public."

Chad Martin was more specific with his question.

"Mrs. Lanier, what can we expect from the youth pill? That is, how will we be affected? How much longer will we live?"

"Your question is impossible to answer at present. Data will be provided to you on a regular basis from this point forward. However, with chickens we have extended lifespan 17 percent on an average. With aging symptoms we have done even better. Aging of specific organs and certain external physical characteristics has been slowed by 22 percent. That is, the chickens looked younger on an average when they eventually died."

"One more question, Mrs. Lanier," said Martin, "if I were to start taking your pill or Dr. von Offer's pill or some combination *today*, how would I know it was working?"

"We believe the most obvious external signs in humans will be a reduction in the growth rate of fingernails and toenails. Hair may also grow slower. And, if Dr. von Offer is correct in his belief that the aging process can be reversed, then white or grey hair might again turn black, skin tissue would become firmer and wrinkles would tend to disappear. Internal body organs would become stronger instead of weaker."

At this point Hardy Van Zelst assumed the podium, thanked the research teams for their efforts, and a round of applause followed.

"Now," said Van Zelst, "we must face the most complex questions of all. Before we as a company can produce and market a youth pill we must believe in the product . . . not only in the massive evidence that it works, but that it is morally, physically, and ethically right. Toward this end Goodhill will conduct numerous seminars for management and marketing personnel in the next twelve months in which we will attempt to determine the impact of this discovery on ourselves, our families, our friends and neighbors. In other words, ladies and gentlemen, the future is here and we must cope with it. We must learn to survive emotionally before we can ask an unprepared world to do so."

[2]U.S. Food and Drug Administration.

Part 2 – Impact

That evening Chad Martin invited Emory Falk and Tom Porter to his hotel room to discuss what all had heard earlier in the day. Falk and Porter were both market representatives from the South Central Region and worked with Martin.

"Van Zelst certainly doesn't waste any time does he?" said Falk. "We're asked to come to a routine two day quarterly meeting at corporate headquarters and, instead, we hear the disclosure of a century. Then we're told to meet *the very next day* for the first of a series of brainwashing sessions."

"Don't assume it's going to be a brainwashing session," said Martin. "Van Zelst is just as interested in finding out how we feel about this youth pill as he is in developing a company marketing strategy. Our attitudes may have a distinct bearing on future marketing policies."

"Is that why a psychiatrist and a sociologist will be at each twenty man seminar session?" asked Porter.

"I suppose so," said Martin. "They'll be there to facilitate the unstructured discussions and will most likely make their reports on our attitudes to Van Zelst."

"I don't care how they handle the seminars or the marketing," said Porter, "as long as we perfect the pill. Hell, I'm forty-eight years old now. I'll have to get started soon or there will be no hope . . ."

"That's the point of these early seminars," said Martin. "To find out exactly how people will react to the entry of a youth pill into their lives. Through us, the company hopes to establish initial reactions to the drug."

"How can the reaction be anything but universally outstanding to a drug which helps you look younger and live longer?" asked Porter. "I for one will take them by the handful."

"I see all kinds of problems," said Falk. "Will the drug be available by prescription only? If so, how will doctors decide who should get it? Everyone is getting older every day so, as von Offer said, *we all have the same disease!* Conversely, if everyone technically needs the drug, why should it be a prescription item?"

"That's right," said Martin. "It might well be classified in the same category as a vitamin and sold over-the-counter."

"That would get the cost down," said Porter. "If it's a prescription item there will be a natural tendency to make youth possible for only those who can afford it."

"Or should the federal government subsidize the pills for the very poor . . . or maybe give them away to every citizen," offered Martin.

"It does start getting sticky, doesn't it?" said Porter.

"It sure does," said Falk. "Suppose we determine that if a man or woman begins to take the pill at age thirty and takes one pill each day for the rest of his life, he can extend his life expectancy three additional years. With that assumption, should he take two pills per day . . . or five or ten? Perhaps there is some magic number of pills per day which will keep him as eternally young as Dorian Gray?"[3]

"Interesting thought," replied Martin," but more likely, additional doses will yield only diminishing returns. It will probably be a waste of money to take extra doses."

"Who in his right mind would believe that?" asked Porter. "Even if told that repeatedly by the doctor, I'd still double or triple the dosage to be sure."

"And kill yourself?" asked Falk. "The drug could well be toxic in large increments. How could we stop people from taking the pills like candy and then having them drop like flies?"

"Prescription?" ventured Porter.

"I don't think that would solve the problem," said Martin. "Black market traffic in the drug would be sure to develop."

"Here's another problem," offered Falk. "Suppose the pill fails to affect or act on people to the same degree. Imagine the consequences for a newly married couple at age twenty who each take the pill for thirty years. It might act in only a negligible way on the man and have a stronger effect on his wife. The man would eventually become middle-aged in appearance and still be married to a raving beauty, attractive to all the young men."

"I hadn't thought of that," said Martin.

"Now that you bring these things up I can see all sorts of problems," said Porter. "What about those who are very old now? Would they be offered false hopes in their declining years?"

"We would have to totally rethink our moral and religious values," replied Martin.

"Whatever we end up with will force major adjustments in the way we live and our attitudes toward life."

"That's right," said Falk. "We may be close to producing Huxley's SOMA pill.[4] I'm not sure I'm ready for that. Perhaps the company would be wise to discontinue research activities on the youth pill."

---

[3]A fictitious character of a young man who appeared never to age in *The Portrait of Dorian Gray* by Oscar Wilde.

[4]A happiness producing and life extending pill universally used in a future world for maintaining social control. Described in *Brave New World* by Aldous Huxley.

"But that doesn't make any sense," replied Porter. "Someone else will only develop it instead. It's progress. You can't stop progress."

"I used to feel the same way," said Falk. "Now I'm not so sure. Progress in all fields is accelerating at an incredible rate. In only one human lifetime man first flew at Kittyhawk and stepped on the surface of the moon. People are beginning to come apart emotionally because of the impermanence of things, the incredible changes taking place around them, their feeling of utter frustration in a vastly complex society of machines and systems which engulf them daily. I really don't believe we're ready for a youth pill."

Discussion Questions

1. What is the obligation(s) of an organization such as Goodhill Pharmaceutical to prepare its customers for a product which is likely to sharply affect their future lives?
2. What other legal, ethical, moral, or religious problems might arise?
3. What comparisons can be drawn from the present and past? Are comparisons of this type valid?
4. Consider organizations which implement dramatic new operating systems and procedures internally? Do they (should they) prepare workers for the emotional changes which may be involved? Can you cite specific examples?
5. What obligations (if any) will future organizations have in assisting employees to cope with the realities of impermanence and change even if these changes are not products of the organization itself?
6. How should schools and universities begin to alter their curricula to prepare students for a life of "future shock"?

Special Project

Prepare a well-documented research paper on the subject of *The Management of Change* with heavy emphasis on human behavior in future complex organizations.

Selected References

Books
Birren, J. E. (Ed.). *Handbook of Aging and the Individual*. Chicago, Illinois: University of Chicago Press, 1959.
Toffler, A. *Future Shock*. New York: Random House, 1970.

Anthologies
Koontz, H., and O'Donnell, C. *Management: A Book of Readings*. New York: McGraw-Hill, 1968.
  Lorig, A. W. "Where Do Corporate Responsibilities Lie?" p. 651.
McKinsey and Company (Eds.). *The Arts of Top Management*. New York: McGraw-Hill, 1971.
  Hertz, D. B. "The Successful Innovators," p. 308.
Preparing Tomorrow's Business Leaders Today. Englewood Cliffs, New Jersey: Prentice-Hall, 1969.
  Powers, J. J. Jr. "The Multi National Corporation," p. 171.

Articles

Allison, D. "Measuring the Good and the Bad of New Technology," *Innovation*, Number Nine, 1970, p. 44.

Hollomon, H. "The Markets Of The 70s Are Community Markets," *Innovation*, Number Fourteen, 1970, p. 26.

Marquis, D. G. "The Anatomy of Successful Innovations," *Innovation*, Number Seven, 1969, p. 29.

Peterson, W. H. "The Future and the Futurists," *Harvard Business Review*, November–December 1967, p. 168.

Yaney, J. P. "The Management of Innovation," *Personnel Journal*, March 1970, p. 224.

CASE STUDY CROSS REFERENCE

Although located elsewhere in this book, the following problem situations are also valuable in the study of Section 10:

Looking Backward

It had not been a particularly good week. On Tuesday, February 9, 1971, at 6:02 a.m., the San Fernando Valley section of Los Angeles was rocked by the first and sharpest of a series of earthquakes. I was fortunate. My home had been spared from damage and my office, nearer to the epicenter, was only littered with fallen books and materials.

The effect was more mental than physical. Like many others, I felt it as an additional psychological depressant for a part of the country already concerned and confused by high unemployment and rising prices.

The next day was no better. On Wednesday the bankruptcy of England's Rolls-Royce Corporation forced the Lockheed Aircraft Corporation of Burbank to terminate the employment of over 6500 persons. To the weakened Southern California economy it was an immediate, staggering shock of yet undetermined effect. For me it was the loss of a significant amount of on-going consulting work in industrial education with Lockheed. By Thursday I had written off the week as one I'd like to forget.

On Friday, February 12, I received an unexpected phone call from upstate New York. The caller identified himself as Dr. Lester M. Cone, Jr., a consulting editor for Pergamon Publishing Company of New York.

"I've read your ideas for a casebook in the behavioral sciences," said Cone. "And I'm going to recommend to the Pergamon Editorial Board that they undertake the project. With a few structural changes we might develop a useful resource document for the college level in addition to the industrial education market (as I had originally intended)."

Funny how one's outlook can change so quickly. Suddenly, the earthquake and local economic problems took a back seat to warm and ego building thoughts of successful authorship. Only a minor step remained — to write the manuscript!

Here is a message. Preparation of this manuscript has been both an enjoyable and intellectually challenging task from which I have drawn great personal satisfaction and identity. I have had an opportunity to create, to build, and to broaden my horizons. I have experienced feelings about the nature of work itself (embodied in many cases) which only strengthen my beliefs in the need to restructure jobs to best utilize human resources.

Here is a second message. To bring the manuscript to this point has required the trust, support, counseling, critical advice, and understanding of Dr. Lester M. Cone, Jr., who has employed sound management practices throughout in supervising this entire project. In retrospect, through him, I see even more clearly the need for the contemporary manager to set high goals for himself and mutually with his employees. I see the need for honesty, frank criticism of sloppy work, and redirection of effort, combined with endless trust, support, and recognition.

LOOKING FORWARD

We want your reactions to *Encounters*, positive and negative, regarding any situation, characterization, or concept. We would like to know if the questions after each case assisted you in understanding the principles or concepts. Where Special Projects were used, did they amplify the classroom learning or add reality and credibility? Were the individual cases believable, understandable, and interesting?

In particular, we would like to know which cases were most useful and meaningful to you as an educator, manager, or student and which you feel should be modified or deleted. With your help we can make future editions even more valuable.

Please send your comments to:

Mr. Gerald Deegan
Managing Editor
Pergamon Publishing Company
Maxwell House
Fairview Park
Elmsford, New York 10523

General References

Athos, A. G., and Coffey, R. E. *Behavior in Organizations: A Multi-Dimensional View.* Englewood Cliffs, New Jersey: Prentice-Hall, 1968.

Bass, B. M. *Organizational Psychology.* Boston, Massachusetts: Allyn & Bacon, 1965.

Davis, K. *Human Relations at Work, The Dynamics of Organizational Behavior.* New York: McGraw-Hill, 1969.

Dubin, R. *Human Relations In Administration.* Englewood Cliffs, New Jersey: Prentice-Hall, 1961.

DuBrin, A. J. *The Practice Of Managerial Psychology.* New York: Pergamon Press, 1972.

Haire, M. *Psychology in Management.* New York: McGraw-Hill, 1956.

Koontz, H., and O'Donnell, C. *Principles of Management,* Fourth Edition. New York: McGraw-Hill, 1968.

Leavitt, H. J. *Managerial Psychology.* Second Edition. Chicago, Illinois: University of Chicago Press, 1964.

McClelland, D. C. *The Achieving Society.* Princeton, New Jersey: Van Nostrand, 1961.

McLarney, W. J., and Berliner, W. M. *Management Training—Cases and Principles.* Homewood, Illinois: Richard D. Irwin, Inc., 1970.

Maier, N. R. F. *Psychology in Industry.* Third Edition. New York: Houghton Mifflin, 1965.

Sayles, L. R., and Straus, G. *Human Behavior In Organizations.* Englewood Cliffs, New Jersey: Prentice-Hall, 1966.

Schein, E. H. *Organizational Psychology.* Englewood Cliffs, New Jersey: Prentice-Hall, 1965.

Smith, H. C. *Psychology of Industrial Behavior.* New York: McGraw-Hill, 1964.

Tannenbaum, R., Massarik, F., and Weschler, I. R. *Leadership and Organization: A Behavioral Science Approach.* New York: McGraw-Hill, 1961.

Tiffin, J., and McCormick, E. *Industrial Psychology.* Englewood Cliffs, New Jersey: Prentice-Hall, 1965.

Whyte, W. F. *Organizational Behavioral Theory and Application.* Homewood, Illinois: Irwin Dorsey, 1969.

THE PRACTICE OF MANAGERIAL PSYCHOLOGY
Concepts and Methods for Manager and Organization Development
Pergamon Management and Business Administration Series, Volume 1
By Andrew J. DuBrin, College of Business, Rochester Institute of Technology, New York

Based upon the author's research and practical experience as a consultant, this volume presents a variety of innovative, conceptual schemes to enable the practitioner, student, and manager to understand the underlying factors that will determine if and to what degree psychological intervention will be beneficial, meaningless, or harmful to an organization. Requiring only a basic background in business or psychology, the book offers such new conceptualizations as a list of behavioral changes needed by managers, the Conflict Matrix, the developmental Goal X Level Integrator, managerial motivational schema, and helpful interventions for managerial obsolescence. A unique Managerial Psychology Matrix specifies the proper conditions for applying such techniques as sensitivity training, performance appraisal, psychological assessment, team development meetings, organizational analysis, and super-subordinate counseling.

THE CYBERNETIC SOCIETY
Pergamon Unified Engineering Series, Volume 15
By Ralph Parkman, San Jose State College, San Jose, California

Provides a unified, interdisciplinary study of some of the basic interactions between modern technology and human society, and traces the roots of these interactions in industrial history. Special attention is given to certain developments in computers and other communications technologies with particular regard to possible advantages of trying to employ them for the organization of large scale systems of men and machines, and also to the potential threat to individual freedoms or initiative resulting from these kinds of approaches.

CLIMATE FOR CREATIVITY
Report of the Seventh National Creativity Research Conference held in Greensboro,
North Carolina. Supported Jointly by the National Science Foundation and the Smith
Richardson Foundation, Inc.
Pergamon General Psychology Series, Volume 9
Edited by Calvin W. Taylor, the University of Utah

This volume offers a multidimensional investigation of the problems of identifying and
establishing proper "climates" or settings for creativity. Part I concentrates on organizational
settings for creativity, including papers on the identification and use of creative abilities
in industry, scientific organizations, major weapon systems innovations, and the U.S. Civil
Service Commission. Part II examines more general creativity climates and studies, discussing
predictors and criteria of creativity; the maintenance of creative output through the years;
programming creative behavior; intellective, non-intellective, and environmental correlates
of mechanical ingenuity; and a holistic approach to creativity.

**STUDIES IN DYADIC COMMUNICATION: Proceedings of a Research Conference on the
Interview**
Pergamon General Psychology Series, Volume 7
Edited by Aron W. Siegman, University of Maryland (Baltimore County Campus) and the
Psychiatric Institute, University of Maryland School of Medicine and Benjamin Pope,
The Sheppard and Enoch Pratt Hospital, Towson, Maryland

The result of a special conference held at the Psychiatric Institute of the University of
Maryland in 1968, this volume includes a number of diverse studies based on both experimental and naturalistic interviews, experimental dialogues and free speech samples. The
papers explore such aspects of the interview as the effectiveness of various interviewing
styles, the role of the interviewer-interviewee relationship, the synchrony phenomenon
or reciprocal modeling, the role of auditory feedback in the control of spontaneous speech,
and speech patterns in patient groups. **Studies in Dyadic Communication** will be a valuable
textbook and reference source for graduate students and research workers in psychology,
communication, psycholinguistics, interviewing, psychotherapy, and counseling.

THE PSYCHOLOGICAL EXPERIMENT: A Practical Accomplishment
Pergamon General Psychology Series, Volume 22
Edited by Harold B. Pepinsky, The Ohio State University, and Michael J. Patton,
University of Utah

Based on the thesis that the reality of an empirical world exists for the participant only
through the methods he and others use to make that world evident to each other, this
volume focuses on reports of six psychological experiments involving counseling processes
and negotiation. The editors examine each of these experiments in retrospect and analyze
how the experimenter and fellow participants contrived to develop the experiment from
its original prospectus into a completed, published document.

THE STRUCTURAL APPROACH IN PSYCHOLOGICAL TESTING
Pergamon General Psychology Series, Volume 4
By Marvin L. Kaplan, University of Windsor, Windsor, Canada, Nick J. Colarelli, St. Louis University, Ruth Brill Gross, University of Cincinnati, Donald Leventhal, Bowling Green State University and Saul M. Siegel, The Ohio State University

Integrating a variety of concepts endorsed by the ego oriented psychoanalysts with those of cognitively oriented psychologists, including Rapaport and Holt, this important work thoroughly describes the structural approach in psychological testing and ties it historically to developments in general and clinical psychology.
CONTENTS: The Place and Importance of the Structural Approach in Psychological Evaluation. Psychoanalytic Foundations of the Structural Theory. Structural Concepts in Test Analysis and Personality Description. Schizophrenia: Faulty Ego Systhesis. Mechanical Man. Kaleidoscopic Ego. Vacillation Between Reality and Psychosis. A System of Warding off Confusion.

THE SOCIAL SELF
Pergamon General Psychology Series, Volume 35
By R.C. Ziller, University of Florida

An examination of the concept of the self as extended to include other persons such as a
friend, your father, your teacher, work group, and someone you know who is unhappy.
The relationships are expressed through geometric arrangements of objects representing the
self and others. These arrangements represent components of the social self and include
such factors as self-esteem, social interest, self-centrality, etc. The three special features of
the book include: the new multi-component definition of the self concept, the unique
non-verbal approach to the measurement of the self concept, and the sweeping Helical
Theory of Personal Change.

EMOTION IN THE HUMAN FACE: Guidelines for Research and an Integration of Findings
Pergamon General Psychology Series, Volume 11
By Paul Ekman, University of California, San Francisco and Langley Porter Neuropsychiatric Institute, Wallace V. Friesen, Langley Porter Neuropsychiatric Institute, and Phoebe Ellsworth, Stanford University

Can facial behavior be controlled or disguised? Can two or more emotions be shown simultaneously? Can judgements of emotion from facial behavior be accurate? What are the similarities and differences in facial behavior across cultures? These and other major questions which have been asked about human facial expression of emotion are examined here in **Emotion in the Human Face**, the first volume to evaluate and integrate critically all quantitative research conducted since 1914 on this particular psychological phenomenon. Including results from yet unpublished studies, the volume also provides conceptual and methodology guidelines for future research.